The Ultimate HSPSAA Guide

UniAdmissions

Copyright © 2017 *UniAdmissions*. All rights reserved.

ISBN 978-1-9998570-6-6

No part of this publication may be reproduced, stored or transmitted in any form or by any means, electronic or mechanical, including photocopying, recording, or by any information retrieval system without the prior written permission of the publisher. This publication may not be used in conjunction with or to support any commercial undertaking without the prior written permission of the publisher.

Published by *RAR Medical Services Limited*
www.uniadmissions.co.uk
info@uniadmissions.co.uk
Tel: 0208 068 0438

This book is neither created nor endorsed by HSPSAA. The authors and publisher are not affiliated with HSPSAA. The information offered in this book is purely advisory and any advice given should be taken within this context. As such, the publishers and authors accept no liability whatsoever for the outcome of any applicant's HSPSAA performance, the outcome of any university applications or for any other loss. Although every precaution has been taken in the preparation of this book, the publisher and author assume no responsibility for errors or omissions of any kind. Neither is any liability assumed for damages resulting from the use of information contained herein. This does not affect your statutory rights.

About the Author

Rohan is the **Director of Operations** at *UniAdmissions* and is responsible for its technical and commercial arms. He graduated from Gonville and Caius College, Cambridge and is a fully qualified doctor. Over the last five years, he has tutored hundreds of successful Oxbridge and Medical applicants. He has also authored twenty books on admissions tests and interviews.

Rohan has taught physiology to undergraduates and interviewed medical school applicants for Cambridge. He has published research on bone physiology and writes education articles for the Independent and Huffington Post. In his spare time, Rohan enjoys playing the piano and table tennis.

The Ultimate HSPSAA Guide

400 Practice Questions

Rohan Agarwal

UniAdmissions

The Basics 7
General Advice 8

Section 1 10
Approaching Section 1 13
Section 1 Questions 14

Section 2 174
Annotated Essays 180
Example Essay Questions 196

Answer Key 198
Worked Solutions 200

Final Advice 244
Your Free Book 246
Oxbridge Interview Course 247

The Basics

What is the HSPSAA?

The Human, Social, and Political Sciences Admissions Assessment (HSPSAA) is a 2 hour written exam for prospective Cambridge applicants for HSPS.

What does the HSPSAA consist of?

Section	Timing	FORMAT	Questions
ONE	60 Minutes	1A: Thinking Skills	36 Multiple Choice Questions
TWO	60 Minutes	Essay Task	One Essay from a choice of Eight

Why is the HSPSAA used?
Cambridge applicants tend to be a bright bunch and therefore usually have excellent grades. The vast majority of applicants score greater than 90% in all of their A level subjects. This means that competition is fierce – meaning that the universities must use the HSPSAA to help differentiate between applicants.

When do I sit HSPSAA?
The HSPSAA takes place in the first week of November every year.

Can I resit the HSPSAA?
No, you can only sit the HSPSAA once per admissions cycle.

Where do I sit the HSPSAA?
You can usually sit the HSPSAA at your school or college (ask your exams officer for more information). Alternatively, if your school isn't a registered test centre or you're not attending a school or college, you can sit the HSPSAA at an authorised test centre.

Do I have to resit the HSPSAA if I reapply?
Yes - you cannot use your score from any previous attempts.

How is the HSPSAA Scored?
In section 1, each question carries one mark and there is no negative marking. In section 2, your answer will be assessed based on the argument and also its clarity.

How is the HSPSAA used?
Different Cambridge colleges will place different weightings on different components so it's important you find out as much information about how your marks will be used by emailing the college admissions office.

In general, the university will interview a high proportion of realistic applicants so the HSPSAA score isn't vital for making the interview shortlist. However, it can play a huge role in the final decision after your interview.

General Advice

Start Early

It is much easier to prepare if you practice little and often. Start your preparation well in advance; ideally by mid September but at the latest by early October. This way you will have plenty of time to complete as many papers as you wish to feel comfortable and won't have to panic and cram just before the test, which is a much less effective and more stressful way to learn. In general, an early start will give you the opportunity to identify the complex issues and work at your own pace.

Prioritise

Some questions in section 1 can be complex – and given the intense time pressure you need to know your limits. It is essential that you don't get stuck with very difficult questions. If a question looks particularly long or complex, mark it for review and move on. You don't want to be caught 5 questions short at the end just because you took more than 3 minutes in answering a challenging question. If a question is taking too long, choose a sensible answer and move on. Remember that each question carries equal weighting and therefore, you should adjust your timing in accordingly. With practice and discipline, you can get very good at this and learn to maximise your efficiency.

Positive Marking

There are no penalties for incorrect answers in the HSPSAA; you will gain one for each right answer and will not get one for each wrong or unanswered one. This provides you with the luxury that you can always guess should you absolutely be not able to figure out the right answer for a question or run behind time. Since each question provides you with 4 to 6 possible answers, you have a 16-25% chance of guessing correctly. Therefore, if you aren't sure (and are running short of time), then make an educated guess and move on. Before 'guessing' you should try to eliminate a couple of answers to increase your chances of getting the question correct. For example, if a question has 5 options and you manage to eliminate 2 options- your chances of getting the question increase from 20% to 33%!

Avoid losing easy marks on other questions because of poor exam technique. Similarly, if you have failed to finish the exam, take the last 10 seconds to guess the remaining questions to at least give yourself a chance of getting them right.

Practice

This is the best way of familiarising yourself with the style of questions and the timing for this section. You are unlikely to be familiar with the style of questions when you first encounter them. Therefore, you want to be comfortable at using this before you sit the test.

Practising questions will put you at ease and make you more comfortable with the exam. The more comfortable you are, the less you will panic on the test day and the more likely you are to score highly. Initially, work through the questions at your own pace, and spend time carefully reading the questions and looking at any additional data. When it becomes closer to the test, **make sure you practice the questions under exam conditions**.

Past Papers

The HSPSAA is a very new exam so there aren't many sample papers available. Specimen papers are freely available online at www.uniadmissions.co.uk/HSPSAA. Once you've worked your way through the questions in this book, you are highly advised to attempt them.

A word on timing...

You have 60 minutes to complete section one which means that you will have around 100 seconds per question; this may sound like a lot but given that you're often required to read and analyse long passages - it can often not be enough. Some questions in this section are very tricky and can be a big drain on your limited time. **The people who fail to complete section 1 are those who get bogged down on a particular question.**

Therefore, it is vital that you start to get a feel for which questions are going to be easy and quick to do and which ones should be left till the end. The best way to do this is through practice and the questions in this book will offer extensive opportunities for you to do so.

> *"If you had all day to do your HSPSAA, you would get 100%. But you don't."*

Whilst this isn't completely true, it illustrates a very important point. Once you've practiced and know how to answer the questions, the clock is your biggest enemy. This seemingly obvious statement has one very important consequence. **The way to improve your HSPSAA score is to improve your speed.** There is no magic bullet. But there are a great number of techniques that, with practice, will give you significant time gains, allowing you to answer more questions and score more marks.

Timing is tight throughout the HSPSAA – **mastering timing is the first key to success.** Some candidates choose to work as quickly as possible to save up time at the end to check back, but this is generally not the best way to do it. HSPSAA questions can have a lot of information in them – each time you start answering a question it takes time to get familiar with the instructions and information. By splitting the question into two sessions (the first run-through and the return-to-check) you double the amount of time you spend on familiarising yourself with the data, as you have to do it twice instead of only once. This costs valuable time. In addition, candidates who do check back may spend 2–3 minutes doing so and yet not make any actual changes. Whilst this can be reassuring, it is a false reassurance as it is unlikely to have a significant effect on your actual score. Therefore it is usually best to pace yourself very steadily, aiming to spend the same amount of time on each question and finish the final question in a section just as time runs out. This reduces the time spent on re-familiarising with questions and maximises the time spent on the first attempt, gaining more marks.

It is essential that you don't get stuck with the hardest questions – no doubt there will be some. In the time spent answering only one of these you may miss out on answering three easier questions. If a question is taking too long, choose a sensible answer and move on. Never see this as giving up or in any way failing, rather it is the smart way to approach a test with a tight time limit. With practice and discipline, you can get very good at this and learn to maximise your efficiency. It is not about being a hero and aiming for full marks – this is almost impossible and very much unnecessary (even Oxbridge will regard any score higher than 7 as exceptional). It is about maximising your efficiency and gaining the maximum possible number of marks within the time you have.

Top tip! Ensure that you take a watch that can show you the time in seconds into the exam. This will allow you have a much more accurate idea of the time you're spending on a question. In general, if you've spent more than 2 minutes on a question – move on regardless of how close you think you are to finishing it.

Section 1

This is the first section of the HSPSAA and as you walk in, it is inevitable that you will feel nervous. Make sure that you have been to the toilet because once it starts you cannot simply pause and go. Take a few deep breaths and calm yourself down. Remember that panicking will not help and may negatively affect your marks- so try and avoid this as much as possible.

Whilst section 1 of the HSPSAA is renowned for being difficult to prepare for, there are powerful shortcuts and techniques that you can use to save valuable time on these types of questions.

Section 1 is the multiple choice section. In the exam, you will be presented with several passages of varying lengths and be asked approximately 2-12 questions per passage. There is a total of 60 minutes for this section and you cannot use any of the time for Section 2 in Section 1 – you only have a maximum of 60 minutes.

The aim of this section is to test your comprehension, interpretation and deduction skills.

This tests your ability to understand the different parts of a passage. It is important to understand what constitutes a good argument:
1. **Evidence:** Arguments which are heavily based on value judgements and subjective statements tend to be weaker than those based on facts, statistics and the available evidence.
2. **Logic**: A good argument should flow and the constituent parts should fit well into an overriding view or belief.
3. **Balance:** A good argument must concede that there are other views or beliefs (counter-argument). The key is to carefully dismantle these ideas and explain why they are wrong.

Sometimes, the question requires you to consider whether an argument is 'strong' or 'weak'. All arguments include reasons (premises) which aim to support a conclusion. Here, we are considering whether the reasons provide weak or strong support.

The parts of an argument:
An argument is an untimely attempt to persuade with the use of reasons. This can be distinguished from an assertion, which is simply a statement of fact or belief.

Assertion: It is raining outside.
Argument: I can hear the continuous sound of water splashing on the roof. Therefore, it must be raining outside.

The argument involves an attempt to persuade another that it is raining and it includes a reason as to why the speaker thinks it is raining, which is the splashing on the roof. The assertion, on the other hand, is not backed up with a reason – it is simply a statement.

An argument involves a premise and a conclusion.
A premise is simply a statement from which another can be inferred or follows as a conclusion.
A conclusion though is a summary of the arguments made.

For example:
> **Premise 1:** All dogs bark.
> **Premise 2:** My pet is a dog.
> **Conclusion:** My pet barks.

The conclusion here follows from both of the premises.

Explanation

Sometimes, it will be necessary to distinguish an argument from an explanation and you will need to be careful here as it can be difficult to distinguish sometimes. In essence, an argument will always involve an attempt to persuade the reader as to a point of view. Explanations, on the other hand, do not. Explanations may describe why something is the way it is or account for how something has occurred.

For example:
1. **Explanation:** We can hear the sound of water drops because the tap is leaking.
2. **Argument:** We can hear the sound of water drops. Therefore, we need to call the plumber.

Example 1 just accounts for *why* water drops can be heard – there is no attempt to persuade the reader that there are either water drops or that the tap is leaking. The tap leaking is just asserted as an explanation for the sound of the water drops.
In example 2, the author is advancing an argument as the author is making the case to call the plumber. The premise being the sound of water drops.

Premise vs. Conclusion

- A **Conclusion** is a summary of the arguments being made and is usually explicitly stated or heavily implied.
- A **Premise** is a statement from which another statement can be inferred or follows as a conclusion.

Hence, a conclusion is shown/implied/proven by a premise. Similarly, a premise shows/indicates/establishes a conclusion. Consider for example: *My mom, being a woman, is clever as all women are clever.*

Premise 1: My mom is a woman + **Premise 2:** Women are clever = **Conclusion:** My mom is clever.

This is fairly straightforward as it's a very short passage and the conclusion is explicitly stated. Sometimes the latter may not happen. Consider: *My mom is a woman and all women are clever.*

Here, whilst the conclusion is not explicitly being stated, both premises still stand and can be used to reach the same conclusion.

You may sometimes be asked to identify if any of the options cannot be "reliably concluded". This is effectively asking you to identify why an option **cannot** be the conclusion. There are many reasons why but the most common ones are:

1. Over-generalising: *My mom is clever therefore all women are clever.*
2. Being too specific: *All kids like candy thus my son also likes candy.*
3. Confusing Correlation vs. Causation: *Lung cancer is much more likely in patients who drink water. Hence, water causes lung cancer.*
4. Confusing Cause and Effect: *Lung cancer patients tend to smoke so it follows that having lung cancer must make people want to smoke.*

Note how conjunctives like hence, thus, therefore, and it follows, give you a clue as to when a conclusion is being stated. More examples of these include: "it follows that, implies that, whence, entails that".
Similarly, words like "because, as indicated by, in that, given that, due to the fact that" usually identify premises.

Assumptions

It is important to be able to identify assumptions in a passage as questions frequently ask to identify these.

An assumption is a reasonable assertion that can be made based on the available evidence.

A crucial difference between an assumption and a premise is that a premise is normally mentioned in the passage, whereas an assumption is not. A useful way to consider whether there is a particular assumption in the passage is to consider whether the conclusion relies on it to work – i.e. if the assumption is taken away, does that affect the conclusion? If it does, then it's an assumption.

> *Top tip!* Don't get confused between premises and assumptions. A **premise** is a statement that is explicitly stated in the passage. An **assumption** is an inference that is made from the passage.

Fact vs. Opinion

Sometimes you will be required to distinguish between a fact and an opinion. A fact is something that can be tested to be true or false. An opinion, on the other hand, cannot be tested to be true or false – it is someone's view on something and is a value judgement.

For example: "Tuition fees were reduced by the Welsh government in 2012. Many viewed this as a fair outcome."
Fact: Tuition fees were reduced by the Welsh government.
Opinion: It is a fair outcome.
> What one person sees as being 'fair' may not be 'fair' to another person – even if many people see a particular policy as fair. It is a normative statement that cannot be tested as true or false.

Correlation vs. Causation

Just because two incidents or events have occurred does not mean that one has caused the other. For example: "French people are known for having a glass of wine with dinner and they have a larger life expectancy than we do. Therefore, we should consume wine to be healthier."

This argument is flawed. There are 2 events: (i) French people known for having wine and (ii) French people having a larger life expectancy. There is no suggestion in the extract that (i) wine is causally related to (ii) or that having wine actually leads to a longer life. Accordingly, in itself, the premises do not adequately support the conclusion – there could be other reasons such as diet or exercise.

Approaching Section 1

The Passage

Take every fact in the passage as true and your answer must be based on the information in the passage only – so do not use your own knowledge, even if you feel that you personally know the topic. For example, if the question asks who the first person was to walk on the moon, then states "the three crew members of the first lunar mission were Edwin Aldrin, Neil Armstrong, and Michael Collins". The correct answer is "cannot tell" – even though you know it was Neil Armstrong and see his name, the passage itself does not tell you who left the landing craft first. Likewise, if there is a quotation or an extract from a book which is factually inaccurate, you should answer based on the information available to you rather than what you know to be true.

Read the Questions First

Different strategies work well for different people but indeed, having a look at the questions before going through the passage can help you focus on the important details in the passage in the first reading of it, thereby saving you time. It's best to try this strategy with some of the passages in this book to see if it works for you.

Timing

Even if you finish the questions before 60 minutes run out, you **cannot** use any of this extra time on Section 2 – you can only use this 60 minutes on Section 1 so you might as well go back through any questions that you found difficult or whether you were uncertain in any areas.

Common Types of Questions

- What unstated assumption is being made?
- Which of the following is an assertion?
- What is the main idea in the passage?
- What is the main argument in the passage?
- Which of the following is an argument in favour of...?
- What is meant by?
- What conclusion is reached by the author?
- Which of the following weakens or strengthens the writer's argument?
- Which of the following is an assertion of fact?

Reading Non-Fiction

As well as critically analysing the passages in the book, a brilliant preparation for the HSPSAA is to engage in further non-fiction reading and to consider some of the following questions:
- What issues are being raised?
- What assumptions are made?
- What is the conclusion?
- Is there adequate support for the conclusion?
- Whose perspective is it coming from?
- How would you create a counter-argument?

Critically reading non-fiction, such as in a quality newspaper, will not only help improve your Section 1 performance but would also improve your knowledge bank for the Section 2 essay.

Top tip! Though it might sound counter-intuitive, it's best to read the question *before* reading the passage. Then you'll have a much better idea of what you're looking for and are therefore more likely to find it quicker.

Section 1 Questions

Passage 1 – Controlled Drugs

There is a consensus among Parliamentarians that the current drug policy is simply not working. Approximately 1 in 12 adults in the UK have taken an illicit drug in the last year (amounting to 2.8 million people) and 1 in 5 young adults have taken an illicit drug. It is thus clear that the Government needs to do more. However, while it is clear that there needs to be a shift in policy, politicians cannot agree on what changes are needed.

Possessing a banned drug is a criminal offence but how can it be that all these individuals are potentially criminals? Is it moral to label these individuals as criminals? Around the world, there have been growing calls for the legalisation of drugs. In 2001, Portugal legislated to decriminalise the use of small amounts of drugs. Since then, drug consumption in Portugal has been below the European average and the percentage of young people aged 15-24 consuming drugs in Portugal has decreased. It is clear that the legalisation of drugs has not had the effect that opponents of the policy claimed it would have. Accordingly, decriminalising drugs may be a pointer in the right direction for the UK.

A key justification for criminalising the possession of drugs is that it would reduce the propensity of drug consumption (or deter people from consuming drugs). However, there is no strong evidence to support this notion. Once a person is in possession of a controlled drug, they have committed a criminal offence, yet this has not deterred the 2.8 million users. Further, a study by the European Union's Drugs Monitoring Agency found no correlation between harsher punishments for drug offences and lower drug consumption. This makes the argument for legalisation much more compelling.

Moreover, drug consumption in itself is a victimless crime in that it doesn't harm anyone apart from the drug user. Furthermore, the majority of users only consume drugs in small amounts which are unlikely to harm themselves. Any negative health effects that can be incurred are limited to the individual. This is in contrast to smoking, where 'passive smoking' can have a serious impact on others.

Opponents of legalisation have suggested that a drug addiction can lead to other crimes, such as theft and robbery, as the individual resorts to secondary crimes to fund their expensive addiction. Accordingly, they argue that taking controlled drugs can be criminogenic. However, this misses the point. The underlying reason for which individuals participate in such secondary crimes (e.g. robbery or theft) is the very high prices of controlled drugs, which are, in turn, a consequence of their prohibition. The very fact that they are illegal means that only criminal gangs end up supplying the controlled drugs, leading to the high prices. If the prohibition is removed, the increase in supply would reduce the price of the drugs and thus, reduce the 'need' to resort to crimes such as theft or robbery.

Legalisation is preferable to criminalisation but that is not to say that legalisation alone would suffice. Excess drug use should be seen as a public health issue, rather than a problem for the criminal law. While a drug addiction can lead to medical issues, so too can excess alcohol. Is it not incoherent for a society to allow any amount of alcohol consumption and yet totally prohibit the smallest consumption of controlled drugs? Accordingly, the freedom that individuals have to choose whether to consume alcohol should be accorded to them in regard to drugs.

1. What is the meaning of **criminogenic** in its context in this passage?
   A. That consuming a controlled drug is a crime
   B. That taking controlled drugs can lead to other crimes being committed
   C. That taking controlled drugs is a victimless crime
   D. That criminalisation is not the best response to reduce the consumption of drugs
   E. Crimes such as theft or robbery

2. Which of the following is presented as being *paradoxical* by the author?
   A. That smoking is not prohibited and yet drugs are prohibited
   B. That alcohol is not prohibited and yet drugs are prohibited
   C. That drug consumption is a victimless crime
   D. That it is not drugs per se that lead to robbery or theft but the high prices of the drugs
   E. That a justification for criminalising drugs is to reduce the consumption of drugs but there is no strong evidence to support that point

3. What is the main argument in the passage?
   A. Drug use is a public health issue, rather than a problem for the criminal law
   B. Drug consumption is victimless
   C. Drug consumption is not criminogenic
   D. That controlled drugs should be regulated
   E. That controlled drugs should be legalised

4. What practical effect does the author believe would come about if the consumption of drugs were legalised?
   A. Drug consumption would fall
   B. Drug consumption would increase
   C. Drug users would take part in fewer secondary crimes (such as robbery and theft)
   D. It makes society fairer
   E. Drug use would be seen as a public health issue

5. Which of the following would most weaken the author's main argument?
   A. Drug consumption has a tendency to increase one's propensity for violence
   B. Criminalisation is moral
   C. Drugs have more negative health effects than alcohol
   D. Drug dealers could turn to other crimes – such as people trafficking
   E. It is not clear that there isn't a deterrent effect of criminalisation

Passage 2 – Sweeney Todd

Despite the fact that some associate musicals with cheesy joy, the genre is not limited to gleeful stories, as can be demonstrated by the macabre musical, 'Sweeney Todd'. The original story of the murderous barber appears in a Victorian penny dreadful, 'The String of Pearls: A Romance'. The penny dreadful material was adapted for the 19th century stage, and in the 20th century was adapted into two separate melodramas, before the story was taken up by Stephen Sondheim and Hugh Wheeler. The pair turned it into a new musical, which has since been performed across the globe and been adapted into a film starring Johnny Depp.

Sondheim and Wheeler's drama tells a disturbing narrative: the protagonist, falsely accused of a crime by a crooked judge, escapes from Australia to be told that his wife was raped by that same man of the court. In response, she has committed suicide, and her daughter - Todd's daughter - has been made the ward of the judge. The eponymous figure ultimately goes on a killing spree, vowing vengeance against the people who have wronged him but also declaring 'we all deserve to die', and acting on this belief by killing many of his clients; men who come to his barbershop. His new partner in crime, Mrs Lovett, comes up with the idea of turning the bodies of his victims into the filling of pies, as a way of sourcing affordable meat - after all, she claims, 'times is hard'.

Cannibalism, vengeance, murder, and corruption - these are all themes that demonstrate that this show does not conform to a happy-clappy preconception of its genre.

Sondheim and Wheeler's musical has been adapted into a number of formats over the years, including the film 'Sweeney Todd: The Demon Barber of Fleet Street' directed by Tim Burton. The nature of a film production necessitated a number of changes to the musical. Burton even acknowledged that while it was based on the musical, they were out to make a film and not a Broadway show. Accordingly, a three-hour musical was cut into a two-hour film, which brought a number of challenges: some of the songs and the romance between Todd's daughter and Anthony (a sailor) had to be removed.

There was initially concern though as the film actors, while critically acclaimed in their profession, were not professional singers. However, that turned out to be a non-issue as the film's soundtrack received glowing reviews, in particular, Depp's voice which received positive critical appraisals.

6. Which of the following statements are best supported by the above passage?
    A. Sondheim is a brilliant musician and lyricist
    B. Most musicals deal with morbid themes
    C. Wheeler is an avid penny dreadful fan
    D. Generalisations can be misleading
    E. Film adaptations lead to fundamental changes in the storyline

7. All the adjectives below are explicitly supported by the passage as ways of describing the crimes described within it, except:
    A. Comic
    B. Culinary
    C. Vengeful
    D. Sexual
    E. Disturbing

8. Which of the following statements best sums up Todd's belief?
    A. Bad people should die so good can live and prosper
    B. Good people should die because the bad have basically taken over
    C. All men should die
    D. All humans merit death
    E. Death is unavoidable

9. Which of the following statements is best supported in the above passage?
    A. There are four themes in 'Sweeney Todd'
    B. Legal corruption is the predominate theme of 'Sweeney Todd'
    C. Several 'Sweeney Todd' themes are morbid
    D. There is nothing positive in 'Sweeney Todd'
    E. Sadness is the focus of Sweeny Todd

10. Which of the following is true?
    A. Mrs Lovett and Sweeney Todd are in a romantic relationship
    B. All of the songs from the musical were removed or adjusted
    C. The storyline of the film adaptation was fundamentally different to the musical
    D. The film did not receive positive critical acclaim
    E. The film actors did not have professional musical experience

Passage 3 – Youth Unemployment

Youth Unemployment -that is: those young people who are in search of work but are unable to get into work -is disturbingly high. The current youth unemployment figure for the UK is at an unsettling 12%. This is much higher than that of other developed countries such as Germany and Switzerland and the societal implications of this are greater than what the politicians acknowledge. The longer a young person is unemployed, the less likely they are to find a job at all. This has destructive effects on the country: it increases the government's spending on welfare pay-outs, reduces the economy's capacity and increases the likelihood of crime. The personal impact of youth unemployment is equally devastating; lower quality of life, low self-esteem, and lack of confidence and even depression, which can lead to a never-ending cycle of unemployment. It is, thus, clear that youth unemployment is a dangerous virus that demands immediate government attention.

There are a number of reasons for the high youth unemployment rate, such as the sluggish state of the economy and the global financial crash in 2007/08. When the economy is not doing well, businesses tend to lay off workers in response to a lack of sales. This happened in 2008 when the economy slumped and unemployment drastically increased. Since then, the economy has only recovered lethargically.

However, this alone does not account for the entirety of the youth unemployment rate. Since the economic slump of 2008, total unemployment has reduced to 5.4%, while youth unemployment is at a much higher 12%. Why is there such a big difference? Is it just an inherent feature of society? Do businesses not want young people? A number of young people report that there aren't enough jobs for them. Yet at the same time, businesses say they are desperate to find skilled young people. They just can't find young people with the right skills to suit their needs. For example, Dulux, the paint manufacturer, has pointed out that there simply aren't enough skilled painters and decorators. In London, two-thirds of construction firms have had to turn down work as they don't have enough practical and skilled workers. And herein lies the problem – many young people do not have the skills that businesses are looking for.

That is not to say that it is the fault of those who are unemployed. The root of the problem is the lack of courses that are geared to the kind of skills that businesses want and the existing structural inadequacies within our education system. The head of Ofsted recently pointed out that the lack of high-quality vocational courses in England is a concern. Vocational courses have traditionally been seen as a 'second-rate' option in the country, with the academic A Levels being the 'gold' standard. This view must change – not everyone is destined for academia and vocationally trained individuals have an important role in our society. Would you rather have a well-read English graduate or a vocationally trained engineer fix your central heating? Thus, the government must make high-quality vocational provision a priority. Vocational education tends to be incorrectly seen as second-rate by students and this must change. Putting an emphasis on vocational courses will address the skills shortage in the UK, make the UK more productive, and crucially improve the prospects of our young generation. In addition, the education sector and businesses should engage with each other more closely to ensure that skill deficits are addressed in the national curriculum.

A report from the Institute for Public Policy Research (IPPR) suggests that youth unemployment tends to be lower in countries where there is a vocational route into employment and not just an academic one. This shines a lot of light on the situation in the UK.

11. Which of the following is **not** a potential personal impact of youth unemployment?
    A. Lower quality of life
    B. Increases the government's spending on welfare pay-outs
    C. Lack of confidence
    D. Low self-esteem
    E. Depression

12. Which of the following is the underlying reason for the high youth unemployment rate?
    A. The global financial crash of 2007/08
    B. Not enough jobs for young people
    C. Lack of skills
    D. The head of Ofsted
    E. The lack of high-quality vocational courses

13. Which of the following is implied but **not** stated in the passage?
    A. There is a mismatch between the skills that young people have and the skills that employers are looking for
    B. Young people don't have the skills that businesses are looking for
    C. Teachers should encourage young people to undertake vocational courses
    D. Businesses should provide training to improve the skills of young people
    E. Unemployment is bad

14. Which of the following is the author's main argument in the passage?
    A. An increased emphasis should be placed on vocational courses
    B. An increase in the skills of young people needs to be brought about
    C. Better jobs for young people are needed
    D. That unemployment has caused a lack of skills
    E. That there aren't enough skilled young people

15. According to the author, what can businesses do to reduce youth unemployment?
    A. Create more jobs
    B. Increase young people's skills
    C. Engage with the education sector
    D. Train more young people
    E. Create vocational courses

Passage 4 – The English Reformation

In the early 1500s, King Henry VIII set the English Church on a different course forever. Henry was undoubtedly a devout catholic when he took the throne. Indeed, he was a staunch defender of Catholicism in the face of threats from religious reformers, such as Luther. Impressed by Henry VIII's defence, the Pope gave him the title 'Defender of the Faith'. So how did Henry come to separate from the Roman Church?

Although historians are not universally in agreement, many put Henry VIII as the key driver behind separating the Church of England from Rome. Henry was disappointed in his marriage with Catherine of Aragon as, in spite of multiple pregnancies, they only had one daughter together. Henry though was desperate to conceive a son. He had a monumental ego and was, thus, concerned about his legacy. In order to secure his dynasty and ensure that the Tudor reign remained strong, he needed a legitimate son. Accordingly, he was eager to secure a divorce with his current wife and marry Anne Boleyn with the aim of having a legitimate son with her. The English church was under the authority of the Roman Catholic Church (of whom the Pope was the leader) and in order to separate from Catherine, Henry needed to obtain an annulment from the Pope. Despite the mammoth efforts of Henry's right-hand man, he was unable to secure an annulment of the marriage from Rome, which would have been the straightforward option. It became clear that Rome was not going to budge on this and from then, Henry began to pursue a separation from the Roman Church.

Historians also point to another reason for Henry's desire to break away from Rome. He liked the idea of being the only head of the church and the supreme leader. His ego influenced many of his key decisions, such as engaging in wars abroad, and this decision was no different.

A number of historians suggest that Thomas Cromwell was the man behind the separation. Indeed, Cromwell played a significant role in engineering it. With control of the King's parliamentary affairs, he persuaded Parliament to enact a supplication pronouncing Henry as 'the only head' of the church, establishing the doctrine of royal supremacy. This was in clear conflict with Papal authority and began the process of breaking away from the Roman Church. But while it is clear that Cromwell had a vital role in the break from Rome, the obvious must still be repeated – were it not for Henry's desire of a break, there would not have been such a break.

Through a series of Acts of Parliament over two years, the break from Rome was secured and ties between the English church and Rome were severed. One such Act of Parliament in 1934, the Act of Supremacy, declared the King as 'the only Supreme head in earth of the Church of England.' This drastic change put the English church on a new course and while there were no major day-to-day changes initially, it planted the seed for the differences we see today between the Roman Catholic Church and the Church of England.

HSPSAA SECTION A — QUESTIONS

16. What was the ultimate cause of the Church of England's breakaway from Rome?
    A. Henry VIII's ego
    B. Rome wouldn't grant him a divorce
    C. Henry wanted a son
    D. Royal Supremacy
    E. Religious reasons

17. What does 'dynasty' mean in the Passage?
    A. Family
    B. Henry's control of the Kingdom
    C. Succession of people from Henry's family to the throne
    D. Exertion of dominion by the Tudors
    E. The power of Henry VIII

18. Why did Henry want a son?
    A. To secure Royal Supremacy
    B. He wanted to divorce Catherine
    C. To secure the Tudor reign
    D. Males were preferred in the 16th Century
    E. None of the above

19. Which of the following is an unstated assumption?
    A. Henry had an ego
    B. There was no opposition to the reformation
    C. The public was supportive of the break from Rome
    D. Henry needed Cromwell to make the break from Rome
    E. Henry believed that he couldn't get a divorce through Rome

20 What is the Royal Supremacy?
    A. The breaking away from Rome
    B. The idea of the King being the supreme authority
    C. The King becoming the leader of the church
    D. The authority of the Pope over the Church
    E. The Act of Supremacy 1934

Passage 5 – Charities and Public Schools

What constitutes a charity is a matter of public significance, but also an important issue in determining the taxable income a charity receives. In the popular sense, charities are seen as institutions which primarily help the poor, however, a question has been raised as to why public schools should be considered as charities considering the fees required to attend them.

In order to be classified and registered as a charity, it is necessary for an institution to demonstrate that its purposes are for the public benefit. Once accorded charity status, the institution gains a number of fiscal benefits from the government. For example, no corporation tax is paid on most types of income. In contrast, corporation tax, which currently stands at 20% of all profits, is paid by all other private businesses. The law should not allow a 'free-for-all' where any profit-making company can be a charity by just doing a minuscule charitable act, as this would have a negative impact on the public purse. Nonetheless, charitable status is highly sought out by many organisations for these reasons and has become highly controversial in the case of public schools.

Public schools charge a fee for admission, in contrast with state schools, which are funded by the Government. Accordingly, as public schools are private institutions, becoming charitable will help their finances. Whether this should be possible hinges on what acting for the public benefit means and requires in the context of education.

In 2011, the Independent Schools Council (ISC), representing public schools, sought a judicial review of the Charity Commission's guidance on what is required for a public school to demonstrate a 'public benefit'. The ISC argued that they did provide a public benefit, but they did face opposition. The Education Review Group, who helped draft the Commission's disputed guidance, also intervened in the case, advancing arguments in the trial. Ultimately, the tribunal held that the Commission's guidance was wrong as a matter of law and required them to change it. The trial judge decided that in order to operate for the public benefit, a sufficient section of society must directly benefit from the education provided, which he said must include children whose parents would be unable to afford the fees without assistance.

In the trial, a number of arguments were advanced on either side of the issue. One such argument was that independent schools are a net cost to society as they remove able pupils from state schools and present barriers to social mobility. However, the tribunal did not consider such an argument as it related to a 'political' issue, rather than a judicial one.

Further, private education provision can provide a multitude of benefits to society. Indeed, it educates the children whose parents pay for the provision. While this may not seem inherently charitable because parents are paying for the education, there are public benefits too. Firstly, the provision of education in itself is a benefit – having an educated population benefits not only the individuals through enabling them to enjoy a higher living standard, but also the general economy. More taxes will be paid and there will be less crime. That is not to say that we should ignore the gap between public schools and state schools. Indeed, state schools that are struggling should be willing to receive help from public schools and public schools should, in accordance with their public duty, offer such help.

21. Which of the following is definitely true based on the passage?
    A. Any institution that provides a public benefit gains fiscal benefits from the government
    B. Every organisation would rather be a charity than a private company
    C. If an organisation is not a charity, it does not provide a public benefit
    D. Charities may not have to pay corporation tax
    E. The law should not allow a free-for-all

22. Which of the following is required if an organisation is to become a charity?
    A. To help the poor
    B. Nothing
    C. To exist for the public good
    D. To demonstrate that the fiscal benefits gained would be for the public benefit
    E. To not make private profits

23. Who is most likely to have advanced the argument that public schools are a net cost to society based on the passage?
    A. The Independent Schools Council
    B. The tribunal judges
    C. State schools
    D. The Education Review Group
    E. The government

24. Which of the following is an opinion as opposed to a fact?
    A. The tribunal did not consider the argument that there was a net cost to society
    B. No corporation tax is paid on most types of income
    C. Public schools charge a fee for admission
    D. The law should not allow a free-for-all
    E. A charity has to demonstrate that it operates for the public benefit

25. Which of the following would have adequately supported the argument that there is a public benefit from public schools before the tribunal?
    A. Public schools educate the children whose parents pay for it
    B. Public schools provide scholarships to others who can't afford the fees
    C. Public schools can make better use of money, as opposed to it being paid through tax
    D. Public schools are better than state schools
    E. State schools can learn from public schools

Passage 6 – Amazon vs. Hachette

The public does not normally witness corporate trade negotiations or disputes. They are generally held behind closed doors and in private for the mutual benefit of the companies in the dispute. However, there was an exception in the dispute between the international publisher, Hachette, and Amazon in 2014. Both of them are powerful organisations with market power, however, this episode has shown that one is more powerful than the other.

It is first necessary to go into the background of this dispute. The sale of a book involves three main protagonists. Arguably the most important, the author writes the book. The publisher prints and distributes the book. The retailers then act as the point of sale to consumers. In the US, there are five very large publishers who have enjoyed significant market dominance. When distributing their books, publishers want them in the biggest retailers and crucially, the biggest of them all by far is Amazon. It is estimated by some that 50% of all book sales (both printed and electronic) across the US go through Amazon. It is the most dominant bookseller and, therefore, it is imperative for publishers to get their books on Amazon. In order to do this though, each publisher needs to enter into a legal contract with Amazon, which is normally a private arrangement.

In 2014, Hachette and Amazon were in negotiations to renew their contract for the pricing and distribution of Hachette's books. While the exact issues in the negotiations remain private, it became clear that the negotiations weren't going well. Amazon stopped selling a number of Hachette's books and delayed deliveries of many by weeks. Famous books such as those by *JK Rowling* were delayed. Was this just business? Or did Amazon go too far? It infuriated both Hachette and the authors of the books that Hachette publish. It showed the length that Amazon would go to in order to get what they want. Hachette's authors, who normally stayed out of publisher-retailer contracts, weighed in and criticised Amazon. Amazon had used their enormous market power to restrict the sales of the books from Hachette to try to get their way and many authors argued that Amazon had abused their market power. However, it was only a minority of authors (and mainly the successful ones) that spoke out.

In reality, Hachette and their authors are not the innocent victims in all of this. Hachette, with their market power in publishing, conspired with the other major US publishers and Apple to fix the prices of eBooks (i.e. to keep them artificially high) in 2012. When the US Department of Justice sued, the publishers (including Hachette) made a settlement for $164m. So it's a bit rich for Hachette to complain about Amazon's aggressive price strategy.

In regard to individual authors, the major publishers haven't always been friendly either. It is a monstrous task for an up and coming author to get even a small book deal with a publisher. Publishers generally have a narrow view as to what a suitable book is and are primarily focused on what they think the monetary returns will be. Amazon, though, has taken a new step. They have introduced a suite of services that allows authors to self-publish their work through Amazon. It allows individuals to publish both an eBook and a print book. Amazon, with their vast resources, are also able to offer a 'print-on-demand' service whereby Amazon prints each book to order. This bypasses the need for traditional publishers or any need for a large pot of cash to fund a print run. Surely, this genius innovation should be applauded. It allows many more small-time authors to self-publish their works and disrupts the unfairness that the big publishers created. Yes, Amazon has excessive market power, but at least they're using it to the benefit of small authors, unlike the traditional publishers. So let them engage in whatever tactics they want to with Hachette.

26. What is the author's view as to the balance of power between Amazon and Hachette?
    A. Hachette is more powerful than Amazon
    B. Amazon is more powerful than Hachette
    C. They are both powerful
    D. The author doesn't have a view as to which
    E. They have both exerted market power

27. The author stated that it is 'a bit rich for Hachette to complain about Amazon's aggressive strategy'. What is he suggesting about Hachette's complaint?
    A. It attacks Amazon's views
    B. It's ironic
    C. It's unfair
    D. It's sarcastic
    E. It's awkward

28. What is the main conclusion of the author's article?
    A. That Amazon has a lot of market power
    B. That Hachette has a lot of market power
    C. Amazon are disruptive
    D. Amazon has done more for small-time authors than Hachette has done
    E. Amazon's actions against Hachette are just business

29. What did the author imply by the use of the word 'monstrous' in the passage?
    A. That the publishers are monsters
    B. That it's a big task to get a book deal
    C. That it is unacceptably too tough to get a book deal
    D. That authors have to work hard
    E. That authors have to act like monsters

30. Which of the following would, if true, most undermine the author's argument in the final paragraph?
    A. Amazon charge high fees to authors for their 'self-publishing' services
    B. Amazon is not the first company to offer services in self-publishing
    C. Hachette offers the same 'self-publishing' services
    D. Amazon has caused a loss to some authors from their aggressive negotiations with Hachette
    E. Amazon are taking away business from the publishers

31. Which of the following would the author most likely disagree with?
    A. It would be easier for authors to use Amazon's services than that of a traditional publisher
    B. Hachette and Amazon have a lot of market power
    C. Amazon has abused their market position
    D. Hachette has abused their market position
    E. Authors have been given a hard deal by the main publishers

Passage 7 – Online Courts

There are two main ways to resolve a private dispute concerning a question of law. Firstly, you can come to a private settlement with the person you disagree with – this can either (i) just be between the two sides of the case or (ii) involve a third party as a mediator. Alternatively, if that doesn't work, you can sue the other person and seek redress from the courts. It is well known, though, that the court system in the UK is expensive, inefficient, and not suited to the needs of the ordinary person.

Let's say, for example, that you are having an electrician complete some wiring in your house at a price of £300. You pay the electrician and he leaves, but it then transpires that he completed the task erroneously and you want your money back. How do you go about getting it back? Would you go to court? The court fee alone is £35 for each side in the case though and any legal advice from a solicitor would cost approximately £200 per hour. It must be noted that there is a well-established principle that the losing side in a civil case pays the winning side's legal costs. However, in the event that you don't win the case, you could potentially lose even more money from having to pay the winning side's (the electrician's) legal costs.

The cost is disproportionately high here in relation to the value of the claim and herein lies a flaw in the justice system. The high cost limits access to justice. The existing court process takes too long, involves too much paperwork and unnecessarily involves the use of expensive lawyers. Lord Dyson, a leading judge in the Court of Appeal (the second highest court in the UK), echoed these comments. Crucially, there are ways to make the system more efficient and the best way is to introduce an online court.

Firstly, we must accept the truth: lawyers aren't always needed for small-time disputes. We can look to eBay for inspiration. eBay is a well-renowned online auction site where private individuals can sell goods to other individuals. It is not always smooth sailing, however, and frequently disputes arise (for example, when a damaged defective item is sold). When disagreements arise, the seller and buyer are encouraged to negotiate online. If negotiation fails, eBay offers an online resolution service whereby an eBay official decides on the case and makes a binding decision. No lawyers and not even any face-to-face interaction with the eBay official. For simple matters, it would be unnecessary and inefficient to hire a lawyer to complete the task. Crucially, this means much lower costs than in a courtroom.

This system should be used by the justice system for small claims. There should be an online mediation system to allow each side to negotiate in an online discussion area.

Anyone watching the ITV hit television show, 'Judge Rinder', would realise that small-time claims don't require a lawyer. The setting for the show resembles a courtroom where small-time disputes are heard before a 'judge' who mediates between each side. The 'judge' then makes a decision that binds each side. There are no lawyers and each person represents him or herself. While there are a wealth of differences between the TV show and actual court proceedings, it does show that lawyers are not always needed to resolve disputes.

Accordingly, the Government should go one step further and establish an online court to resolve small-time legal disputes. This would involve real judges from the judiciary deciding cases online. They would review the documentary evidence submitted online by the parties and, if necessary, conduct a hearing via video link. While it would cost a lot to set up the online system, it would, in the long run, result in significant cost efficiencies both to the government and to the users of the online court.

32. Which of the following most undermines the author's argument in the second and third paragraphs?
    A. For small claims, people don't need to go to court to resolve disputes – there are alternative methods (such as private mediators)
    B. Such small cases are normally successfully settled outside of court
    C. The UK's justice system is cheaper than that of many other countries in the world
    D. The losing party pays the winning party's legal costs
    E. Solicitors fees for court cases are greater than their fees for out-of-court settlement

33. Assume that you and the plumber go to court. You each take 1 hour of legal advice from a solicitor. How much are the total legal fees for the losing side in the case?
    A. £35
    B. £200
    C. £235
    D. £300
    E. £470

34. Which of the following is an assertion of opinion?
    A. '60 million disagreements between traders and buyers are settled online'
    B. 'the seller and buyer are encouraged to negotiate online'
    C. 'this means much lower costs than in a courtroom'
    D. 'This system should be applied by the justice system'
    E. None of the above

35. Which of the following is implied but not stated about the TV show 'Judge Rinder'?
    A. Judge Rinder decides real cases
    B. The two sides are not represented by lawyers
    C. It is fake
    D. The TV show is not set in a real courtroom
    E. It is innovative

36. Which of the following was not argued by the author?
    A. That an online court should be introduced
    B. The online court should be modelled on the 'Judge Rinder' TV Show
    C. The online court should be modelled on eBay's dispute resolution system
    D. That existing legal costs are too high
    E. Lawyers are not always needed for legal disputes

37. The author argues that the justice system is inefficient. Which of the following best describes why his argument is weak?
    A. It involves a generalisation – the author only referred to small claims but this does not necessarily mean that the whole justice system is inefficient
    B. People don't have to use the justice system to reach a settlement
    C. Only one judge's approval was cited
    D. The author did not say how much the online court would cost
    E. eBay and the justice system are not comparable

Passage 8 – Cars

We live in a world of technological change and it seems that nothing is immune from it. Our phones, computers, kitchens, gardens and cars are all undergoing significant change. If businesses want to keep the custom of consumers, they must engage in technological change and find new, innovative ways to improve their products.

Ever since the introduction of the car over 100 years ago, one thing has remained constant: a human being has always driven the car. While the look, feel, and efficiencies of cars have improved enormously, cars have always required a human being to drive them. Indeed, the law requires human beings to be in control of cars. However, all of this is going to change.

Car companies – and some traditionally non-car companies – have been developing 'driverless cars' at a monumental rate. Famously, TopGear presenter Jeremy Clarkson tried an autonomous BMW around their race track in 2011. While driving on a race track is not comparable to driving on busy roads, there have been significant developments since. Google, for instance, have been testing autonomous cars on open roads in California. A key feature of autonomous vehicles is that they are capable of sensing their environment without human input.

Driverless cars are expected by industry experts to be the norm within 20 years. According to the Society of Motor Manufacturers and Traders, the market for autonomous car technology is expected to contribute £51 billion to the UK economy and over 300,000 jobs. A lot needs to happen in the meantime, though. Car companies need to rigorously test their cars on open roads and the public need to be convinced of their utility. Testing on open roads will allow companies to develop the accuracy and safety of the technology used. Indeed, such testing is essential to develop autonomous cars – how else can we be sure that they will be safe in the real world?

The current law requires a human being to be in control of a car. However, governments have issued special dispensations to car companies wanting to test autonomous cars on public roads. The UK government allow autonomous vehicles to be tested as long as a driver is ready to take over in the case of a system fault. The government has also announced that 40 miles of road in Coventry is to be equipped with technology to aid autonomous vehicles. The significance of the government's support is that it will accelerate the development of autonomous cars and will encourage worldwide car companies to set up permanent research facilities in the UK to test autonomous cars. If the UK can become a world leader in autonomous vehicles, the industry may well contribute a lot more than the expected £50 billion to the UK economy.

However, not everyone is convinced of the success of the driverless car. The CEO of Porsche, a luxury car company, recently dismissed the use of driverless cars, saying that his cars are meant to be driven. That may well be correct for the luxury car market – people want to drive the cars they spend £100,000+ on. However, it does not follow that it's the same for the rest of the car market. People will see that the benefits of autonomous cars outweigh the use of traditional cars. Firstly, autonomous cars are expected to be safer than traditional cars. For instance, a computer system can react much faster than a human to a dangerous situation. Secondly, the driver becomes a passenger and can do something else with his time – the age old saying that time is money still rings true today. This alone will encourage drivers to buy driverless cars. While people may find driverless cars strange initially, they will get used to them. The first desktop computer seemed strange but it is now virtually ubiquitous. So peculiarity should actually be an incentive to development.

38. What is the **main** point the author is making by using the first desktop computer analogy [final paragraph]?
    A. Desktop computers are strange
    B. The public should adapt to the driverless car
    C. People find new things strange
    D. People eventually adapt to new things
    E. The public will adapt to the driverless car

39. What is the underlying **assumption** that the author made in using the first desktop computer analogy?
    A. That people will adapt to new things
    B. People find new things strange
    C. Desktop computers are strange
    D. The public should adapt to the driverless car
    E. Peculiarity should actually be an incentive to development

40. What does the Top Gear autonomous BMW test suggest about the potential for autonomous cars on roads?
    A. It shows that autonomous cars can work on public roads
    B. There would not be accidents from the use of autonomous cars
    C. Autonomous cars will be well received by the public
    D. It would appeal to celebrities, such as Jeremy Clarkson
    E. None of the above

41. What is an underlying theme of the article?
    A. To describe the advent of the driverless car
    B. The autonomous car industry will contribute £50 billion to the UK economy
    C. The public will want to drive an autonomous car
    D. Development of driverless cars has been at a fast rate
    E. There are arguments for and against the adoption of driverless cars

42. Which of the following most undermines the author's argument in the final paragraph?
    A. The fact that driverless cars will be expensive
    B. Cars are meant to be driven
    C. The public would not be convinced by the safety of it
    D. A survey showed that many people are doubtful of the uptake of the autonomous car
    E. The CEO of Porsche is correct

Passage 9 – Beauchamp and Childress

Euthanasia, derived from the Greek word for 'easy death', involves the purposeful killing of a sick patient where the actual death is caused by a third party. Assisted suicide is the purposeful killing of one's self, made possible with the support of another person. So the individual takes the final action to end their life (e.g. injecting lethal drugs) but there is assistance from another person (e.g. a doctor providing the lethal drugs). Both assisted suicide and euthanasia involve at least a second person in the death whereas suicide just involves the deceased person. For this reason, assisted suicide and euthanasia are more controversial.

Beauchamp and Childress highlight four principles (Autonomy, Beneficence, Non-maleficence and Justice) that they believe should have a role in the decision-making process of medical ethics. These can conflict with one another and also, each principle can potentially conflict with itself.
Autonomy is the ability to self-govern one's own actions. The obvious point is that in order to respect autonomy, people should have the right to decide for themselves if they would like to die, for whatever reason. Otherwise, it would not accord sufficient respect to their position as autonomous human beings capable of reason.

However, when a person is mentally ill to the extent that their capacity to understand their own situation and determine their own actions is diminished, the ability to be autonomous is effectively lost. Therefore, no decisions relating to their own death should be taken by them. But still, this view is only relevant if the person is suffering from some form of mental incapacity.

However, the Society for the Protection of the Unborn Children suggests that a "patient's freedom entails a responsibility to act ethically" thereby implying a condition (or a limit) is attached to a person's autonomous abilities. Thus, they believe that refusing a patient's request for assisted suicide or euthanasia would not restrict the person's autonomy as, in making such a request, the person is not adhering to their responsibility.

However, this definition of autonomy is not universally accepted and incorporates an artificial condition. Further, it follows from the Society's argument that they would argue that suicide should become illegal.

The overruling idea is that patients should be able to make decisions regarding assisted suicide and euthanasia for themselves.

On the other hand, the principle of **non-maleficence** is that there is a commitment by medical professionals to do no harm. This may be seen as a very clear reason not to cause or assist in a death and militates against allowing euthanasia and assisted suicide. However, the principle should also be interpreted to mean: do not cause pain. Not yielding to a patient's own wish of death may prolong their suffering and, thus, result in further pain. Hence, "harm" can be interpreted in two different ways here to support opposing views.

These principles can be useful in deciding whether to allow an assisted suicide. When deciding on particular cases, certain arguments can be ruled out or be more relevant and thus, have more weight placed on them to come to an overall conclusion.

For example, the court in the case involving Diane Pretty in 2002 did not allow her husband to assist in her death. The court arguably gave priority to the principle of non-maleficence over personal autonomy. Yet still, in the case of Miss B, she won the case for her treatment to be withdrawn (a ventilator to be turned off) with the intention of letting her die without it - this is because it was different from Pretty's case. Here, the second person would not actually be 'acting' or causing harm. The hospital simply didn't act (in not providing treatment). Hence, it appears that the principle of non-maleficence had a significant weighting in both these cases as a dangerous precedent might have been set if a second party was allowed to participate in a killing because of the consequences for the exploitation of the vulnerable.

43. What does the Society for the Protection of Unborn Children assume about an intentional killing?
    A. It is not a function of autonomy
    B. It is unethical
    C. It is a crime
    D. It goes against autonomy
    E. It involves harm to the patient

44. Which of the following constitutes an explanation of why there is a gap in the author's argument that it follows from the Society's argument that suicide should become illegal?
    A. Suicide is not necessarily unethical
    B. Assisted suicide and euthanasia can't be assimilated with suicide
    C. Suicide is not illegal
    D. The Society did not argue that suicide should be illegal
    E. Suicide is not wrong

45. According to the passage, what is the implicit argument that the Society is making?
    A. Assisted suicide and euthanasia should not be allowed
    B. Assisted suicide and euthanasia are unethical
    C. Assisted suicide and euthanasia are illegal
    D. Suicide is illegal
    E. Suicide should be illegal

46. Which principle has priority according to the author?
    A. Autonomy
    B. Non-maleficence
    C. Euthanasia
    D. Assisted Suicide
    E. No principle has priority over another

47. According to the author, why did the court allow treatment to be withdrawn in the case of Miss B?
    A. The principle of non-maleficence was satisfied
    B. In order to respect the patient's autonomy
    C. It was not euthanasia
    D. The patient was not vulnerable
    E. The patient made the choice out of her own free will

Passage 10 – The IMF

The International Monetary Fund (IMF) is an international organisation, with 188 member countries whose main goal is to encourage monetary cooperation and secure financial stability across the world. It was formed in 1944 in response to the issues raised by the Great Depression in 1930. The IMF's most well-known feature is the ability to make loans to countries in need. All the member countries contribute money to a pool of funds, which can be distributed to any country experiencing difficulties. Indeed, this has saved many countries from financial ruin but the IMF's policy of attaching conditions has been severely criticised by many economists.

The IMF, among other things, operates a formal policy known as 'Surveillance', which involves reviewing each member's economy and their economic policies. The organisation then provides an assessment of each government's policies and gives suggestions as to what policies governments should take. Surveillance is also designed to warn countries of risks to their economies. In spite of this, no one at the IMF predicted the global financial crash which affected the entire world in 2007. What this made clear is that the IMF is unable to determine what the true risks in the world are. This surely would have dented confidence in the IMF and given their incompetence on this front, it would be unsurprising if countries don't rely so heavily on their advice.

When countries have financial difficulties – for example, when they have run out of money or have run up huge debts to international creditors – the IMF can step in and provide a loan. These are not the run-of-the-mill bank loans which consumers get from banks. Crucially, the IMF is the last port of call and can prevent a country from going into bankruptcy. For instance, Ireland was hit very badly by the recession, unemployment dramatically increased, the government ran out of money and they had difficulty in borrowing money. The IMF stepped in (with others) and provided a bailout loan to Ireland. This proved to be what Ireland needed and they have since made a solid economic recovery, which just shows what the IMF can do.

However, it has not always been plain sailing. Another debt crisis unfolded in Greece in 2010, where the Greek government also ran out of money. The situation was more serious than in Ireland though, as the Greek government had spent even more money than what they had, borrowed a lot of money and then they couldn't afford to meet the repayments on their loans. The IMF (and the EU) did come along to bail them out with a loan but they imposed strict conditions, such as a requirement that the Greek government reduced spending significantly. These conditions differentiate an IMF loan from an ordinary bank loan. Banks don't dictate what borrowers can spend in their lives but the IMF dictates what proportion of a loan countries can spend. Many economists criticised the IMF for requiring this as it meant that the Greek government could not stimulate their flailing economy. Indeed, the economy did get worse and the IMF must take some responsibility for it.

While the IMF has an important role to play in the world, they must not attach such strict conditions to the loans they give. Doing so can potentially make a bad situation even worse, as it did in Greece.

48. The Passage does not suggest:
    A. That the IMF could have done better
    B. That the IMF has caused some problems for countries
    C. The IMF should be replaced
    D. The IMF should be improved
    E. The IMF has been incompetent

49. Which of the following does the author portray as a positive intervention by the IMF?
    A. Giving a loan to Greece
    B. Giving advice to countries
    C. Making loans to countries in need
    D. Attaching conditions to loans
    E. Giving a loan to Ireland

50. According to the Passage, what was the root cause of the Greek debt crisis?
    A. The IMF's strict conditions on its loan to Greece
    B. The global financial crisis
    C. The government spent more money than what it had
    D. The IMF requiring the Greek government to reduce spending significantly
    E. The IMF's loan

51. Which of the following would the author be least likely to agree with?
    A. The IMF needs to change its procedures
    B. The IMF has only been beneficial in the world
    C. The IMF should have a replacement
    D. The IMF made a positive difference in Ireland
    E. The IMF made a negative difference in Greece

52. Which of the following is implicit in the author's assertion that the IMF is incompetent?
    A. The IMF should have been able to give a warning about the financial crisis
    B. The IMF should be replaced
    C. The IMF is useless
    D. The IMF failed to warn countries about the global financial crisis
    E. The IMF did not help in the Greek debt crisis

Passage 11 – The European Convention

The Human Rights Act in the UK has caused significant controversy and there have been calls from figures within the government to scrap it. While it has accorded many basic rights and freedoms to individuals, there have been instances where it has led to controversy. This has dented public confidence in it.

To understand the position, it is necessary to look at the background story. After the atrocities of World War II, European countries got together and signed the European Convention on Human Rights (ECHR) in 1950 and it came into force in 1953. There are 46 signatories to the Convention. This is an international treaty which contains a number of rights and freedoms which every person is entitled to in their countries (these rights are colloquially known as the 'Convention rights'). It included articles guaranteeing liberties such as the right to a fair trial, right to life and a prohibition on discrimination. From then on, all the States that signed up to the treaty were bound to uphold the rights of their citizens. The treaty also established a Court based in Strasbourg, known as the 'European Court of Human Rights', which can determine whether a State has breached a person's human rights and can hear cases from aggrieved citizens. If they find that a State has breached a person's human rights, they can award compensation (an award which the particular government must satisfy). So since 1953, if the UK government made a law that infringed a person's human rights, that person could take the UK government to the European Court and seek redress. However, international law operates differently to national law and UK citizens could not make a claim in the UK courts for a breach of the ECHR. They could only make a claim against the government in the European Court. This meant that people had to incur significant and unnecessary expenses if they were to vindicate their human rights. This changed at the beginning of the millennium, though.

In 1998, the UK Parliament passed the Human Rights Act, which came into force in 2000. This incorporated the Convention rights into domestic law. Crucially, this means that where the government breached the European Convention on Human Rights, UK citizens could sue in domestic courts (rather than just the European Court in Strasbourg). The domestic courts can quash government decisions and instruments that are inconsistent with the Convention rights and the Act it makes human rights a part of the law of our country.

There have been concerns though that the European Court has given too much protection to dangerous individuals. In the case of Abu Qatada, the UK government wanted to deport a terrorist suspect to Jordan to face criminal prosecution for terrorism offences. However, the European Court of Human Rights had a different say on the matter and effectively blocked the move, saying that it would be a breach of his right to a fair trial. It determined that there was a real risk of evidence obtained from torture being used in Qatada's trial in Jordan. The UK wanted to deport him nonetheless and appealed the ruling. It ended up taking over 10 years, numerous appeals, and a treaty between Jordan and the UK, by which it was agreed that evidence from torture would not be used, to send Qatada back to Jordan. In another instance, the European Court held that prisoners in the UK, who are currently not allowed to vote, should get the right to vote. Both these matters were given enormous press coverage, compared to other cases involving human rights. In particular, newspapers focused on the fact that most of the judges in the European court are 'foreign' and 'unelected'. The fact that Abu Qatada claimed £700,000 in legal aid from the government to pay for his numerous appeals further infuriated the public, but arguably that was an issue relating to the domestic government and not the Convention.

These are just two isolated cases, though. In the vast majority of instances, there have been more positive cases, which have not been reported as widely. For example, the Court has held that the security services can't shoot to kill without good reason. After 9/11, it was held that it is inconsistent with human rights to imprison a terror suspect (or, indeed, any suspect) indefinitely without a criminal charge. In 2015, the Court of Appeal held that the Convention requires the police to investigate rape allegations. Can anyone disagree with these judgements? They are just a few examples of the numerous instances in which the European Convention on Human Rights has helped give rights to the ordinary person in the UK while balancing concerns for national security. Indeed, the European Court may not be perfect – but what system (or person) is perfect?

53. Which of the following is an unstated assumption in the second paragraph?
    A. European countries were disgusted at World War II
    B. That the UK was a participant to the European Convention on Human Rights
    C. That the UK introduced the Human Rights Act
    D. A person whose human rights were infringed could sue to the government abroad
    E. The European Court of Human Rights can award compensation

54. Since which year could UK citizens seek protection of their Convention rights through domestic law?
    A. 1950
    B. 1953
    C. 1998
    D. 2000
    E. The year in which the Human Rights Act was introduced

55. Which of the following is an argument made by the author?
    A. The European Court of Human Rights were wrong in the Abu Qatada case
    B. The European Convention on Human Rights has caused endless problems for the UK
    C. The European Convention on Human Rights is not beneficial to the UK
    D. The European Convention on Human Rights has benefited UK citizens
    E. If a State breaches the Convention, they can be sued

56. According to the author, why did the UK not deport Qatada back to Jordan for over 10 years?
    A. The European Court of Human Rights didn't allow it
    B. They were unsure as to whether the European Convention on Human Rights prevented it
    C. The possibility of torture in Jordan
    D. There was a risk that evidence from torture would be used against Abu Qatada in a trial in Jordan
    E. The UK did not want to give Abu Qatada a fair trial

57. What is the author's main point about the 'more positive' cases in the final paragraph?
    A. Positive cases do not receive as much attention as the negative cases
    B. The Human Rights Act does not lead to bad outcomes
    C. The European Convention is not perfect
    D. The benefits of the European Convention outweigh the negatives
    E. The European Court is unelected

58. Which of the following would be a suitable main conclusion to the article?
    A. The UK should keep the European Convention on Human Rights
    B. The UK should not keep the European Convention on Human Rights
    C. The European Convention on Human Rights should be altered
    D. The European Court of Human Rights needs to be improved
    E. There are drawbacks to the European Convention on Human Rights

Passage 12 – Business Objectives

Most institutions in the country are businesses – shops, factories, energy companies, airlines, and train companies, to name a few types. They are the bedrock of society, employ most people in it and it is, thus, crucial that we examine their values.

The overriding objective of businesses is to make the most profit (i.e. maximise on revenue and minimise on costs). The notion was first popularly expounded by Adam Smith in his book, 'The Wealth of Nations' in 1776. Furthermore, his view was that if an individual considers merely their own interests to create and sell goods or services for the most profit, the invisible hand of the market will lead that activity to maximise the welfare of society. For example, in order to maximise profits, sellers will only produce and sell goods that society wants. If they try to sell things people don't want, no one would buy it. This is how the free market works. Indeed, the focus on profit is the basis on which companies operate and encourages them to innovate and produce goods that consumers want, such as iPhones and computers. So there are clear benefits to the profit maximisation theory.

This is a more effective society than, for example, a communist society where the government decides what to produce – as the government has no accurate way of deciding what consumers need and want. Arguably, the poverty that communist regimes such as the Soviet Union created have instilled this notion further.

However, were companies left to their own devices to engage in profit maximisation, what would stop them from exploiting workers? What would stop them from dumping toxic chemicals into public rivers? Engaging in such practices would reduce their costs of production, which would increase their profits. However, this would be very damaging to the environment. Accordingly, other objectives should be relevant. Businesses can also do other bad things to make a profit as well. For example, selling products to people who don't want or need them.

Corporate social responsibility entails other possible objectives for businesses, such as a consideration of the interests of stakeholders. A stakeholder is, in essence, anyone who is significantly affected by a company decision, such as employees or the local community. One business decision can have huge impacts on stakeholders. For example, a decision to transfer a call centre from the UK to India would likely increase profits, as wage costs for Indian workers can be much lower than that of British workers. This increase in profits would benefit the shareholders, however, it negatively harms other stakeholders. It would make many employees redundant. Here, there is arguably a direct conflict between profit maximisation and employees' interest. Nonetheless, moving call centres abroad does not always work. Given the different cultures and accents, companies have received complaints from frustrated customers. This, in fact, led BT to bring back a number of call centres to the UK.

However, the objective of profit maximisation has not always led to maximum welfare for society. Arguably, as banks sought to maximise their profits, they lent money to individuals who could not afford to pay it back. Eventually, many borrowers stopped meeting their repayments and lost banks enormous amounts. This led to a need for banks to be bailed out by the government and Lehman Brothers; one of the largest US banks that collapsed. Arguably, though, this was more due to idiocy rather than profit maximisation alone – in the end, the banks lost billions.

59. What literary technique did the author use by referring to an 'invisible hand'?
    A. A simile
    B. A metaphor
    C. An organisation that ensures that welfare for society is maximised
    D. Irony
    E. Analogy

60. Which of the following groups is a stakeholder in a business that was implicitly mentioned in the passage?
    A. Employees
    B. People
    C. Shareholders
    D. Pressure Groups
    E. Business rivals

61. Why does the author discuss the example of call centres?
    A. To argue that businesses are bad
    B. To show that call centres should not be moved abroad
    C. To show that moving call centres abroad can harm UK jobs
    D. To show the consequences of profit maximisation
    E. Because the author is against call centres moving abroad

62. Which of the following best encapsulates the author's position?
    A. Profit maximisation should be abandoned
    B. Adam Smith is wrong
    C. Profit maximisation works
    D. Profit maximisation should not be the only business objective
    E. Employees should have a greater role in businesses

63. What is Adam Smith's view according to the Passage?
    A. Profit maximisation arose because of the invisible hand
    B. The invisible hand had an important role in establishing profit maximisation
    C. Profit maximisation leads to the invisible hand
    D. Profit maximisation maximises welfare for society
    E. Profit maximisation is the best option for society

Passage 13

Global oil prices have fallen over the past year to rock bottom – from over $100 per barrel in 2013 to $30 at the dawn of 2016. At the possible peril of oil producers, there appears to be no let-up in the oil price. The ultimate reason for this is a simple matter of demand and supply. The so-called 'shale boom' in the US, where fracking was used to extract oil in an alternative way, meant that there was a lot more oil in the world – i.e. the supply of oil was boosted. This reduced the need to import oil into the US and other sellers (like Saudi Arabia and Nigeria) had to sell their oil elsewhere. However, there was no one else to sell it to and thus, to get rid of it, the price had to be reduced.

A major problem for oil companies is that the oil price reduction has drastically reduced their revenues by over 70%. Crucially, the revenue reduction has harmed the profitability of many oil companies. BP have even run a loss of £4.5 billion in 2015 – a dangerously high figure which has led them to cut 7,000 jobs. Indeed, job cuts are the staple response to low profits. In particular, many skilled North Sea oil workers have been made redundant, thereby increasing unemployment in Northern Scotland (particularly in Aberdeen). This has had devastating impacts on families, some of whom may require state benefits until new work is found. There would also be knock-on effects in the local community. As significantly fewer people have an income from work, much less money will be spent in local shops. Instead, 7,000 people paying taxes to the government will end up seeking unemployment benefits from the government. Unfortunately, there seems to be little other option for businesses like BP where their woes were brought on by the oil price. They're losing money and must cut costs, including employees, in order to survive. Otherwise, the loss-making Oil Company will eventually go bust. What now needs to happen is that the government must provide adequate support to those made redundant and sponsor retraining schemes where required.

The low oil price has caused other problems as well. Many oil businesses are highly 'leveraged'. In other words, they have borrowed significant amounts of money from banks. Such money was borrowed in order to fund new projects and new oil rigs, but they are less likely to be profitable now. If, as is the case with many at the moment, an oil company is making a loss, they will no longer be able to pay back their loans to the banks. Given this new likelihood, many loans previously seen as 'safe' are seen as significantly risky and could cause monumental losses for banks exposed to oil companies. This requires incredibly careful attention from financial regulators as this may have wider effects on the economy.

It doesn't stop there. Oil companies engage many other businesses (or contractors) to build projects or to help with maintenance. Unlike consumer businesses (like Tesco or Sainsbury) who deal with millions of customers, these contractors only deal with a few customers (such as oil companies). Accordingly, those contractors who only supplied the oil industry will find lower business and might potentially end up bust themselves (which means that they will have to make their employees redundant too).

All this will involve work for law firms. While they may get less work from advising on exploration projects and on buying oil rigs, they will, at least, get more work from administrators advising on insolvency, from banks for the restructuring of debts, and from oil companies looking to merge with one another to save on costs.

The low oil price has already had immediate impacts on consumers. Fuel (both diesel and petrol) comes from oil. Therefore, the lower oil price should influence the fuel prices as it will cost much less to produce the fuel. This would benefit consumers. Again, fuel is a significant factor in airline ticket prices so there should be a corresponding impact there too. Finally, as fuel gets cheaper, transportation costs will fall. As such costs have a significant impact on imported goods (such as electronics and computers from China), there should be price drops there too.

64. According to the author, who has the most to gain from the low oil prices?
    A. Oil contractors
    B. Business rivals
    C. The government
    D. Law firms
    E. Consumers

65. What is the immediate reason given in the passage for the unemployment resulting from the cuts made by BP?
    A. Low oil prices
    B. Demand and supply
    C. Many workers have been made redundant
    D. A loss of £4.5 billion
    E. Low revenues

66. What unstated assumption is made when the author states that the 7,000 unemployed individuals will end up 'seeking unemployment benefits' from the government?
    A. Those individuals have become unemployed
    B. The government has unemployed benefits to give
    C. Those individuals will not find work elsewhere initially
    D. That the low oil price has caused the unemployment
    E. That the low profits has caused the unemployment

67. What was the main reason for the reduction in the price of oil?
    A. Lack of demand
    B. People aren't interested in buying as much oil anymore
    C. The 'shale boom' in the US
    D. Saudi Arabia couldn't sell their oil in the US, but couldn't sell it elsewhere either
    E. The peril of oil producers

68. According to the author, why do some oil companies have little option but to make the redundancies that they have made?
    A. Low oil prices
    B. Workers are no longer useful
    C. Redundancies are necessary to boost profits
    D. US fracking
    E. Survival

Passage 14 – Nuclear Energy

Energy is ubiquitous in all of our lives, such that life without it would be very different. Where our energy comes from and the consequences of using it has come centre stage in the last half century. Non-renewable energy comes from energy sources that will run out in our lifetimes. Examples include fossil fuels: such as coal, oil, and natural gas. Accordingly, the current over-reliance on these sources is not ideal as they will run out, maybe not in our lives, but certainly in our children's and grandchildren's lives. Therefore, we must take action to develop renewable energies in order to give future generations a sustainable future.

A further and more significant consequence of fossil fuels is that they pollute the atmosphere. Their use involves the emission of carbon into the atmosphere, which most scientists believe contributes to global warming over time. Many also believe that upsetting the carbon balance in the atmosphere will lead to more unforeseen weather patterns. Given that 80% of the UK's energy came from fossil fuels in 2013, it is necessary to further develop cleaner alternatives.

Nuclear power, already an important source of energy, has been a government priority recently. In fact, in 2015, the government have even offered very significant subsidies for nuclear power with ministers proclaiming that nuclear power is the future for the UK's energy needs, being the most beneficial source of energy. The big attraction of nuclear power is that it is a clean form of energy – it does not emit carbon into the atmosphere. It just emits harmless water vapour. Crucially, the increased use of nuclear power can help the UK meet its obligations under international treaties to reduce carbon emissions. However, the use of nuclear power raises some significant concerns.

Harnessing nuclear energy involves a complex process and numerous steps to ensure that it is done in a safe manner. Nuclear materials emit dangerous radioactive material, which has the potential to kill or cause serious injury. The danger of radiation can be seen from the disaster at Chernobyl, where an explosion took place at a nuclear power plant. This led to 31 immediate deaths and an estimated 4,000 deaths due to cancer, resulting from the radiation. The surrounding area, of approximately 1,600 square miles, has been declared uninhabitable for 20,000 years. While there are significant safeguards to prevent such an accident happening again, such that we can consider nuclear power effectively safe for the most part, the risk of an accident cannot be ruled out. In 2011, another serious radiation release occurred in Japan.

Producing nuclear energy leads to 'nuclear' waste which is officially separated into three categories: low-level waste, medium-level waste, and high-level waste. High-level waste includes the by-products of the reactions inside the nuclear reactor and this stays highly radioactive, and, thus, dangerous, for many thousands of years. Accordingly, safe disposal is critical. Suitable storage is at an enormous cost and requires effective government planning. Yet it does not seem that the government always consider the long term implications of nuclear waste. In 2007, for example, the High Court quashed the government's decision to build new nuclear power stations because of inadequate and misleading consideration given to waste disposal. This is worrying. If the government were to account for the implications and the true cost of dealing with nuclear waste, they would see that it's not necessarily the 'economical' future for the UK's energy needs.

69. Which of the following is not true based on the passage?
    A. All the non-renewable energy sources emit carbon into the atmosphere
    B. Carbon emissions are harmful to the atmosphere
    C. There is currently an over-reliance on fossil fuels
    D. The UK is under an obligation to reduce carbon emissions
    E. Nuclear waste can be dangerous

70. Which of the following does the author argue the passage?
    A. Nuclear power has been a government priority recently
    B. Nuclear power stations will kill or cause serious injury
    C. Nuclear power should be made into a clean form of energy
    D. Society should develop clean renewable energies
    E. Nuclear power is economical

71. Which of the following would the author most likely agree with?
    A. Nuclear power is worse than fossil fuels
    B. Nuclear power is the most beneficial to society
    C. There should be greater focus on renewable energy sources (such as solar and tidal power) that do not create dangerous waste
    D. The government should consider the cost of nuclear waste
    E. Nuclear power is unsafe

72. What did the author refer to as 'worrying'?
    A. That the High Court quashed a government decision
    B. That the government wanted to build new nuclear power stations
    C. The high cost of dealing with nuclear waste
    D. The fact of the government giving inadequate consideration to nuclear waste disposal
    E. Nuclear waste disposal

73. Which of the following most weakens the government's argument that nuclear power is most beneficial to society?
    A. Other forms of energy are cheaper
    B. Other types of energy are important
    C. There are cheaper and cleaner alternatives
    D. The disaster in Chernobyl caused mass damage
    E. The High Court's decision

Passage 15 – Equal Pay

Figures from the Office for National Statistics show that there is a 14% difference in average pay between men and women in full-time jobs. Yet since the Equal Pay Act in 1970, it has been unlawful for an employer to pay differential wages to men and women doing the same work. So why, 45 years since then, are women earning less than men?

Essentially, it is against the law for an employer to directly discriminate on the grounds of gender. If a woman can show that they're being paid less than a man for doing exactly the same value of work for the same employer, they can sue their employer in an employment tribunal. However, the effectiveness of this has been inhibited by high tribunal fees, which act as a disincentive to women to bring forward their claims. Some have also reported fears of career progression being hindered by bringing a claim. Accordingly, it would be more effective for a governmental body to identify and bring prosecutions against employers who discriminate, rather than leaving it to individuals.

Nonetheless, direct wage discrimination does not entirely account for the gender gap in average pay in the whole of the UK.

The average salary for a male in an executive role is £40,625 whereas the average for a female in an executive role is £30,125. It does not conclusively follow that there is direct discrimination by individual employers on wages – executive roles differ from organisation to organisation and so do their pay structures.

A particular issue highlighted by the Fawcett Society is that 47% of women are in low paid jobs whereas the figure for men is just 17%. A reason for this is that women tend to be in lower paid sectors – for example, 80% of care and leisure workers are women while only 10% of those in better paid skilled trades are women. This cannot necessarily be attributed to discrimination. The reasons for entering lower paid professions are multi-factorial, and can include discrimination in recruitment, especially in traditionally male-dominated sectors. Indeed, traditional stereotypes may well permeate the career decisions of both girls and boys – traditionally, boys have tended to take up STEM subjects, particularly Physics, whereas girls have tended to take more of the Arts and Humanities subjects.

Even within sectors, women tend to occupy lower positions than men, which inevitably leads to lower salaries. Out of all the FTSE 250 directors, only 19.6% are female. Figures from HMRC further highlight that women are underrepresented in the top jobs as only 27% of women are higher rate tax payers. It is, thus, clear that women do not get as far in the world of work as men do, which is deeply concerning. Whatever the reason for the pay differential is, it needs to change as women are equally as talented as men.

While current laws may well be making a difference, they can't, in their current form, change attitudes. What can the government do about all of this? Some have suggested a mandatory minimum of women in certain roles. While this will undoubtedly help the figures, it may just be sticking a plaster on the wound. Yes, companies will improve the number of women represented in the workforce but it may not lead to the culture change that is required. It may further cause resentment and doubt as to whether those who reached those positions did so on merit.

The government has, alternatively, proposed to require any organisation with more than 250 employees to report the pay gap between men and women in their workforce. They will be legally required to show the number of men and women in each pay range, which will highlight the pay gaps within the organisation. The government then propose to create a league table of the best and worst employers. This would likely lead to significant public pressure on employers to improve the pay gaps within their organisation. Crucially, this would be more likely to stimulate the culture change required – from recruitment to promotions - while also helping the enforcement of existing laws by notifying employees of when there may be potential discrimination. If companies do not address the issue after this, it may, in fact, become necessary for the government to impose a mandatory minimum number of women in higher positions.

74. What is the author's preferred option for tackling the gender pay gap?
    A. Strengthen discrimination law
    B. Implement a reporting obligation
    C. A mandatory minimum number of women in higher positions
    D. Reduce tribunal fees
    E. The government should bring prosecutions against discriminatory employers

75. Which of the following is an argument made by the author?
    A. Women are equally talented as men
    B. Lower tribunal fees are necessary
    C. Current laws are not making a difference
    D. Maternity leave should be increased
    E. The government should prosecute employers who directly discriminate

76. Why does the author prefer a reporting obligation as opposed to a mandatory minimum?
    A. A reporting obligation will help change the culture
    B. A reporting obligation may be more effective
    C. It will reduce the gender pay gap
    D. It does not require people to pay high tribunal fees
    E. It allows the companies to take action themselves first

77. Which of the following are reasons for the differential in *average* pay between genders?
    A. Discrimination
    B. There are more women in lower paid sectors
    C. Men occupy higher positions in the same sector
    D. A, B, and C
    E. Resentment

78. What is the author's concern with the current discrimination laws?
    A. They do not make a difference
    B. The government needs to enforce it better
    C. Direct discrimination is only one part of the problem
    D. They only work in cases of discrimination by one employer
    E. The high costs of bringing a claim (high tribunal fees) under current discrimination laws

Passage 16 – Trade

We enjoy TVs, phones, computers, electronics, and clothes, but we do so at our eventual risk.

International trade is an enormous advantage to the entire world – it allows people in the world to enjoy goods made in other countries. However, it does benefit some countries more than others. The UK has for some time been a net importer of products from the rest of the world. Importing involves buying goods from abroad, whereas exporting involves selling goods abroad. Put simply, we buy more from other countries than we sell to them.

For consumers in the UK, importing may seem beneficial – we can benefit from televisions, phones, computers, food, and other cheaper goods from other countries. In particular, the development of low-cost manufacturing in China and India in the last 30 years has meant that it's much cheaper to produce goods there rather in the UK. It's not so much an innovation but more an expansion, due to the ability to pay workers much lower wages. While the UK is a net exporter of services (in particular financial services), it is a net importer of physical goods and when considering both goods and services together, the UK is a net importer.

Importing goods mean that British money is going abroad to foreign companies as opposed to British companies, but this is not a problem in itself. As long as Britain exports to the rest of the world as much as it imports, which economists call a 'trade balance', the position is satisfactory.

Oddly, even in spite of a weakening currency, the country is nowhere near to having a trade balance. In 2014, we imported £34bn more than what we exported. This means that £34bn leaves the UK each year. If that was instead spent on UK goods (rather than foreign goods), it would boost British businesses, British jobs, and reduce our reliance on debt.

Indeed, debt is a direct consequence of being a net importer. How do we, as a country, fund these extra £34bn purchases from abroad? Debt. The UK borrows a lot of money and these debts are held by foreign investors, which is fine in the short run but eventually, that money will have to be paid back and with interest.

Being a net importer (which is the same as not exporting enough) is also a symptom of a wider problem in the UK. Due to the process of de-industrialisation in the 1980s, the UK has produced significantly fewer manufactured and semi-manufactured goods. Given the lack of investment in those industries, it costs a lot more to manufacture those goods in the UK when compared to, for example, Germany. It is also a symptom of a poorer skills base among UK workers. Simply, when we are not as skilled as those in other countries, it costs more to produce things here and, thus, we have to sell our products at higher prices. In this global marketplace, people can simply get products more cheaply from other countries. This, in turn, reduces our exports.

79. What should a weakening currency ordinarily achieve according to the author?
    A. Lead to more imports
    B. Not lead to a trade balance between imports and exports
    C. Lead to a trade balance between imports and exports
    D. More trade
    E. £34bn of net imports

80. Which of the following best explains what a 'trade balance' is?
    A. When there is a balance in trade
    B. When there are no imports
    C. When exports are greater than imports
    D. When the level of exports is the same as the level of imports
    E. When there is a satisfactory level of trade

81. Why does the UK not have a trade balance?
    A. Foreign debt from abroad coming into the UK
    B. The UK's imports are much greater than their exports
    C. Cheap Chinese goods
    D. International trade
    E. De-industrialisation and a poor skills base among UK workers

82. Which of the following is the author's purpose in writing the article?
    A. To explain the UK's import and export levels
    B. To argue that the UK should not import as much
    C. To argue that the Chinese low-cost goods are bad for the UK
    D. To show that the UK have net imports of £34bn
    E. To show that the UK owes money to foreigners

83. Based on the last paragraph, why would an overseas individual buy a manufactured good from Germany as opposed to the UK?
    A. A preference for German goods
    B. Germany produces more goods than the UK
    C. The individual is German
    D. There is a lack of investment in the UK manufacturing sector
    E. The prices of German goods are cheaper than UK goods

Passage 17 – Star Wars

Star Wars has stormed back onto the box office, just 10 years after the last one. In 2012, Disney famously bought the rights to the Star Wars franchise from the original founder, George Lucas. With the intention of producing another trilogy, Disney released the first film, "Star Wars: The Force Awakens" in December 2015 to the delight of fans.

A few suggested that the film was based too much on the old style, but they were few and far between. The majority of cinema goers pronounced the film a success on social media and it immediately received positive critical acclaim. You know you've created a successful film when hard-to-please and meticulous critics give it a good rating. The actors themselves received heaps of praise as two up and coming British actors came into stardom.

The film didn't just achieve success on this front. As a result of being a box office hit, it has reached $2 billion in box office sales, one of only three films to have ever done so. According to analysts, the success doesn't stop there, though. Some suggest that merchandise sales will outstrip the takings from box office sales.

An important part of most successful films is the consumer products that go with them and Star Wars is no exception. Disney exploited the pre-existing goodwill that the first six Star Wars films built up and licensed and created a vast array of products – from toy action figures of the film's characters to remote controlled droids. Significantly, Disney did not create all of these products themselves. They have licensed the Star Wars brand to other companies, who are allowed to use the Star Wars brand on their own goods. This has meant that other companies can use their expertise to produce Star Wars related goods which Disney could not produce. Significantly, in return for using the Star Wars brand, such companies pay Disney a license fee. For example, Electronic Arts, the game software developer was granted a license to produce Star Wars video games. In return, they gave Disney $225 million.

Disney picked an unorthodox time of year to release the Star Wars film but this was another inspired decision, both in terms of film screenings and consumer products. Given the Christmas period, where parents would have been wondering what gifts to buy their children, Disney gave them a clear answer. In releasing the Star Wars products a month before the film, Disney gave fans and, crucially, parents the opportunity to consider buying them for Christmas. Unlike most children's films, many of today's parents were teenagers at the time of the original Star Wars trilogy (in 1977 to 1983) and, thus, would have had a greater inclination towards purchasing the Star Wars goods. It's clear that this merchandising strategy played out well as Star Wars merchandise sales boosted profits in their consumer products section by 23%.

Paradoxically, it seems, Disney's share price has gone down since the release of the film. It appears though that this is due to concerns about a different part of the Disney Company, such as its ESPN network.

84. Why did Disney's share price go down after the release of the latest Star Wars film?
    A. Some people did not like the film
    B. The film did not get as much revenue as expected by investors
    C. Concerns about the next Star Wars film
    D. Investors are concerned about other areas of the Disney company
    E. Disney's performance has been poor

85. Which of the following is an opinion rather than an assertion of fact?
    A. The film received positive critical acclaim
    B. Disney mobilised a commercial enterprise
    C. Many of today's parents were teenagers at the time of the first trilogy
    D. The new Star Wars trilogy is a resounding success
    E. Parents were wondering what gifts to buy their children

86. What prediction does the author specifically make about Star Wars merchandise?
    A. Other companies will produce Star Wars branded products
    B. That merchandise revenues will exceed box office revenues
    C. Parents will be interested in buying Star Wars merchandise
    D. It will make the Star Wars film a success
    E. The Star Wars merchandise will get good reviews

87. Which of the following would be a view held by the author?
    A. The Star Wars film was based too much on the old films
    B. Disney's share price should not have gone down
    C. Any successful film would have significant merchandising from toys
    D. The success of the merchandising contributed to the success of the Star Wars film
    E. The success of the Star Wars products created by other companies should not be credited to Disney

88. Which of the following is definitely false based on the passage?
    A. Disney licensed all their merchandise to other companies
    B. The film was successful
    C. The founder of Star Wars played a role in the new film
    D. The film was not a British film
    E. The film was not a success in the eyes of a few people

Passage 18 – Marriage

In 2014, the Marriage (Same Sex Couples) Act 2013 brought a revolution in society where, for the first time, individuals of the same sex could enter into a marriage. Previously, marriage was only exclusively available for opposite-sex couples (a man and a woman), a fundamental part of marriage for hundreds of years. In 2004, same-sex couples were allowed to enter into a civil partnership, being a marriage in all but name. Some see this as insignificant. Others argue that, by giving same-sex couples a different label, their relationship would be seen as different. Whether this is a legitimate difference was and is a matter of debate. In any event, Parliament took the bold step in 2013 by legislating to allow same-sex marriage. The institution of marriage has now evolved to allow both opposite-sex and same-sex couples to marry.

Some opponents of same-sex marriage argue though that marriage is, by definition, a relationship between a man and a woman. Therefore, it should remain as just between a man and woman. However, this reasoning is circular. Such reasoning follows as such: a marriage is between a man and woman, therefore, it's between a man and woman. It adds nothing to the argument at stake and does not address the question of what a marriage should be. It is an extraordinarily shallow argument.

In considering what marriage is, many opponents base their view on marriage being a religious construct. Marriage ceremonies frequently, but not exclusively, take place in churches and other places of worship. In Christianity, the institution of marriage is a sacrament. Crucially, the main denominations of Christianity do not recognise same-sex marriage. Accordingly, on religious grounds, it is opposed.

Significantly, the Marriage (Same Sex Couples) Act guarantees the availability of a civil (non-religious) marriage and allows a religious marriage if the particular place of worship wishes to allow it.

Some opponents take the position that marriage can only be between a man and a woman because of biological or 'natural' reasons. This is because, in order to procreate (i.e. to produce a child) naturally, there must be a man and a woman. However, as the courts have highlighted in a different context, the essential feature of being in an opposite-sex relationship does not necessarily involve children – a number of opposite-sex couples are married but without children. Same-sex relationships can have exactly the same qualities of intimacy, stability, and interdependence that opposite-sex couples can have. Further, a marriage cannot be nullified by a lack of children.

Proponents of same-sex marriage indeed base their argument on the view that marriage is a social construct. Accordingly, as society evolves to accept that there is not a relevant distinction between opposite-sex and same-sex couples, same-sex couples should be accorded the same rights as opposite-sex couples – i.e. to marry should they so wish.

Whether the modern institution of marriage is a religious construct or a social construct is a matter of debate. Some proponents of same-sex marriage have pointed out that marriage is no longer a religious construct, but a matter for society as a whole. Opponents though insist on the continuing significance of religion. These two views are not as inconsistent as they first seem. It is indeed true that marriage started out as solely a religious construct, with its origins being in the 12th Century.

Marriage was still a social construct though – the vast majority of society was religious and religion had a ubiquitous role in daily life. On this basis, it had significant social relevance. That's not to say that religion is not important today – it certainly still is. That said, it is not as universal now and ever since 1837, marriages need not have taken place through a religious ceremony.

What has been a constant though since the 12th Century and now is that the institution of marriage has reflected society and has continued to evolve in order to do so.

HSPSAA SECTION A — QUESTIONS

89. What is the author's belief as to the availability of same-sex marriage?
    A. It should be allowed
    B. It should not be allowed
    C. The concerns raised of same-sex marriage are valid
    D. That same-sex marriage is a religious construct
    E. None of the above

90. What is the author's concern in the second paragraph?
    A. Marriage is not just between a man and woman
    B. Marriage should not just be between a man and a woman
    C. It is illogical to suggest that marriage is just between a man and a woman
    D. The reasoning employed by the opponents' argument here was circular
    E. Marriage should be open to same-sex and opposite-sex couples

91. Which of the following best encapsulates the author's view as to marriage?
    A. It is not a religious concept
    B. Religion should not be relevant in marriage
    C. Marriage has always been a social construct
    D. Religion should not inform marriage
    E. Not as many people are religious in the 21st Century

92. What did the author imply about the state of marriage before 1837?
    A. Society was entirely religious
    B. It was only possible to get a marriage through a religious ceremony
    C. Marriage started out as a religious construct since the 12th Century
    D. It was different
    E. More individuals took it seriously

93. Based on the whole passage, what does the author imply about marriage today in the final sentence?
    A. Marriage is a social construct
    B. The acceptance of same-sex marriage is a reflection of society
    C. Religion is not relevant anymore
    D. Marriage has evolved to reduce the relevance of religion
    E. Same-sex marriage should be allowed

Passage 19 - Sugar Tax

According to an analysis in the Global Burden of Disease Study, 67% of men and 57% of women are obese or overweight. According to the study, the UK has one of the highest levels of obesity in Western Europe, which carries severe consequences for the population, health services, and the economy.

One proposal under consideration by the government is to impose a tax on sugary products, in proportion to the amount of added sugar in a particular beverage. This is particularly relevant as most adults and children consume too much sugar.

The government currently recommends that sugars should be limited to 5% of the total energy an individual consumes in a given day. This means a recommended maximum of 30g of sugar per day. Significantly, anyone who consumes a full can of ordinary coke is instantly above the recommended maximum. The government hope that their recommendations influence people's behaviour but given the high obesity rates in the UK, it is clear that it has not solved the problem. Accordingly, stronger action is clearly required but a sugar tax has led to controversy.

Being overweight and obese causes significant health issues such as diabetes, heart disease, and cancer. It not only reduces the quality of life but also one's life expectancy. It, thus, has major implications. Even though there are labels on products displaying the amount of sugar, people tend not to look at them and even when people do, they're not aware of the significance of it. Arguably, as individuals do appreciate an immediate or short-term negative health consequence of sugary food and drinks, many may not see it as a serious issue until they actually develop health problems. Not only are there serious personal consequences but the total social cost of obesity is at a mammoth £47 billion.

Imposing a sugar tax should both dis-incentivise excessive sugar consumption and make sure that those who are likely to add to the social cost of obesity contribute more to society.

It is sometimes attested that a sugar tax or any limit on sugar infringes on people's freedom, as the government is intervening in people's lives to reduce what they can consume. If an individual wants to consume sugar, they should be free to do so, with an absence of government interference. However, this argument can be countered by the fact that consumers can still consume sugary foods should they wish, they will just pay an extra tax which reflects the costs to society of obesity. Surely it is better that they pay for the health costs they cause than for the whole of society to pay, which is what currently happens. Accordingly, it would be fair to impose the sugar tax.

It is, finally, arguable whether a choice to consume sugary drinks involves the exercise of free will. Our decisions to consume say, a can of fizzy pop, are heavily influenced by advertising campaigns and the social acceptance of it. However, this does not necessarily lead to informed consent to the consequences of obesity and being overweight. A large swathe of society is ignorant of the health consequences so it appears that the public does not truly understands the risks of consuming too much sugar.

However, imposing a tax is not the end of the government's problems and as the chief nutritionist at Public Health England pointed out: obesity does not have a 'single bullet solution'. Other actions such as education are vitally important but whatever the cost of these policies, their benefits must surely outweigh the cost of picking up the pieces. It's better to put up a fence at the top of the cliff rather than an ambulance at the bottom.

HSPSAA SECTION A — QUESTIONS

94. Which of the following best accords with the main idea in the article?
    A. Obese individuals are to blame for their health consequences
    B. Sugar should be taxed
    C. Sugar should not be taxed
    D. There are other policies which should be done
    E. To consider the pros and cons of a sugar tax

95. Which of the following would, if true, most weaken the author's argument?
    A. A sugar tax is immoral
    B. A sugar tax affects the poor
    C. A sugar tax would lead to public protest
    D. A sugar tax would increase prices
    E. People would not reduce consumption in response to an increase in prices in sugary products

96. Which of the following would undermine the 'fairness' argument made by the author [sixth paragraph]?
    A. Some people would disagree with the sugar tax
    B. The sugar tax would not reduce the consumption of sugary products
    C. People are unaware of the health consequences of sugary products
    D. Sugar doesn't necessarily cause health problems in people, particularly when they consume small quantities
    E. Not everyone is ignorant of the health consequences

97. Which of the following is not true based on the passage?
    A. Around the world, more men are obese than women
    B. Social cost of obesity is estimated at £47 billion
    C. Being overweight causes health problems
    D. All cases of obesity can be blamed on excess sugar consumption
    E. Many individuals are ignorant of the health consequences of obesity

98. Which of the following is an <u>unstated</u> assumption in the passage?
    A. Sugar consumption is a cause of obesity and heart disease
    B. The social cost of obesity is £47 billion
    C. A full can of coke exceeds government sugar recommendations
    D. The government proposed the sugar tax
    E. A sugar tax will not solve all of the problems

99. Which of the following best illustrates the final sentence of the passage:
    A. The government should not provide health assistance to those who suffer from obesity
    B. The government should focus entirely on stopping people from consuming sugar
    C. Preventing a high consumption of sugar is more effective than trying to cure the health consequences of it
    D. Education is better than taxes
    E. Someone is falling off a cliff

Passage 20 – Tour de France

The Tour de France was established in 1903 to increase sales of the newspaper L'Auto, yet it went on to become the world's biggest cycle race and arguably the toughest sporting challenge on the planet. The modern version is a 23-day event, consisting of 21 days of racing where the competitors cycle at least 100 miles on each day. On half of the stages, the cyclists go up a number of mountains, including those in the Alps. Such a feat is absolutely astonishing both for seasoned fans and particularly for the uninitiated. It is, thus, easy to forget that the competitors themselves are human. Crowds line the streets in support of their favourite cyclists or just to see the spectacle. It is something that the whole of France and the world of cycling gets behind. So its humble beginnings would naturally surprise most people.

While the exact route of the Tour de France changes from year to year, the finish line is always at the heart of Paris on the world famous Champs-Elysées. The person with the fastest time wins the competition and is awarded the coveted Yellow Jersey.

What makes this sport even more intriguing is its structure. Approximately 200 cyclists take part and each rider is part of a team. In each team, there are nine riders. The team provides mechanical support, race support, medical assistance, massages after the race, and food specifically prepared for the demands of the race. The team's race director determines the strategy for each day of racing and for the competition as a whole. Gaining a place on a team is, some say, even harder than actually doing the race itself. The team must be convinced that you will be able to complete the course, that you're dedicated to the success of the team and if you're not going to be the team leader, that you'll sacrifice yourself for the leader.

It is not the organisers nor an official qualification round that determines who enters the competition; it is the teams. The teams have the freedom to choose who races for them. Cycling looks like a deceptively easy sport to understand – after all, what is there to a bunch of men racing around France for 3 weeks?

On flat stages, most of the cyclists tend to stay together in a group (or 'peloton' in French) for most of the day, which has a major influence on the team's racing strategy. Further, each team of cyclists has one individual designated as the team leader, which the others must support.

A significant factor in cycling is the slipstreaming effect. This effect is not just in cycling – it occurs whenever two objects move in space with one closely followed by the other. It applies to motor racing as well. It also explains why birds fly in a V-formation. When one cyclist follows another very closely, the cyclist behind saves a significant amount of energy. Conversely, that means that the cyclist in front uses up more energy. For these reasons, the cyclists tend to stay together in the races – each cyclist can take it lighter by being behind someone.

That leads on to a crucial point. The team chooses one rider to be the leader – it is simply determined on who, in their opinion, is the best cyclist at the time of choosing. The rest of the riders in the team are expected to support the lead cyclist in the race. They do this by, among other things, making sure the leader is behind them. As this happens with all teams, it is, in essence, each 'lead' rider against each other, each of whom is supported by their teammates. While this is the convention, it isn't always crystal clear how the best is chosen.

For example, when Team Sky had two very strong cyclists in 2012, a supporting rider demonstrated superior vigour on many of the stages. The leader of the team won the whole race but it was not without its controversy.

Given the extra amount of energy used up by the supporting cyclist in order to help his team leader, if they were going head-to-head, it would not be possible to say that the result would have been the same. That would have also led to a far more exciting spectacle as well. Interestingly enough, while the team leader won the race, in the end, the 'supporting rider' came 2nd, beating all the other team's lead cyclists – something unheard of in the historic sport. And yet, unlike every team leader (including his own), he didn't have the support that team leaders have.

100. Which of the following is an opinion?
    A. [The Tour de France] 'has become the world's biggest cycle race'
    B. It is the 'toughest sporting challenge on the planet'
    C. The competitors are human
    D. The route is 3000km
    E. A condition for becoming part of the team is that one would be willing to make sacrifices

101. Why does the lead rider in a team benefit from being the lead rider?
    A. The leader has the support of the team management
    B. The leader can beat the riders from the other teams
    C. The leader is the best of the rest in his team
    D. He is more likely to win the race
    E. He is dominant over his teammates

102. Why do the cyclists stay in a group in the races on flat stages?
    A. It is the best team strategy
    B. The slipstreaming effect
    C. It is the team's racing strategy
    D. To support the team leaders
    E. They are supported by riders at the front

103. Which of the following is implied but not stated by the author in the final paragraph?
    A. The correct result was reached in the 2012 race
    B. Team Sky's choice of leader was not correct for them
    C. A different result may have been reached in an equal race
    D. The slipstreaming effect meant that the supporting rider was a better rider
    E. The supporting cyclist may have been stronger in the 2012 race

104. Based on the passage, why would the supporting cyclist in the 2012 Tour de France have used extra energy?
    A. He was inefficient
    B. He was a better cyclist
    C. He was helping the team leader win, with the slipstreaming effect
    D. He was not as good a cyclist
    E. He was racing against the team leader

Passage 21 – Criminal Justice

The principle of equality before the law is a fundamental part of our justice system and the rule of law. While this has many facets, one is that people should not be treated more severely on account of their race or colour. Yet the treatment of ethnic minority individuals has been a never-ending concern due to the disproportionate numbers of ethnic minorities in prison. It has now reached the top of government and the Prime Minister has ordered a government review into discrimination against black and ethnic minority people in the criminal justice system.

Statistics from the Home Office indeed show that 25% of the prison population are ethnic minorities, and yet they only account for 14% of the UK population. Ethnic groups also receive longer custodial sentences than for white offenders. These are troubling statistics. It is, therefore, imperative to find out what the root cause of this is, and the government's review will hopefully go in depth enough to shed more light onto the matter.

Once a person is found guilty of a criminal offence, the courts then consider what their 'sentence' or punishment should be. Judges have discretion in choosing what sentences to give to offenders, even among those convicted of the same offence, and are required by law to consider a number of factors in making up their minds. For example, aggravating factors such as violence, previous offences, and pre-meditation, can increase the sentence the judge gives. Likewise, cooperation with the police may reduce the sentence. A guilty plea at the start of the trial leads to an automatic reduction of a third of the sentence. These factors explain why those convicted of the same offence can receive different sentences.

However, a study in 1992 by Roger Hood found that 7% of the over-representation of ethnic minorities in prison came from a higher use of custody than would have been predicted from legally relevant factors, which indicates discrimination in the exercise of judicial discretion. Indeed, other possible reasons also abound.

Cultural differences play a significant role. For example, admitting guilt in a criminal case (officially termed a 'guilty plea') can lead to a significant reduction in the sentence given (up to a third in some cases). Ethnic minority offenders, though, are significantly less likely to plead guilty than white offenders and are less likely to opt for legal advice. This may be a significant reason for the longer sentences. On the face of it, this does not appear to be discrimination. Given that judges are legally required to give the sentencing 'discount' for a guilty plea, it may be necessary to consider whether this discount should remain.

Finally, a black individual is six times more likely to be stopped and searched by police than a white person. The racial disparity in stop and searches are particularly disturbing given that the chances of arrest are not different for a black or white person. This may be for a number of reasons. It could be due to a police force's priority in high-crime rate neighbourhoods. However, a number of researchers have found that racial stereotypes exist, consciously and subconsciously, among police officers which could lead to a greater targeting of ethnic communities. Increased targeting, whether subconscious or conscious, would naturally lead to an increase in the numbers of ethnic minority offenders arrested. Accordingly, the significance of the disparity in stop and searches among racial groups requires urgent attention in the government's review. The government have already been encouraging police forces to reduce the disparity but it appears that more needs to be done. These figures in themselves do not conclusively demonstrate discrimination but may be indicative of it.

105. Which of the following is an opinion as opposed to an assertion of fact?
    A. The disparity requires urgent attention
    B. There is an over-representation of ethnic minorities in prisons
    C. Ethnic minority offenders are less likely to plead guilty
    D. Judges are required to give a sentencing discount for a guilty plea
    E. A black person is more likely to be stopped and searched than a white person

106. What is the implication of the second paragraph?
    A. More ethnic minorities are criminals
    B. There are a disproportionate number of ethnic minorities in prisons
    C. The government needs to find out the cause of it
    D. The statistics are not ideal
    E. There is racism in the criminal justice system

107. Which of the following is true, based on the passage?
    A. The higher sentences given to ethnic minorities is a breach of the rule of law
    B. Judges have a discretion to giving a guilty plea discount
    C. Ethnic minorities are more likely to have longer sentences than white individuals
    D. Judges consciously discriminate against ethnic minority defendants
    E. Socio-economic factors are not related to the longer sentences of ethnic minorities

108. What is the main reason for those convicted of the same offence being given different sentences?
    A. Discrimination
    B. Judicial discretion
    C. A different level of harm is caused
    D. More stop and searches of ethnic minorities
    E. The legal requirement to consider aggravating factors

109. How could the final paragraph explain the disproportionate number of ethnic minorities in the prison population?
    A. More ethnic minorities commit crimes
    B. The police are discriminating against ethnic minorities
    C. The increased targeting means that ethnic minority offenders are more likely to be caught than white offenders
    D. The chances of arrest do not differ between white and black individuals
    E. The government should act to reduce the number of ethnic minorities in prison

110. What is implied by the author in the final paragraph?
    A. There may be discrimination in the police
    B. The government needs to take further action
    C. There needs to be further investigation into the reasons for the disparity
    D. The reason for the disparity is multi-factorial
    E. Judicial discretion is not a factor for the disproportionately high % of ethnic minorities in prison

Passage 22 – Tax Incentives

Tax inversions have been on a trend throughout 2015. A well-known instance is when Pfizer, a large pharmaceutical company, made a deal to buy Allergan, a much smaller drug company which produces Botox. A tax inversion is where a company purchases a smaller company in a different jurisdiction so that it can relocate its headquarters to benefit from a lower corporate tax rate. A number of American companies have taken this route, to the annoyance of the US Government.

This also leads to another issue. A number of countries have offered competitive tax regimes or tax incentives to encourage foreign companies to set up there. A tax incentive involves the reduction or exemption of a tax liability. In particular, it appears that the UK are taking this approach in their tax policy – in 2015, the UK government announced a reduction in the corporate tax rate from 20% to 18% by 2020.

In the US in contrast, the corporate tax rate is at 35% for most companies and uniquely, it is on both the profits earned in the US and abroad. Both these features make the US rate one of the highest in the world.

Concerns have been raised about companies moving around to take advantage of competitive taxes in other countries. Such moves may well improve the profitability of companies and their returns to shareholders. However, the tax inverters still maintain their activities in the country that they left. Lower contributions from corporations mean that individual citizens have to pick up the tab and that the government has to reduce spending in society.

A further issue is that it may lead to unfairness to smaller companies, who have a limited ability to do a tax inversion, which in turn gives them a competitive disadvantage. On the other hand, though, supporters of tax inversions argue that the benefit of tax competition means that multinational companies can pass savings on to customers and invest more. The CEO of Pfizer claimed that their merger with Allergen will allow them to invest more in the US.

Proponents of low tax rates argue that regardless of geography, complex and high taxes are inefficient and stifle investment. Accordingly, taxes should be lowered and simplified in order to stimulate business activity and growth. When businesses grow, so too can jobs, wages, and prosperity generally. An incidental point is that the drive to attract business can encourage more efficient tax regimes. These can apply to both large and small business, and take forms such as the UK's wholesale reduction of corporation tax to 18%.

Famous businessman, Warren Buffett, has pointed out that on the contrary, investors want good roads, an educated and healthy workforce, and the rule of law - all of which help prosperity, but inextricably mean tax is needed.

111. Which of the following is true based on the passage?
    A. There were no tax inversions before 2015
    B. Tax inversions are bad
    C. Tax inversions always lead to more investment
    D. The Pfizer-Allergen deal will benefit society
    E. Allergen is in a different country to Pfizer

112. Which of the following is a defining feature of a tax inversion?
    A. A company buying another company
    B. Moving to another country
    C. A company making more profit
    D. A company moving its headquarters to a lower-tax regime
    E. A company evading tax

113. What is the main motivation for American companies buying companies in other countries?
    A. To expand reach to other countries
    B. To benefit customers
    C. To have lower taxes
    D. To leave America
    E. To benefit from simpler tax regimes

114. Which of the following is stated as a benefit to society of a company doing a tax inversion?
    A. Lower tax rate
    B. An efficient tax system and lower tax rate
    C. More jobs
    D. Lower taxes to both big and small businesses
    E. More businesses being attracted to the society

115. Which of the following is an argument that is implied but not stated in Warren Buffett's statement?
    A. The US should keep increasing its tax rate
    B. The UK's tax rate is too low
    C. Taxes are good for businesses
    D. Taxes should be raised
    E. Businesses should pay their taxes

Passage 23 – Black Death

In the Middle Ages, most people tended to form small communities on a feudal manor, which consisted of a village, church, and a castle presided over by a lord. Peasants typically held some land in the manor and in return, had to provide some services to the lord. While they could occupy a property, they were not allowed to leave the manor without permission.

The high mortality of the Black Death shocked medieval British society in more ways than could have been predicted at the time. Although historians disagree on the precise mortality rate, a number of estimates put the decline in population size at 50%. Perversely, this might have actually been to the benefit of the peasants that remained.

The decrease in population reduced the supply of labour and, thus, wages rose and peasants were able to demand higher wages. This allowed them to enjoy a higher standard of living. Due to the massive death rate, many vacant land holdings became available when people died without an heir. This transformed the position of peasants, as they could now move to different manors. Due to the labour shortage, the lords wanted the peasants to stay and were willing to increase wages and improve conditions. For example, some labourers were given a hot meal as opposed to a cold one. However, this increase in wage costs meant that lords could not farm as much of their demesne and had to change the way in which it was used.

This change in bargaining position shifted the economic balance of power and marked the breakdown of the feudal system. An example can be shown in Great Waltham and High Ester, where 7 in 51 marriages before the Black Death took place without merchet being paid. After the Black Death, though, this increased to 20 out of 46. Accordingly, it is clear that the power of the lords in the manorial system had weakened and they no longer held ultimate control over their peasants.

Peasants at the bottom of the social hierarchy were marked by a greater individualism. Their labour to the lord was no longer determined by their ties to the land or by custom but by market forces – i.e. which lord was offering the best pay. Given the greater availability of land, those who were doing well, such as merchants and clothiers, could also buy it and improve their status. This is remarkably reminiscent of a capitalist society as opposed to a feudal one.

Interestingly, women were valued a lot more and their wages increased. The Black Death's high mortality meant that much of the workforce was dead and needed to be replaced. However, there was not much of a transformation in society as the general attitudes towards women remained.

It is not a ubiquitous view though that the Black Death caused this change in the balance of power between peasants and the lords.

The Great Famine had already started the reduction of the population that led to increasing wages. Accordingly, some see the Black Death as an accelerator of social change, rather than an initial cause. Others also question the very basis of the view that the Black Death 'caused' the increase in entrepreneurialism among the lower orders in society. In order for a move from feudalism to capitalism to occur, there must surely be a change in attitudes (such as an increase in risk taking) – otherwise, even the death of half the population would not change things. Accordingly, some view the Black Death as merely giving an opportunity for the shift in the balance of power.

116. Which of the following fits in logically with the third paragraph?
    A. Peasants were previously tied to their manor
    B. Peasants transformed society
    C. Peasants were poor
    D. The power of the lords increased
    E. Peasants became more powerful than the lords

117. Why did women get higher wages?
    A. Women were valued a lot more
    B. Attitudes in society changed
    C. There were more women than men
    D. There was a shortage of labour
    E. The end of feudalism and a move to a capitalist society

118. Which of the following is true based on the passage?
    A. Peasants had permission to move to different manors
    B. The lords were happy for peasants to leave
    C. The Black Death caused the social change that was described
    D. The Black Death triggered the end of the manorial system
    E. Peasants were able to demand higher wages

119. Which of the following is an assumption made about the Great Famine?
    A. It reduced the population
    B. It had an impact on wages
    C. It occurred before the Black Death
    D. It was more severe than the Black Death
    E. It was a bigger cause of the shift in the balance of power

120. What is a common feature among the views in the final paragraph?
    A. The Great Famine had a role in shifting the balance of power
    B. The Black Death had a role in the shift of the balance of power
    C. The Black Death did not impact the shift in the balance of power
    D. Black Death was just an accelerator of social change
    E. Society was going to change even without the Black Death

121. Which of the following, if true, most weakens the author's argument in the fourth paragraph?
    A. In most manors, there was not a reduction in the number those paying merchet
    B. Most peasants were still paying merchet
    C. The lords still owned the land which was being used
    D. The lords still decided the wages to pay peasants
    E. The shift in the balance of power was small

Passage 24 – Cohabitation

Out of the 18.6 million families in the UK, 12.5m consist of married couples, and this has traditionally been the most common family type in the UK. However, cohabitation is on the rise, with statistics displaying an increase of 30% in cohabitation since 2004, thereby making cohabitation the fastest growing type of family in the UK. Accordingly, this should raise concerns as to whether the current legal regime for families is still suitable for society.

A difference between marriage and cohabitation is that, as a legal construct, many legal rights and responsibilities flow from the fact of being married. No additional legal rights flow from the fact of being a cohabitant.

In essence, a cohabitation is where two adults live together as a couple in an intimate and committed relationship. Strictly speaking, there is no legal definition of cohabitation – it is simply whenever people are living together in a relationship but are not married. It's more a descriptor denoting a relationship, which may be like a marriage, but is not formally one.

For example, a key difference is when one partner dies without creating a will. In the instance of a married couple, most of the property would pass to the spouse. Alternatively, the partner in a cohabitation would not automatically receive such property, unless it was stated in the will. Indeed, it is easy for a cohabiting couple to get round this by simply creating a will but thinking about the consequences of death is not particularly common among couples.

Furthermore, the process of separating is markedly different for a married couple compared to a cohabiting couple. An unmarried couple can just go their own ways and separate informally. On the other hand, separation from a marriage requires the consent of the court (although that is a mere formality) but crucially, the courts can, and frequently do, transfer property between spouses on divorce. For example, in the high-profile divorce between Heather Mills and Paul McCartney, Mills was awarded £24.3 million out of McCartney's estate. No such award would have been made had they been cohabitants.

While some have argued for such legal rights, both on death and separation, to be accorded to cohabitants, there are serious issues with such assertions. The most serious issue is that of consent. In regard to cohabitation, it is not possible to say that the parties consented to giving each other additional rights and responsibilities in respect of the other. Accordingly, it would infringe the parties' freedom and autonomy. Or would it? Campaigners retort that 58% of cohabiting couples believe their rights are the same as that of married couples anyway.

However, given that the rest of the couples surveyed do not consent to having new legal duties, surely the law should not impose that on them against their wishes. The law also becomes significantly more uncertain in giving rights and responsibilities to cohabitants: at what point do people living together become cohabitants? A legal definition would be required, which would descend into arbitrariness. In particular, it must be decided how long it would take for a couple to legally become a cohabitee. Further, to determine whether one is a cohabitee, it would likely be necessary to undertake an inquiry of a couple's relationship, which would hardly be an easy and inexpensive task.

While the status quo may not entirely reflect the public's understanding, improving the latter as opposed to forcing individuals to undertake greater legal duties and responsibilities would surely be the ideal solution.

122. How does a marriage and cohabitation differ?
    A The individuals in cohabitation are not committed to each other for life
    B The legal rights and obligations are lower for a cohabitation than a marriage
    C The courts have given more rights to cohabitees recently as opposed to married couples
    D In cohabitation, the partners can separate
    E Married couples tend to have children

123. How can a cohabiting couple put themselves on the same legal basis as a married couple in the event of a death of one of the parties?
    A They cannot under the current law
    B They need to get married
    C They need to separate
    D Write a will
    E Write a contractual agreement

124. What would the argument of the 'Campaigners' in the [final] paragraph most likely be?
    A For cohabitants to get all the same legal rights and responsibilities as married couples
    B Having legal rights and responsibilities would infringe the cohabiting couple's freedom
    C Having legal rights and responsibilities would not infringe the cohabiting couple's freedom
    D That 58% of cohabiting couples believe their rights and responsibilities are the same as married couples
    E The parties' freedoms should not be infringed

125. Which of the following policies would the author most likely agree with?
    A Making cohabitation a legal concept
    B Give cohabiting couples rights and responsibilities in regard to each other
    C Banning cohabitation
    D Require cohabiting couples to enter into a marriage
    E A campaign to raise awareness of the differences between cohabitation and marriage

126. Which of the following does the author disagree with?
    A Cohabitation
    B Legal rights and responsibilities
    C That 58% of cohabiting couples consent to the same rights as in marriage
    D Imposing additional legal rights and responsibilities on cohabiting couples
    E The £24.3 million settlement for Heather Mills

Passage 25 – F1

Formula 1, the pinnacle of motorsport, should epitomise the best racing the world has to offer and yet television viewing figures are decreasing and the outcomes of races are more predictable than ever. Worryingly, a survey in 2015 of over 200,000 fans highlighted significant disquiet over the way the sport is going. One of the top three descriptors of the sport was 'boring' and 89% of fans said that F1 needs to be more competitive. This should not be a surprise given that one team has dominated since 2014 but hopefully, this will be a wakeup call. At the same time, costs in F1 are spiralling out of control, which make it difficult for smaller teams to catch up.

F1 has tried to project an image of being environmentally friendly by requiring all teams' engines to have a capacity of 1.6 litres, much smaller than in previous regulations, and electrical and kinetic energy recovery systems in order to harvest energy that would have otherwise been wasted. Indeed, an object of this was to attract more commercial partners. In particular, if F1 regulations are more relevant to road cars, manufacturers would be more likely to enter, or remain in, Formula 1 as it would have a greater relevance to their commercial operations. A corollary of this is that costs of engines have doubled, coming into the region of £18 million for a year's supply. This is double that of the previous engines and is the biggest single expense for the teams. Such costs are significantly inhibiting for smaller teams.

It is not just the cost of engines that is large – the entire budgets of teams stretch to 100s of millions. Red Bull is estimated to have the largest budget at over €460 million with Mercedes close behind. While these large operations can add to the prestige of the teams, it doesn't necessarily add to the excitement of the sport. Arguably the latter is more important and serious issues in F1 remain.

Since the new regulations were introduced, one team, in particular, the Mercedes F1 team have by all accounts dominated the sport with very few drivers from other teams winning. While Mercedes have undoubtedly produced the best car and thus, are deserving of their success, it has led to accusations that the spectacle has become boring. It is mostly clear which team is going to win before the race has even started. This issue always abounds when one team dominates and may make a Grand Prix more of a procession than a race.

Mercedes have received criticism for their continued winning streak. Indeed, a famous driver from a rival team, Sebastian Vettel, has suggested that this is why the sport is boring. However, dominance is not a new phenomenon in F1 though, it has happened before – Vettel himself enjoyed a number of years in a dominant Red Bull with little competition from the other drivers. In 2000-2004, Ferrari dominated F1. It is thus clear that dominance is a key feature in Formula 1.

Accordingly, Mercedes should not be criticised for doing what every other team is doing, which is building the best F1 car they can. Mercedes built the best of the rest which is why they're winners. However, the tendency of F1 to produce a dominating team should not be attributed to the Mercedes car, but to the nature of some of the rules and regulations of the sport. The rules must be created in such a way as to promote competition. While the drive for environmentally friendly engines did not aim to achieve this, it did not help and may have even hampered competition.

Rule changes should include making it easier for cars to overtake, reducing engine costs and even reducing the total costs of teams. Such changes would reduce the large disparity between teams and make for closer racing. Whether the F1 rulers can make such changes depends on their will but it is in their interest too. Ultimately, change is required as should television numbers continue to drop, F1 will no longer be a draw on sponsors' and TV companies' money. In the long run, at least, F1's success is inextricably linked to the fans and the powers that be in F1 should recognise that.

127. What does the word 'corollary' mean in the context in which it is used?
    A. A benefit
    B. A consequence
    C. An incidence
    D. Cost
    E. Price

128. Which of the following is an opinion as opposed to a fact?
    A. The entire budgets of teams stretch to 100s of millions
    B. One of the top three descriptors of the sport by fans was 'boring'
    C. Engine costs have doubled
    D. F1 is the pinnacle of motorsport
    E. Mercedes should not be criticised

129. Based on the whole passage, how might the drive for environmentally friendly cars have hampered competition?
    A. It caused the dominance of Mercedes
    B. It led to slower engines
    C. It increased engine costs, which hit smaller teams harder
    D. It reduced the excitement of racing
    E. It has led to a procession rather than a race

130. To what does the author attribute the success of Mercedes?
    A. Mercedes building the best car
    B. The rules and regulations of F1
    C. The engine changes
    D. The drive for environmentally friendly engines
    E. Spending the most money

131. Why is there dominance in F1 according to the author?
    A. The racing is not close enough
    B. Mercedes' winning streak
    C. The new environmentally friendly engines
    D. Large spending
    E. The rules and regulations of F1

Passage 26 – Reparations

The transatlantic slave trade lasted approximately four centuries, and Britain played a well-known role in it. Over this period, English ships made slaving voyages to Africa, where Africans were captured and transported to the Americas to be sold as goods. David Richardson, a prominent historian, has calculated that over 3 million enslaved Africans were transported to the Americas. The Royal African Company gave the slave trade a formal royal charter and it has been argued that the slave trade was the richest part of Britain's trade in the 18th century. Karl Marx has argued that the slave trade created the financial conditions for Britain's industrial revolution but the extent of economic benefit to Britain has been heavily disputed. Slavery was formally abolished through The Slavery Abolition Act 1833 across the British Empire.

Recently there have been calls for the UK to pay reparations to compensate for the atrocity of the slave trade centuries ago. On Prime Minister David Cameron's first state visit to Jamaica in 2015, he faced calls from politicians (including the Jamaican leader) for Britain to pay reparations for its involvement in the slave trade. According to calculations by researchers, total reparations could be between $5.9 trillion and $14 trillion.

It is a fundamental moral right of anyone to seek redress for damage caused to them. However, the damage was done centuries ago so many question whether modern Brits should be subject to reparations when no actual damage was done by them. They committed no wrong.

Indeed, one line of argument is that we embrace our history in other aspects, such as the success of Britain in World War II. The British government has also apologised for tragic events such as the Hillsborough tragedy. Accordingly, when embracing our history, we should surely embrace our full history. Indeed, Germany has paid over €89 billion in reparations to compensate Jewish victims of Nazi war crimes in World War II in the 60 years after it. However, opponents of reparations suggest that this is not analogous to giving reparations for the slave trade.

If it was decided that Britain should pay reparations, critics argue that it is not clear who should be paid. Did countries such as Jamaica suffer the entirety of the damage? From another perspective, the damage was done to individuals specifically as opposed to just the countries as a whole.

In a further argument outlined by Julia Hartley-Brewer, she points out that the majority of slaves were, in fact, sold by African rulers to Europeans in exchange for goods, such as weapons. Accordingly, should the current ruling classes of Africa benefit from reparations? However, even though others had a role in the slave trade, it should not displace any responsibility of one of the main antagonists.

Some argue that it's clear that given Britain's involvement, they owe a clear and substantial debt to the descendants of slaves who were harmed. However, opponents of reparations dispute the idea that the damage of slavery continues to the present day.

132. Why might the German reparations not be analogous to reparations for the slave trade?
    A. The Nazi war crimes were more recent
    B. The Nazi war crimes were worse
    C. Victims of the Nazi war crimes themselves were being paid
    D. More died from Nazi war crimes than through the slave trade
    E. Modern Brits are not at fault for the slave trade

133. Which of the following best *illustrates* the implicit argument made when considering who Britain should pay reparations to [5th paragraph]?
    A. A company should not claim damages when its employee is injured by another person
    B. When an employee is injured, its descendants should be able to claim damages
    C. When an employee is injured, the community should benefit
    D. When a company suffers damage, its employees should benefit
    E. When an employee suffers harm, they should be compensated by the community

134. What was the author's purpose in writing this article?
    A. To argue for reparations for the slave trade
    B. To argue against reparations for the slave trade
    C. To point out and consider arguments for and against giving reparations for the slave trade
    D. To argue for the position of modern British people
    E. To argue that Britain was not wholly responsible for the slave trade

135. What is the author's view as to Julia Hartley-Brewer's point [penultimate paragraph]?
    A. African rulers were to blame for the slave trade and not Britain
    B. The slave trade was wrong
    C. It should not affect the UK's responsibility
    D. The UK was the main antagonist
    E. That it is incorrect

Passage 27 - Animal Experimentation

Animal experimentation has become significantly controversial in recent years. With the advocacy of groups such as the National Anti-Vivisection Society, public discourse on animal testing has taken on a new light. Extremist animal rights groups have taken to violent demonstrations and the harassment of employees engaged in animal testing. Indeed, the arguments for animal rights are important but extremist actions tend to shut off the oxygen for such debate. Many animal rights groups tend to believe that any animal testing is unacceptable and cruel, without being willing to consider a balanced view, though. That's not to say that their arguments are not useful, but that there must be consideration of the benefits of animal testing.

Reasonable scientists do not aim to make animals suffer if unnecessary. In fact, the law does not allow that. The current legal position, as laid out in the Animals (Scientific Procedures) Act, is more restrictive than one may first envisage. Firstly, animal testing is not allowed unless a license is granted by the government to the researcher carrying out the testing, to the particular project as a whole and for the place at which the work is carried out. When deciding whether to grant a license, there must be a clear potential benefit to either people, animals or the environment. In essence, the potential costs and benefits are weighed up. Animal rights groups even disagree with this, though. Ultimately, animal testing is not undertaken unless necessary and harm is minimised at all points in the process. Crucially, the legal position makes sure that there is a net benefit to society from the use of animals in research. Furthermore, strides in technology reduce the need to use animal experimentation.

The benefits of using animal testing cannot be understated – there are approximately 120,000 sufferers of dementia in the UK, to which animal testing is being used in the development of treatments to mitigate against the symptoms of it.

Of course, that's not to say that a blanket allowance should be given – licenses should only be given where there are no other possible treatments. Developments in technology and computer modelling have meant that the need to engage in animal testing may well reduce.

Public opinion also appears to be on the side of animal researchers -a 2005 poll by MORI showed that 89% of the public accept the need to use animals, so long as animals do not suffer unnecessarily.

In the instance of tinnitus, which affects approximately 10% of the UK population, the use of animals in research has the potential to improve the quality of lives of millions of people. Testing has involved a wire being inserted into the brains of mice and sounds being played to gauge their neurological response to sound. The mice are sedated with anaesthetic and given pain killers. Crucially, animal research does not always necessarily involve harm to animals, which makes the uncompromising position of animal rights groups untenable.

136. Which of the following is true based on the passage?
    A. Reasonable scientists do not make animals suffer
    B. Animal testing is always necessary
    C. The government considers the costs and benefits of engaging in animal testing
    D. Not enough animal testing is done
    E. Scientists are reasonable

137. What is the author's view as to the use of animal testing?
    A. Animal testing should be allowed
    B. Animal testing should not be allowed
    C. Cannot tell
    D. Animal testing is not necessary for society
    E. Animal rights groups should be banned

138. Which of the following is an opinion?
    A. Reasonable scientists do not aim to make animals suffer unnecessarily
    B. Animal testing is not allowed unless a license is granted
    C. Tinnitus affects 10% of the UK population
    D. 89% of the public agree with the need to use animals in testing
    E. There are 120,000 sufferers of dementia in the UK

139. What is the author's objection to animal rights groups?
    A. They advocate against animal testing, which is beneficial
    B. They take an absolutist position
    C. They do not understand the benefits of animal testing
    D. They are out of step with public opinion
    E. They do not help those with serious diseases, such as Parkinson's

140. Which of the following most undermines the author's viewpoint?
    A. The estimated benefit of animal research is far higher than the actual benefit derived
    B. Animals can feel harm
    C. The public is misinformed as to the ability of animals to suffer harm
    D. There are other methods of research that could be usefully used
    E. Patients may not know that they're being treated with animal-tested products

Passage 28 – Copyright

Copyright is a significant form of intellectual property right. It is a legal right that is accorded to the creator of, among other things, films, soundtracks, and original literary, artistic, dramatic and musical works. It lasts for 70 years after the death of the author and any person who copies, sells or distributes a copyrighted work without authorisation can be sued by the author. The author can claim damages for a loss of earnings and seek a court injunction to stop the individual infringing the author's rights. Breach of this would be a contempt of court, which carries, even more, consequences for the individual.

However, the relevance of copyright in the modern world has been questioned more than ever. It is meant to protect song artists, but illegal downloading is all too prevalent in the world. Indeed, within a day of Kanye West's latest album release, there were reports of over 500,000 unlawful downloads, with an estimated cost of $10 million to West. A particular concern is whether the law is now out of touch, particularly when improvements in technology have meant that enforcement of copyright is significantly more arduous. For example, it is harder to close down websites, and this allows them to operate above the law. In the meantime, record labels have been developing technology to help inhibit infringement. However, the very nature of digital products, such as songs, means that preventing the illegal use of them will continue to be laborious.

Accordingly, copyright is now more relevant than ever. Removing copyright protection would leave artists' incomes even more in peril of the morals of the population. It would legalise an immoral act and mean an even greater amount of free downloading. The fact of copyright protection indicates to society that it is wrong to download music without paying for it, or without authorisation. Removing that protection will increase unauthorised use.

Indeed, a prime justification of copyright protection is the natural rights theory, first advanced by Locke. The premise here is that every person 'has property in his own person'. Accordingly, when using your labour with things from nature, those things become yours. Using labour confers natural rights over the resultant output of that labour. Therefore, allowing copyright protection is vital to recognising those rights.

Locke's approach though is only superficially satisfying in regard to copyright protection. Many critics point out that copyrighted works, such as books and songs are not the complete creation of the author. The author's work may well have been influenced by other creators and works that had an impact on the author. Further, academics Alpin and Davies suggest that 'labour' alone is too imprecise to determine the boundaries of intangible goods.

Nonetheless, an alternate theory put forward by Hettinger may provide the answer. Based on the utilitarian theory, as founded by Bentham, Hettinger suggests that laws should promote the creation of valuable intellectual works, such as music, books, and films. Accordingly, this requires artists to be granted copyright protection in what they produce in order to incentivise the production of such works. The provision of copyright allows authors greater control over what they can do with their work – they can decide on its sale and distribution and at a price of their choosing. If anyone tries to sell their work without their consent, that person can be taken to court. However, a concern with Hettinger's view is that it is not clear whether empirical evidence exists to back this up or even whether it would be possible to acquire such legitimate evidence.

141. What have improvements in technology done?
    A. Allowed illegal downloading to be stopped
    B. Discouraged illegal downloading
    C. Made illegal downloading free
    D. Made illegal downloading unfair
    E. Allowed illegal websites to evade authorities

142. What effect does the writer believe that removing copyright protection will have?
    A. Artists' incomes would be at the peril of the morals of the population
    B. Legalise an immoral act
    C. Legalise the free downloading of music
    D. Increase the number of free downloads
    E. Hamper efforts of record labels to increase protection

143. Which of the following is a conclusion which can be derived from Locke's theory of natural rights?
    A. Every person has natural rights
    B. Every person has a right to the things that they create
    C. It would not be right to give one's own creation for free
    D. Copyright protection should be increased
    E. People's creations should not be used without their consent

144. According to Hettinger, why should copyright exist?
    A. To allow authors a fair price for their work
    B. To ensure that a person's creation receives a just reward
    C. To accord with utilitarianism
    D. To incentivise the production of intellectual works
    E. To stop people free-riding

145. Which of the following is implied but not stated in Hettinger's argument?
    A. Having control over one's intellectual creation encourages creation
    B. Author's getting paid for their works encourages creation of their works
    C. There is no evidence backing it up
    D. There is evidence backing it up
    E. Locke's justification should not apply at all

146. Which of the following is common among Locke and Hettinger's justifications?
    A. They both critique the status quo
    B. They both advocate against the use of the law to provide copyright
    C. They both suggest that there should be copyright protection
    D. Authors always want to get paid
    E. Not paying an author for their work is always wrong

Passage 29 – Tax Avoidance

The tax affairs of large corporations have taken centre stage over the last few years, and mostly, but not wholly, through their own fault. While tax is a controversial matter in itself, for corporations, it has become even more significant. Tax reduces a business's paper profits and so businesses indeed have an incentive to pursue lower taxes. There are two main ways to do this directly: tax evasion and tax avoidance. Tax evasion is the illegal reduction of one's tax liability – this can be through misreporting a company's sales or simply not paying the correct liability. Tax avoidance, on the other hand, is the legal reduction of one's tax liability and is basically where a company's tax liability is lower than it should be – sometimes this is quite subjective but it can be obvious at other times. Tax avoidance can occur through setting up offshore subsidiaries, transfer pricing and benefiting from vague tax laws.

Tax rates are deceptively clear. Each company has to pay 20% of all UK profits as corporation tax to HM Revenue & Customs. If a company does not pay the 20% tax on its declared profits, it is breaking the law. Crucially, if no UK profits are made, the company is liable for no tax. However, this is an issue given that the profits that a company can legally declare may not be a sign of their true profits. This is where tax avoidance occurs.

However, Starbucks took headlines in 2012 when Reuters pointed out that since setting up in the UK in 1998, they had paid a meagre £8.6 million corporation tax on £3 billion of sales. In a number of years, they paid zero tax. This revelation led to boycotts and protests at Starbucks stores. Indeed, they were acting within the law, but as one protester pointed out: "They've shown utter contempt for our tax system."

It is unacceptable for such companies to be paying such little tax. In particular, companies that benefit from public infrastructure, such as roads and railway, and from public services, all of which require tax. It's, thus, quite ironic that Starbucks relied on the police to protect their stores from protests and yet they contributed a pittance to the public purse.

However, a significant issue is where the responsibility for such an unacceptable situation lies. Such companies are already acting lawfully and abiding by the rules. Some even question whether companies such as Starbucks are acting immorally, given that they're 'just' following the rules. The government do indeed have responsibility for implementing rules. While it may be quite difficult in this globalised world to establish laws to reduce tax avoidance, it is still the responsibility of world governments to coordinate efficient tax policies and prevent or reduce tax avoidance.

That's not to say that multi-national companies are absolved from responsibility, though. They have benefited enormously from basing their operations in the UK – with £3 billion of revenue in the example of Starbucks. It allowed shareholders to gain wealth while not contributing to society. It is quite simply unfair. Small businesses are less able to avoid tax because they can't shift their profits to subsidiaries abroad or hire expert tax lawyers. Individual citizens also can't avoid tax. So it is quite clear that politicians and companies need to restore balance in the tax system, however hard it may be.

147. What is the difference between tax evasion and tax avoidance?
- A. The public only condemns tax avoidance
- B. Google and Starbucks have only committed tax avoidance
- C. Tax evasion is morally bad
- D. Tax avoidance is moral
- E. Avoidance is legal but evasion is illegal

148. How much profit did Starbucks declare in the years when it paid zero tax?
- A. £8.6 million
- B. £3 billion
- C. 20%
- D. Zero
- E. Cannot tell

149. Why was there a boycott of Starbucks stores in 2012?
- A. Starbucks engaged in tax evasion
- B. Starbucks engaged in tax avoidance
- C. Consumers did not like Starbucks
- D. Too many companies were acting in defiance of the tax rules
- E. Starbucks paid the wrong form of tax

150. What is the implied argument in the fourth paragraph?
- A. Companies should not prioritise profit over tax
- B. Companies should pay for the infrastructure and police
- C. Companies should pay tax
- D. The police should not have protected Starbucks stores
- E. The tax rate should reduce

151. Which of the following is a matter of opinion?
- A. The tax rate
- B. Tax evasion
- C. Tax avoidance
- D. The amount of profit declared
- E. Starbucks had £3 billion of sales in the UK

152. Who holds responsibility, according to the author, for the tax avoidance in the UK?
- A. The tax system
- B. Small businesses
- C. Tax avoiding companies
- D. Government
- E. The government and tax avoiding companies

153. Why is there unfairness in the tax system generally according to the author?
- A. Tax avoidance
- B. Globalisation
- C. Starbucks avoiding tax
- D. Multinational companies avoiding tax while individuals have to pay their way
- E. The corporation tax rate is only 20%

Passage 30 – Susan B. Anthony

At the election of President and Vice President of the United States, and members of Congress in November 1872, Susan B. Anthony, and several other women, offered their votes to the inspectors of election, claiming the right to vote, as among the privileges and immunities secured to them as citizens by the fourteenth amendment to the Constitution of the United States. The inspectors, Jones, Hall, and Marsh, by a majority, decided in favour of receiving the offered votes, against the dissent of Hall, and they were received and deposited in the ballot box. For this act, the women, fourteen in number, were arrested and held on bail and indictments were found against them under the 19th Section of the Act of Congress of May 30th, 1870, (16 St. at L. 144.), independently charging them with the offence of knowingly voting without having a lawful right to vote. The three inspectors were also arrested, but only two of them were held to bail, Hall having been discharged by the Commissioner on whose warrant they were arrested. All three, however, were jointly indicted under the same statute—for having knowingly and wilfully received the votes of persons not entitled to vote.

Of the women voters, the case of Miss Anthony alone was brought to trial, a nolle prosequi having been entered upon the other indictments. Before the trial, Miss Anthony gave lectures in all of the twenty-nine districts in Monroe County, the location of the trial, where she argued that she had a lawful right to vote. US Supreme Justice, Judge Ward Hunt, was persuaded that Miss Anthony might have prejudiced potential jurors and moved the trial to Canandaigua, Ontario County. Miss Anthony continued to give lectures in Ontario County, but the trial was not altered again and set to go ahead.

Upon the trial of Miss Anthony before the U.S. Circuit Court for the Northern District of New York, at Canandaigua, in June, 1873, it was proved that before offering her vote she was advised by her counsel that she had a right to vote; and that she entertained no doubt, at the time of voting, that she was entitled to vote.

154. According to the above passage, how many people in total were arrested due to the group of women voting?
    A. Fourteen
    B. Three
    C. Seventeen
    D. Sixteen
    E. Fifteen

155. Based on the passage only, who was definitely brought to trial over the incident?
    A. Susan B. Anthony
    B. Susan B. Anthony and the inspectors
    C. Susan B. Anthony, Jones, and Marsh
    D. Jones, Marsh, and Hall
    E. None of the above

156. Which of the following best describes initial opinions of the election officers?
    A. United by each member's personal support of the women's votes
    B. Divided in response to the women's actions
    C. Apathetic about the women's actions
    D. United by general disapproval of the women's actions
    E. Unequivocal about the legality of the women's actions

157. Which defence for Susan B. Anthony is mentioned above?
    A. She did not realise she was not allowed to vote
    B. That all people born in the USA should be able to vote for their president
    C. That gender should not prevent her vote
    D. The election officers accepted her vote, showing that the responsibility did not lie with her
    E. The previous law was wrong

158. Why did Judge Ward move the case to Ontario County?
    A. The judge was against Anthony's case
    B. The judge believed that the jury could have been prejudiced in Monroe County
    C. The judge believed that the jury was biased
    D. The judge disagreed with the content of Anthony's lectures
    E. The judge was based in the Ontario County

Passage 31-Birds

The following Passage is found in a book on nature published in 1899:

Five women out of every ten who walk the streets of Chicago and other Illinois cities, says a prominent journal, by wearing dead birds upon their hats proclaim themselves as lawbreakers. For the first time in the history of Illinois laws, it has been made an offence punishable by fine and imprisonment, or both, to have in possession any dead, harmless bird except game birds, which may be possessed in their proper season. The wearing of a tern, or a gull, a woodpecker, or a jay is an offence against the law's majesty, and any policeman with a mind rigidly bent upon enforcing the law could round up, without a written warrant, a wagon load of the offenders any hour in the day and carry them off to the lockup. What moral suasion cannot do, a crusade of this sort undoubtedly would.

Thanks to the personal influence of the Princess of Wales, the osprey plume, so long a feature of the uniforms of a number of the cavalry regiments of the British army, has been abolished. After Dec. 31, 1899, the osprey plume, by order of Field Marshal Lord Wolseley, is to be replaced by one of ostrich feathers. It was the wearing of these plumes by the officers of all the hussar and rifle regiments, as well as of the Royal Horse Artillery, which so sadly interfered with the crusade inaugurated by the Princess against the use of osprey plumes. The fact that these plumes, to be of any marketable value, have to be torn from the living bird during the nesting season induced the Queen, the Princess of Wales, and other ladies of the royal family to set their faces against the use of both the osprey plume and the aigrette as articles of fashionable wear.

159. In 1899:
- A. Women across the USA could be prosecuted for owning ornamental dead birds
- B. There was a significant rise in female arrests in America
- C. Possession of a dead gull could lead to trouble
- D. Americans responded to law by citing the use of jays as ornamentation unfashionable
- E. Delinquency across America increased

160. Ostrich feathers were seen as preferable to osprey plumes because:
- A. Ostriches are less intelligent birds
- B. Ostriches are killed for their meat, so one might as well use their feathers
- C. Queen Elizabeth has an especial love of ospreys
- D. Harvesting osprey plumes was seen as an inhumane process
- E. Ostrich feathers were of superior quality

161. Which of the following is false, based on the passage?
- A. Games birds could be possessed by citizens of Illinois all year round
- B. Possessing a bird was not illegal in every circumstance
- C. Wearing a woodpecker could lead to police action
- D. Possessing certain birds could lead to a fine or imprisonment
- E. All policemen would take action against any person wearing a prohibited bird

162. Banning Osprey plumes in the UK's army was difficult because:
- A. Many uniforms required them
- B. The Princess did not have the authority to implement the ban
- C. Her ultimate support was predominately female, and thus, their concerns seemed to have no relevance from the male domain of the army
- D. It would be hard to differentiate between other regiments within the army, who were already wearing ostrich feathers
- E. The production process of osprey plumes was easier

163. Which of the following could NOT be legally owned in Illinois, according to the passage?
- A. A live bird intended for personal ornamentation
- B. A live bird intended for fighting
- C. A dead bird of prey that had violently attacked you
- D. Feathered garments
- E. None of the above

Passage 32-Books

Gutenberg's father was a man of good family. Very likely the boy was taught to read. But the books from which he learned were not like ours; they were written by hand. A better name for them than books is 'manuscripts,' which means handwritings.

While Gutenberg was growing up, a new way of making books came into use, which was a great deal better than copying by hand. It was what is called block printing. The printer first cut a block of hardwood the size of the page that he was going to print. Then he cut out every word of the written page upon the smooth face of his block. This had to be very carefully done. When it was finished, the printer had to cut away the wood from the sides of every letter. This left the letters raised, as the letters are in books now printed for the blind. The block was now ready to be used. The letters were inked, the paper was laid upon them and pressed down. With blocks, the printer could make copies of a book a great deal faster than a man could write them by hand. But the making of the blocks took a long time, and each block would print only one page.

Gutenberg enjoyed reading the manuscripts and block books that his parents and their wealthy friends had, and he often said it was a pity that only rich people could own books. Finally, he determined to contrive an easy and quick way of printing.

Gutenberg, indeed, found this way and made the first movable-type printing press in Europe, with pieces from lead, tin, and antimony. Crucially. Gutenberg's innovation was confirmed by the production of the 'Gutenberg Bible'; the first major book printed with the movable-type printing press. With the invention came cheaper and higher quality books, thereby encouraging the development of printing presses across Europe, which in turn increased the number of books in supply. A new feature of the movable-type printing press was the advent of oil-based ink, which was more durable. This has been termed the 'Gutenberg Revolution'.

HSPSAA SECTION A — QUESTIONS

164. Which of the following reasons can be inferred from the above passage to explain Gutenberg's desire to create a new way of printing?
    A. It was a lucrative business to go into
    B. He wanted to make text more accessible
    C. He was tired of waiting for each book to be hand-written or block pressed and wanted quicker access to literature
    D. He found the current books too costly for him to continue his reading habit
    E. He wanted to spread his ideas across Europe

165. Which of the following is **NOT** mentioned as a downside to block printing?
    A. It exhausts the carver
    B. It is intricate and demands attention to detail
    C. It is a lengthy process
    D. An individual block has limited utility
    E. It requires the attention of an individual

166. Which of the following statements is definitely true according to the above passage?
    A. Gutenberg was taught to read as a boy
    B. Gutenberg's father belonged to the aristocracy
    C. Block printing was the predominant book manufacturing process whilst Gutenberg was growing up
    D. Gutenberg's family was somewhat social
    E. Gutenberg was deeply religious

167. Which of the following is false, based on the passage?
    A. Printing with the block process was a simple task of inking up the prepared block and pressing it down on a piece of paper, to make one page of the text
    B. The movable-type printing press was the first of its kind in Europe
    C. Oil based ink was not used in block printing
    D. The ink lasted for longer in books made in the movable type printing press
    E. More books were produced

168. Which of the following statements are **NOT** supported by the above passage?
    A. Manuscripts were beautifully crafted
    B. 'Manuscripts' is an appropriate name for what it describes
    C. Block printing is an appropriate name for what it describes
    D. Having well off friends was a good way to expand your reading
    E. It is probable that Gutenberg was educated

Passage 33- Norway

The following is taken from a book about Norway published in 1909:

'In a country like Norway, with its vast forests and waste moorlands, it is only natural to find a considerable variety of animals and birds. Some of these are peculiar to Scandinavia. Some, though only occasionally found in the British Isles, are not rare in Norway; whilst others (more especially among the birds) are equally common in both countries.

There was a time when the people of England lived in a state of fear and dread of the ravages of wolves and bears, and the Norwegians of the country districts even now have to guard their flocks and herds from these destroyers. Except in the forest tracts of the Far North, however, bears are not numerous, but in some parts, even in the South, they are sufficiently so to be a nuisance and are ruthlessly hunted down by the farmers. As far as wolves are concerned, civilisation is, fortunately, driving them farther afield each year and only in the most out-of-the-way parts are they ever encountered nowadays. Stories of packs of hungry wolves following in the wake of a sleigh are still told to the children in Norway, but they relate to bygone times—half a century or more ago, and such wild excitements no longer enter into the Norsemen's lives.

Yet, less ferocious animals give the people trouble enough, and amongst these may be mentioned the lynx and the wolverine, or glutton, each of which will make his supper off a sheep or a goat if he gets the chance. Of the two, the lynx is perhaps the worse poacher and his proverbial sharpness renders him difficult to catch. Not so the glutton, who, if he succeeds in crawling through a hole in the fence of a sheepfold, stuffs himself so full that he cannot get out again. I think that most of us would rather be called lynx-eyed than gluttonous, and certainly a lynx is a much handsomer beast than a glutton.

With the exception of the rabbit, all our English animals are found in Norway—the badger, fox, hare, otter, squirrel, hedgehog, polecat, stoat, and the rest of them. But besides these, there are little Arctic foxes and Arctic hares with bluish-grey coats in the summer and snowy-white ones in the winter. This change of colour is a provision of nature, rendering these particular animals, and some birds also, almost invisible among the snows. The ermine is another instance of this. In summer, he is just an ugly little brown stoat; but in winter, he comes out in pure white, with a jet-black tip to his tail, a skin worth a lot of money.'

169. Which of the following is best supported by the above passage?
    A.   The variety of birds and animals to be found in Norway is unique to that country
    B.   The variety of birds and animals to be found in Norway is common to all European countries
    C.   By having forests, a country is more likely to have a variety of birds and animals
    D.   England and Norway have similar geographical features
    E.   All Norwegian animals can be found in England

170. English people are described as:
    A.   Having been anxious about certain animals
    B.   Sceptical of bears
    C.   Living in fear of wolves
    D.   Developmentally behind the Norwegians
    E.   Worth a lot of money

171. Bears are described as:
    A.   Hunting
    B.   Scavenging
    C.   Damaging
    D.   Man-eating
    E.   Almost invisible

172. Bears are also:
    A.   Numerous in all forest tracts
    B.   Numerous throughout the North
    C.   Numerous throughout the South
    D.   At risk in parts of Norway
    E.   In parts of England

173. The Passage suggests:
    A.   The movement of wolves to the out-of-reach parts of Norway is beneficial
    B.   Wildlife currently threats Norwegian children
    C.   Regret at the loss of adventures
    D.   Norsemen particularly respect their natural surroundings
    E.   It would be preferable to be gluttonous

174. Which of the following is an opinion?
    A. It is better to be called lynx-eyed than gluttonous
    B. The ermine changes colour
    C. Norway has vast forests and waste moorlands
    D. There are a variety of birds
    E. English animals can be found in Norway

Passage 34- Colonialism

Most of the colonists who lived along the American seaboard in 1750 were the descendants of immigrants who had come in fully a century before; after the first settlements, there had been much less fresh immigration than many latter-day writers have assumed. According to Prescott F. Hall, "the population of New England ... at the date of the Revolutionary War ... was produced out of an immigration of about 20,000 persons who arrived before 1640," and we have Franklin's authority for the statement that the total population of the colonies in 1751, then about 1,000,000, had been produced from an original immigration of less than 80,000.

Even at that early day, indeed, the colonists had begun to feel that they were distinctly separated, in culture and customs, from the mother-country and there were signs of the rise of a new native aristocracy, entirely distinct from the older aristocracy of the royal governors' courts. The enormous difficulties of communication with England helped to foster this sense of separation.

The round trip across the ocean occupied the better part of a year, and was hazardous and expensive; a colonist who had made it was a marked man—as Hawthorne said, "the petit maître of the colonies." Nor was there any very extensive exchange of ideas, for though most of the books read in the colonies came from England. The great majority of the colonists, down to the middle of the century, seem to have read little save the Bible and biblical commentaries, and in the native literature of the time, one seldom comes upon any reference to the English authors who were glorifying the period of the Restoration and the reign of Anne. "No allusion to Shakespeare," says Bliss Perry, "has been discovered in the colonial literature of the seventeenth century, and scarcely an allusion to the Puritan poet Milton." Benjamin Franklin's brother, James, had a copy of Shakespeare at the *New England Courant* office in Boston, but Benjamin himself seems to have made little use of it, for there is not a single quotation from or mention of the bard in all his voluminous works. "The Harvard College Library in 1723," says Perry, "had nothing of Addison, Steele, Bolingbroke, Dryden, Pope, and Swift, and had only recently obtained copies of Milton and Shakespeare....Franklin reprinted 'Pamela' and his Library Company of Philadelphia had two copies of 'Paradise Lost' for circulation in 1741, but there had been no copy of that work in the great library of Cotton Mather."

175. Which of the following is true according to the passage?
    A. Over half of the 1750 colonists that lived on the American seaboard had genetic links to immigrants who had arrived a century ago
    B. Most of the books on board ships were Bibles and biblical commentaries
    C. The colonists had poor communication skills
    D. The colonists disliked the English
    E. Many colonists visited England after immigrating to America

176. Which of the following statements is supported by the above passage?
    A. According to Hall, America's population at the date of the Revolutionary War could be entirely traced back to 20,000 immigrants
    B. The population in the 1751 colonies was over ten times the original immigration that moved there
    C. According to Hall, in 1751, the population in the American colonies was one million
    D. According to Hall, 80,000 people led to a population of 1,000,000
    E. Most of the population on the American seaboard immigrated there

177. According to the passage, the new aristocracy that existed in the colonies was:
    A. Similar to the England's
    B. Similar to European aristocratic systems in general
    C. Not based in royal governors' courts
    D. Not based on genetic lines
    E. Based on custom

178. Which of these is **NOT** given as a reason for the sense of separation from England?
    A. Travel between America and England was costly
    B. The English saw the early colonists as backwards
    C. Travel between America and England was slow
    D. Travel between America and England was dangerous
    E. Lack of an exchange of ideas

179. What did the author mean by the word 'allusion' in the passage?
    A. An implication
    B. An illusion
    C. Deference
    D. Thoughts
    E. Reference

Passage 35 - Rorschach

When discussing his famous character Rorschach, the antihero of 'Watchmen', Moore explains, 'I originally intended Rorschach to be a warning about the possible outcome of vigilante thinking. But an awful lot of comic readers felt his remorseless, frightening, psychotic toughness was his most appealing characteristic – not quite what I was going for.' Moore misunderstands his own hero's appeal within this quotation: it is not that Rorschach is willing to break little fingers to extract information, or that he is happy to use violence, that makes him laudable. The Comedian, another 'superhero' within the alternative world of Watchmen, is a thug who has won no great fan base; his remorselessness (killing a pregnant Vietnamese woman), frightening (attempt at rape), psychotic toughness (one only has to look at the panels of him shooting out into a crowd to witness this) is repulsive, not winning. This is because The Comedian has no purpose: he is a nihilist, and as a nihilist, denies any potential meaning to his fellow man, and so to the comic's reader. Everything to him is a 'joke', including his self, and consequently, his own death could be seen as just another gag.

Rorschach, on the other hand, does believe in something: he questions if his fight for justice 'is futile?' then instantly corrects himself, stating 'there is good and evil, and evil must be punished. Even in the face of Armageddon I shall not compromise in this.' Jacob Held, in his essay comparing Rorschach's motivation with Kantian ethics, put forward the postulation that 'perhaps our dignity is found in acting as if the world were just, even when it is clearly not.' Rorschach then causes pain in others not because he is a sadist, but because he feels the need to punish wrong and to uphold the good, and though he cannot make the world just, he can act according to his sense of justice - through the use of violence.

180. Which of the following best describes 'Watchmen'?
    A. A book that contains only vicious characters
    B. An expression of despair when contemplating an imperfect world
    C. An example of how an author's intentions are not always realised
    D. A book that accidentally glamorises violence
    E. A book which highlights the ideal hero

181. Which of the following best accords with the view of the author?
    A. All heroes use a minimum of violence
    B. No hero uses violence
    C. Heroes aim to uphold good
    D. A hero should have a sense of purpose
    E. It is impossible to be both a comedian and a hero

182. Which of the following best articulates the view put forward by Jacob Held?
    A. We find dignity through just actions
    B. If one decides to behave as though the world is fair, this may lead to a discovery of self-worth
    C. It is shameful to view the world as corrupt
    D. Self-value can only be found in madness
    E. All means should be used in the pursuit of justice, including violence

183. What does the passage above argue?
    A. Rorschach breaking little fingers is preferable to the comedian attempting to rape somebody
    B. The comedian's depressing sense of humour has made him unpopular
    C. Rorschach is not actually violent
    D. Rorschach is popular because his aggressive behaviour has a moral intent, and is not just violence
    E. Violence is not a pre-requisite for heroism

184. What does the word 'nihilist' mean in the context of the passage?
    A. Someone who believes there is no meaning to life
    B. Someone who is full of anger at the corruption of society
    C. Someone who is narcissistic
    D. Someone who hates other people
    E. Someone who treats everything as a joke

Passage 36 – Gambler's Fallacy

The gambler's fallacy is a logical fallacy, where an independent event becomes more predictable the more it is repeated and, of course, takes place in the context of gambling. It can be demonstrated with the example of a dice being thrown. On the first throw yielding a score of 5, the second yielding a 5, what is the probability of another 5 coming up? Some may think it nearly impossible. Indeed, the odds are low when considering all 3 throws together but when considering just that third throw, the odds are still 1 out of 6, just as it was for the first and second throws. Crucially, each throw is independent of each other, so a previous throw has no bearing on the next one. Therefore, contrary to instinct, the independent event becomes no less independent on a second try. However, this is a frequently made mistake by gamblers.

Another name for the gambler's fallacy is the Monte Carlo fallacy, which is named after a famous example of it occurring at the Monte Carlo Casino in 1913. The night proceeded as a normal one until it was noticed that the roulette ball had fallen on black for a number of rounds. As it kept on coming on black, more and more gamblers were putting their money in - surely the ball would fall on red soon? It didn't. 26 spins in a row, in fact, fell on black, leading to losses in the millions. Gamblers believed that the odds were stacked in their favour, even after a few black runs. However, as a mathematical probability, it makes no difference how many blacks or reds there are: at each round, there's always a 50% chance of it being either black or white.

The basic laws of probability are taught at GCSE Mathematics level, so it should not be a problem for those who paid attention at school, which raises a question as to why it remains such a prevalent issue. Indeed, research has shown that sub-conscious processes may have a role to play. In the Journal of Experimental Psychology, researchers conducted a study of participants on the gambler's fallacy. The participants were split into two groups: the experimental group and the control group. The gambler's fallacy was explicitly explained to the experimental group and they were told not to rely on previous runs when making guesses. The control group was told nothing about this, though. The researchers then showed the participants a re-shuffled deck of cards and asked them to guess which shape would come next in the sequence. The results showed that the responses did not differ between the different groups, thereby indicating that the experimental group was not swayed by knowledge of the gambler's fallacy.

In particular, though, Roney and Trick showed in 2003 that grouping events, such that the next event appears as if it comes at the beginning of the next sequence, may overcome the gambler's fallacy. In the study, participants were shown a sequence of 6 coin tosses, with the final 3 flips being heads. One group were asked to predict the seventh flip. The other group was asked to predict the first event for the next sequence. Those in the former group tended to predict tails more. Accordingly, viewing independent events as a 'beginning' rather than as part of a sequence can help abate the gambler's fallacy.

185. Which of the following best explains the word 'fallacy'?
    A. A gambling addiction
    B. A belief
    C. A mistaken belief
    D. When a dice falls independently of the previous dice
    E. A lie

186. Which of the following is the best definition for the Monte Carlo fallacy?
    A. A gambling addiction
    B. The events in Monte Carlo in 1913
    C. The view that a previous event influences a future event
    D. The view that a future event is thrown into doubt by a previous event
    E. The circumstances around an independent event

187. Why did gamblers place money on the red in the Monte Carlo Casino incident in 1913?
    A. They knew they were going to get a windfall
    B. The red was more popular than the black in those times
    C. 26 spins in a row were on black
    D. They thought that the fact of the ball falling on black so many times increased their odds of winning on red
    E. They disagreed with the gambler's fallacy

188. Which of the following can be assumed about the research in the Journal of Experimental Psychology?
    A. The experimental group did not listen to what the researchers said to them
    B. The participants represented all areas of society
    C. The gambler's fallacy was tested
    D. Participants were shown at least one card
    E. The researchers were biased

189. Which of the following can be inferred from the third paragraph?
    A. The gambler's fallacy cannot be solved
    B. The gambler's fallacy was proved to exist by that research
    C. The research took place after 1913
    D. Teaching probability does not necessarily alleviate the gambler's fallacy
    E. Researchers conducted a study of participants

190. In the final paragraph, why did those in the first group tend to predict tails more?
    A. There was a head in the time before
    B. They did not believe in the gambler's fallacy
    C. They believed in the gambler's fallacy
    D. The gambler's fallacy
    E. A matter of probability

Passage 37 – Human Organ Sales

In the year 2013/14, over 4,000 organ transplants took place, 1,146 of which consisted of donations from living individuals. Despite recent year-on-year increases, the current rate of organ transplants is not enough to satisfy demand for them, and this has severe consequences: approximately three people die in the UK every day from not having an organ transplant.

NHS Blood and Transplant suggest that there needs to be a revolution in social attitudes towards donation but such a revolution needs a radical change in tactics. A public campaign to increase awareness of joining the organ donation register has taken heed. Indeed, any member of the public can register to donate their organs in the event of death. However, take up has been relatively low. In order to help counter the shortage, the Welsh government have adopted a system of presumed consent such that a person is deemed to consent to their organs being donated unless they have indicated otherwise (in which case, their organs will not be donated). Again, though, whether such a scheme will alleviate the shortage is unclear.

Accordingly, it has been proposed that a marketplace for organs be developed, where people are allowed to provide organs and be paid for them. This would acknowledge that the shortage is a major public health problem and encourage donors to come forward. In response to such suggestions in the past, opponents have maintained that it is immoral, but they tend only to involve either no or superficial consideration of the countervailing policy considerations and critically do not address the shortage of organs. Indeed, one can actually query whether it is moral to allow people to die in circumstances in which death can be avoided.

The positive case for allowing the sale of organs is generally based on the existence of a shortage, but there are other useful considerations too. The libertarian argument is based on the view that adults exercising their free will should be able to decide what to do with their own bodies. Accordingly, should they wish to give their organs in return for a price, there should not be an objection to it unless there are strong reasons against it. Freedom and respect for personal autonomy demand no less.

A regular assertion is that allowing the sale of organs will exploit the poor; they would be in the most need to cash in on their spare organs which could be at the expense of their health. However, they can still give their organs at present via a donation – why should there be a difference in the health risks between getting money for giving your organ and getting nothing for it? If the current risk framework for living transplants was used to determine whether one can sell their organs, giving an organ for money will not be more dangerous and riskier. In fact, providing money for organs is fairer than the current system – the providers of organs are compensated for the organ, the health risks, and their time. The involvement of money should not make it immoral – the surgeons carrying out the transplant, the transportation officers, and nurses are all paid for carrying out a transplant but no one would argue they're immoral.

Far from being immoral, the individual providing the organ would be saving someone else's life. Providing economic compensation should not make a difference. While opponents suggest that the poor would be exploited, it is incumbent on them to elaborate on how this is a different form of exploitation to working in high-risk occupations such as deep-sea diving, in the military or in a coal mine. The health risks of these occupations far outweigh the risk undertaking an operation to remove an organ, such as a kidney. Far from being exploited, people, however rich they are, should be able to give, should they want to.

Of course, this is not to say that any market in organs should be unregulated. In fact, quite the contrary is suggested by proponents of this. A heavily regulated market and safeguards to ensure fully informed consent and protection for the vulnerable are vital. Moreover, the system as proposed by Erin and Harris (2003) would fit well with the current system. There would only be one buyer of organs, the National Health Service, and organs could be distributed in accordance with existing priority rules, based on need and fairness.

This does not make the medical profession less caring or infringe on morality, it is, in fact, our moral imperative to ensure that we protect as many lives as possible. On a consequentialist perspective, the benefits of a market for human organs are clear but the drawbacks are not.

191. In which of the following circumstances would the libertarian argument not support the sale of organs?
    A. Where it is not provable that organ transplants would save lives
    B. Where it is against nature
    C. For those who do not give informed consent
    D. Where there is a risk to the donor
    E. When there is not a shortage

192. Which of the following is true?
    A. The Welsh government impose organ donation on individuals after their death
    B. Organs that are sold will go to the highest bidder
    C. Organ donation is moral
    D. A person can refuse to have their organs donated after death in Wales
    E. A marketplace for organs would be unethical

193. Which of the following is an argument in the passage?
    A. People should be able to sell their organs
    B. Opponents have maintained that it is immoral
    C. A market for organs should not exist
    D. The libertarian argument should prevail over all others
    E. The health risk of organ donation is outweighed by the benefit to the recipient

194. Which of the following is an opinion?
    A. The poor would be exploited
    B. In 2013/14, over 4,000 organ transplants took place
    C. There is a shortage of organs
    D. There are not enough donors to satisfy demand
    E. A public campaign has taken place to encourage organ donations

195. Which of the following is not advanced as an argument, implicit or explicit, by the author?
    A. Poorer individuals should be allowed to donate their organs should they wish
    B. There is little difference between selling an organ and working in a high-risk job
    C. A human organ market would be fair
    D. It would be better for the poor as opposed to the rich, to donate their organs
    E. The health risks are not increased for an organ transplant which is sold

Passage 38 – Free Speech

If someone says something you don't like, what do you do? Stop them from speaking or let them speak, but state your disagreement with them? In day-to-day conversations, either option does not appear to make much difference but on a larger scale, the repercussions for freedom of expression are enormous.

Either course of action has different consequences and implications for society at large. Take the former option and the other person won't be heard – in the event of the latter option, that person may be heard and the public may disagree with it but at least the public would be able to make up their own minds on the matter. Were the public to agree with the position, surely that is a right people have, regardless of your opinion.

Student unions in British Universities have been particularly vociferous in clamping down on speakers who might offend students. Indeed, many question the extent to which a person has a right to offend another. However, as Louise Richardson has pointed out, education is not comfortable. On the contrary, it is about tackling ideas and arguments you don't like, "confronting the person you disagree with and trying to change their mind. This isn't a comfortable experience but it is a very educational one."

Student unions are in a position of significant power in university circles, in being able to organise protests and decide on who speaks in their debates. A number of student unions operate a 'no-platform' policy, where an individual is prohibited from speaking at events. This may be due to the individual holding extremist views, but someone has to make a judgement as to what counts as extremist. This can potentially be a serious infringement of a person's freedom of speech if misused.

Indeed, student union leaders have taken contentious actions recently. For example, controversial writer, Germaine Greer, gave a speech at Cardiff University. While this was accompanied with a protest, the university's student union also started a petition to ban the writer from speaking in the first place. Most individuals may well disagree with Greer's arguments, which indeed are extreme.

What was more surprising, however, was that Peter Tatchell, a gay rights campaigner, was declared transphobic and racist by the National Union of Student's LGBT (Lesbian, Gay, Bisexual and Transgender) officer, who refused to share a platform with him. The officer justified her statement because Tatchell signed an open letter denouncing the NUS' no platform policy and supporting the free speech of individuals such as Germaine Greer. This shows a surprising mind-set in the student's union. If mere opposition alone to the no platform policy makes one subject to the no platform policy, surely that is an extremist policy in itself. Indeed, I, the author of this piece, would not be given a platform to speak on this basis by the student unions.

The increasing tendency for student unions to censor speakers who may offend them is concerning. Certainly, many may not agree with controversial speakers. However, blocking their free expression not only infringes on free speech but reduces the flow of ideas. It epitomises the undemocratic position that the views of those in powerful positions is more important than the views of others. It is only through allowing controversial speakers, and for people to hear a variety of views that one can be sure they have reached an informed view. Restricting freedom of speech, thus, reveals a lack of respect for the personal autonomy of individuals and their freedom to make up their own minds.

If those who seek to ban controversial speakers instead work to formulate counter-arguments, they will find a richer and more fulfilling public discourse.

'Offensiveness' for the purpose of the so-called 'no-platform' policy is vague and can lead to speakers being arbitrarily cut off from discourse at the behest of those leading student unions. Who are they to say whether something, in particular, is offensive? And even if a view offends a few individuals, it should be through debate that it is countered and not by shutting the debate off.

196. What unstated assumption was made by the author in stating that he would not be given a platform to speak?
    A. He would not be allowed to speak by student unions
    B. He agrees with Germaine Greer's views
    C. He would have the same fate as Peter Tatchell
    D. He is a campaigner for gay rights
    E. The officer's views on the no-platform policy are reflective of the student unions

197. Regarding freedom of speech?
    A. It is a human right
    B. Freedom of speech may be countered in circumstances where there are offensive views
    C. Peter Tatchell should not have been blocked from speaking
    D. Respect for personal autonomy requires freedom of speech
    E. There should not have been protests against Germaine Greer's speech

198. Which of the following is an opinion?
    A. Tatchell signed an open letter denouncing the no-platform policy
    B. 'Offensiveness' has a number of different meanings
    C. A number of student unions operate a 'no-platform' policy
    D. Students protested against Germaine Greer's talk
    E. The increasing tendency for student unions to censor speakers who may offend them is concerning

199. Which of the following follows from the passage?
    A. Students are extremists
    B. Students are against free speech
    C. Many students are against free speech
    D. Student unions express the views of the student body
    E. Some student unions have been trying to prevent certain individuals from speaking

Passage 39 - Bering Fur Seal Arbitration

The Bering Fur Seal Arbitration was one of the earliest international environmental law cases between the United States and Great Britain. The conflict arose once the US bought Alaska from Russia and thereafter granted a monopoly to the Alaskan Commercial Company through granting the company the exclusive right of sealing on the Pribilof Islands, at the edge of US territorial waters in the Bering Sea. In the 1880s, however, Canadian ships engaged in killing seals in the water, an activity known as pelagic sealing, just outside US waters. This depleted seal stocks inside US waters and on US land, which led to an international conflict between the United States and Great Britain, acting on behalf of Canada.

The United States wanted the upkeep of fur seals and, after the failure of negotiations with Great Britain, an arbitration tribunal was set up to resolve the issue. In order to be successful, the US needed to assert some type of right to the seals outside their territory. Among the arguments advanced by them at the arbitration, it was claimed that the US had the exclusive jurisdiction to the Bering Sea but this argument was flatly rejected. Alternatively, the US put forward the proposition that they were acting for the benefit of mankind generally to keep up the seal stocks. Additionally, they suggested that sealing on the land, which the US engaged in, was right but that pelagic sealing was illegitimate. This argument, convenient though it was, had never been recognised in any system of law, international or domestic and would have amounted creating new law. Hence, while their counsel displayed ingenuity, they were effectively countered by the counsel for Great Britain, who ended up persuading the tribunal.

In accordance with the terms of the arbitration treaty, the tribunal laid down a number of regulations for the purpose of preserving the fur seal stocks, which were binding on both Great Britain and the United States. The main regulation was the creation of a 60-mile exclusion zone, where pelagic sealing was not allowed except at certain times and in certain ways. One such regulation prohibited the use of firearms and explosives.

200. Why did the US bring the case against Great Britain?
- A. Great Britain had responsibility for Canada at the time
- B. Canadian ships were killing the US' seals
- C. Canadian ships had breached US waters
- D. The seal stocks were being depleted
- E. As they had a monopoly over their seals

201. Who did the arbitration tribunal find in favour of?
- A. The United States
- B. Canada
- C. Great Britain
- D. Alaska
- E. No one

202. Why was the US' argument convenient?
- A. It fitted in well with their case
- B. The US was sealing on land and Canada's was in the water
- C. It was not held to be convenient
- D. It created a new law
- E. It gave them exclusive jurisdiction

203. Which of the following is true?
- A. Sealing was prohibited
- B. The US could not seal on the Pribilof islands
- C. The US were acting for the benefit of mankind
- D. Great Britain was more restricted in sealing in the exclusion zone
- E. Great Britain lost the case

204. Which of the following would the regulation allow?
- A. British ships to seal in the exclusion zone at restricted times
- B. US ships to seal in the exclusion zone at restricted times
- C. US ships to seal on the land on the Pribilof islands
- D. Sealing at all hours, so long as it was without a firearm or explosive
- E. No sealing at all

Passage 40 – Footballers' Pay

In 2012-13, the average yearly salary of a Premier League footballer was £1.6m, while at the same time, the average salary in the UK stood at £26,500. The footballers at the top of the tree earn significantly above the average footballer even, with Wayne Rooney on a reported £13 million contract with Manchester United, thereby earning him over 9 times the average every week. This may seem a lot for kicking a ball and running around a field. Footballers tend to enjoy extravagant lifestyles, which have been brought into public focus in recent times given the tough economic conditions that have affected the rest of society.

In 2008, the Labour Government's Sports minister labelled footballers' salaries as obscene, pointing out the difference when compared to the ordinary worker. The Archbishop of York believes that there must be higher taxes for them. What makes a footballer's occupation more worthwhile to society than that of a doctor or nurse, who goes about saving lives? It is indeed arguable that their success is in a big part due to the talent they have from birth, and that is entirely down to luck. It may, thus, seem unfair that footballers earn over a hundred times more than nurses or doctors, many of whom have to work late shifts and make life-and-death decisions and seem to contribute more value to society.

On the contrary, though, the workings of the free market can be used to explain the seemingly excessive salaries of Premier League footballers. Put simply, there aren't many people with the skills of such footballers – they are in short supply – and at the same time, many people – in fact, millions – want to watch them, either at a football match or on television. Consequently, television broadcasters are willing to pay mammoth sums to have the TV rights to football matches and companies are willing to pay millions to sponsor mainstream football teams. These give the teams the enormous purchasing power with which to pay their players large sums. Given that each team wants to win, they will want the best players and thus, will bid against each other for them, thereby inflating their wages even further.

However, if it's just a matter of luck, is it fair that footballers are paid significantly more than doctors? Indeed, supporters of the status quo point to the fact that their respective wages are determined by the market makes it fair – their wage is reflective of their value to society. Millions of people excitedly tune in to watch football and it is, therefore, argued by supporters that society, by this choice, determines the footballer's wage.

On the contrary, though, opponents point out that the market-determined wage (or the market value attributed to one's skills) is mainly determined by luck and not entirely by oneself. Accordingly, the wage differential is not particularly fair given that someone earning a low wage, such as a junior doctor, may well work much harder than a person, such as a footballer, earning a significantly higher wage.

However, it is wrong to focus this debate solely on footballers. It requires significant political discourse as it goes to the heart of a fundamental part of society: the free market system. How, whether and to what extent this should be reformed are matters for careful political debate. The market system does not just lead to footballers enjoying large salaries, but other sports stars, celebrities in general, bankers, lawyers, chief executives etc. earn wages that are significantly above that of the average too. The position of footballers should be seen as not much different from these other professions. It is, thus, incoherent to consider the position of footballers' salaries and not consider society as a whole

Crucially, 45% income tax is already paid on earnings over £150,000 and it is up to democratically elected governments to consider whether taxation suffices or if a wholesale change of the pay system is warranted, such as imposing 'wage-caps'. When considering the latter, however, it is worth bearing in mind that it is not inexorable that the reduction would go to lower earners and not boost the company's own profits.

205. What do the opponents and supporters agree on?
    A. What the wage rate for footballers and nurses should be
    B. That fairness has different meanings depending on the context
    C. That the existing settlement is fair
    D. That fairness has a role to play in the wage debate
    E. That fairness leads to the current outcome

206. Which of the following is not inconsistent with the arguments of <u>both</u> the opponents and supporters of footballers' wages?
    A. Footballers benefit from luck to have their talent
    B. Footballers have a fair wage
    C. Footballers' wage should be determined by the free market
    D. It is unfair that nurses are paid less
    E. Footballers should be paid less

207. Which of the following is not inconsistent with the author's argument in the passage?
    A. One's hard work is a factor for success
    B. It is obvious that the market-based system needs to be overhauled
    C. Fairness is a definitive concept
    D. Wage differentials reflect hard work
    E. Footballers don't pay tax

208. What does the word 'inexorable' mean in this context?
    A. Unnecessary
    B. Mindless
    C. Sporadic
    D. Random
    E. Unavoidable

209. Which of the following is argued by the author?
    A. The supporters of footballers' wages are incorrect
    B. The opponents of footballers' wages are incorrect
    C. Top footballers are in short supply
    D. It is incoherent to only consider footballers' salaries and not society as a whole
    E. 45% income tax is already paid on earnings over £150,000

Passage 41- The Underground

We are once again facing the possibility of major tube strikes across the capital. It seems that the strikes which occurred last summer were not enough to convince Boris Johnson, Mayor of London, to work with the unions rather than against them in his mission to get the night tube rolled out across the city. The national media and the public at large have again declared themselves outraged at the possibility of further strikes. People fear the misery and inconvenience caused by the last 24-hour walk-out. The Prime Minister has also condemned the strikes as 'unacceptable and unjustifiable'. In fact, a Tory London Assembly member has called for a 'Dad's Army' of retired former Tube workers to 'prop up' the Underground during the industrial action. But is all this outrage really justified or should we think again?

I would ask you to consider how you might feel if your employment contract were suddenly changed without your consent. I would further ask how you would feel if that contract were changed such that your working hours became significantly less convenient without additional remuneration. That is the very real situation in which many tube staff now find themselves. These people do some of the most vital work in London – and it's often a thankless task. We ought to be supportive of them, rather than resentful of trying to ensure they work in suitable conditions and are adequately remunerated for their indispensable services to this country. It seems ridiculous that when junior doctors were striking, there was so little public anger but when tube staff strike, people are so incensed. The double standards here are quite incredible.

Much of the national media have already responded to the story that there may be further strikes – largely with real anger. This is especially the case with more conservative newspapers, tending to fight any action by unions that they possibly can. For example, a scathing article was yesterday published by the Daily Mail. Interestingly, social media, as unrepresentative as it may be, has offered a more sympathetic view. More than 10,000 people have retweeted "The night tube can wait, people should be paid to work late." Others have posted messages in support of tube workers on Facebook, as well as posts highlighting the difficulties faced by those who are forced to work late. Of course, we should hesitate before using social media as a useful poll of public opinion, but it is encouraging that a significant proportion of people are being exposed to less conservative views about the issue.

The right-wing press will always be keen to encourage us to disparage unions, and many of us may have unwittingly taken on the views promulgated in such media. I would suggest, however, that we might benefit from rethinking such views. A more sympathetic viewpoint would encourage us all to be more grateful for those who operate Transport for London every day – and such a viewpoint might even help Boris Johnson to finally get the night tube plan moving.

210. What is the main argument of the Passage?
    A. That the Mayor is being unfair
    B. That we should be more sympathetic to tube drivers and workers
    C. That tube staff should work harder
    D. That strikes are pointless
    E. The night tube is unnecessary

211. What is the inconsistency being highlighted in the Passage?
    A. That the public are not angry about junior doctors' strikes but are angry about tube strikes
    B. That most Londoners don't want the night tube
    C. That the night tube will cost a lot of money but not be worth it
    D. That the public support teachers' strikes but not tube strikes
    E. The right-wing press only disparages unions

212. What view of social media is taken in the Passage?
    A. That most people on it are right-wing
    B. That people on it are cruel
    C. That it may offer a skewed view of public opinion
    D. That it offers a very accurate view of public opinion
    E. People are very active on social media

213. What does the word 'conservative' mean in the Passage?
    A. People who were privately educated
    B. People who are uncaring humans
    C. People who are members of a specific political party
    D. People who are on the right-wing of a spectrum of thought
    E. Unwillingness to accept industrial change

214. What is suggested by the final paragraph?
    A. That we should not listen to newspapers
    B. That we should not listen to Boris Johnson
    C. That we should re-evaluate some of our beliefs
    D. That we should think before we tweet
    E. A different approach will help Boris Johnson to retain his position

Passage 42 - Politics

Not enough people join political parties anymore and it's damaging our political process. Although membership of two major parties surged after the 2015 election, still less than 10% of the UK population are members. There are three ways in which this damages our political process: many people are completely uninformed about politics and have no idea, for instance, as to how to distinguish between left-wing and right-wing parties; unpopular leaders run parties and political parties only speak for a small proportion of the electorate. Because the majority of people refuse to make a choice, the minority makes that choice for them.

A large proportion of the UK population are completely disengaged from politics. A recent survey showed that over 70% of people have never read a political manifesto in their entire life. When the most recent election rolled around, many of my friends had no idea to vote for because they had no idea about what their political convictions were. This is troubling because it means that none of them have ever bothered to vote at a general or local election. Where's the democracy in that? It's not necessarily the case that these friends of mine don't have views on how the country should work – they do – but they have no idea which parties represent those ideas. If they investigated the policies and ideals of the different political parties, read their election manifestos, and then joined political parties, they would not be in such a predicament. As far as politics is concerned, in this day and age, ignorance is certainly not bliss.

Jeremy Corbyn took control of the Labour Party in autumn 2015 despite being very unpopular with the majority of the electorate. Although he obtained a very significant majority within the Labour Party, this is not representative of the rest of the UK's views. Most consider his pacifism to be untenable and found Hilary Benn's approach much more persuasive. However, a silent majority refused to participate in the labour elections, some due to laziness, and others due to the mentality (prevalent amongst many) that their favourite candidate would be selected regardless of whether they voted or not. If more of those who identify with the left had joined Labour and voted in their leadership election, perhaps a more appropriate leader would have been selected.

It is very easy for political parties to speak only for a small proportion of the electorate when so many people do not get involved with them. This fact is glaringly obvious, but, surprisingly, has been missed by many people. Young people often complain that politicians do not care about them or their interests – but, of course, it is very easy for that to be the case when so few of them join parties and force politicians to consider that their interests really do matter. It's vitally important for the young to engage if, for example, they ever want a chance of reversing the Conservative party's tuition fee increases, which so many of them seem to resent.

215. What are the political views of the author?
    A. Conservative
    B. Liberal Democrat
    C. Labour
    D. There is not enough information to tell
    E. Communist

216. Which of the following is an argument made in favour of joining political parties?
    A. Corbyn is a pacifist
    B. If more people joined, inappropriate leaders would be less likely to get selected
    C. Tuition fees are expensive
    D. The author's friends have political views
    E. Many people are uninformed about politics

217. What unstated assumption is being made?
    A. Engagement with politics is a good thing
    B. Corbyn is bad at his job
    C. A lot of the UK population are not engaged with politics
    D. Young people complain a lot
    E. Corbyn's views are not representative of many people's views

218. What is meant by untenable?
    A. Pointless
    B. Unable to stand up against attack
    C. Unfair on some people
    D. Annoying
    E. Understandable

219. What does the writer seek to demonstrate in using the following statistic: "less than 10% of the UK population are members (of political parties)"?
    A. That their friends do not care about politics
    B. That Corbyn is a pacifist
    C. That Corbyn got a large majority of votes in the Labour leadership election
    D. That a lot of people are disengaged from politics
    E. That political activism is more popular elsewhere in Europe

Passage 43 – Gender Equality

Gender equality has, for as long as we can remember, been a serious and troubling issue. Recent studies have shown that a pay gap still exists and many women report incidents of discrimination experienced at work. However, in the UK, there is a growing willingness to tackle the issue of gender equality and this is reflected both through the passing and enforcement of anti-discrimination legislation and through the implementation of various policies by employers in the public and private sectors. In the ongoing struggle for gender equality, one author suggests that the approach to tackling differences between men and women has failed...

"It is sometimes possible to identify existing differences, such as responsibility for childcare and legislate to accommodate for those. It would seem that this might be a major step forward in the struggle for gender equality. Many employers in the private sector now offer schemes which are designed to assist women; for instance, partnership schemes (where an employer buys many places at local nurseries near the workplace for their employees to use) are becoming more and more common. A large proportion of employers also offer women with children flexible working hours and childcare vouchers. In the public sector, assistance to women with children also abounds. Government bodies have been known to buy places with childcare providers before and after school so that employees' children of a relevant age can attend breakfast and after-school clubs. Some may even provide care during the school holidays, which can prove a particularly hard time for employees to get childcare cover. By offering assistance to women who want childcare so they can return to work, governments would seem to be advancing the struggle for gender equality.

However, if such privileges are given only to women, the idea that only women should be responsible for childcare may be perpetuated. In one case, a father was denied access to his employer's subsidised childcare scheme because it was only for female staff. The employer initially maintained that the general policy was justified, notwithstanding the fact that, in that particular case, the father was the sole carer for the child. Fortunately, the employer reached an agreement with that particular employee. However, doubtless many other fathers will find themselves excluded from childcare vouchers and nursery partnership programmes in a similar manner. The aim of the subsidised childcare policy was to allow women to continue working, rather than leaving their jobs after having a child. This was an exception to a general policy of gender neutrality, specifically to tackle the under-representation of women in the banking sector. As the policy was one of "affirmative action", it was not illegal. In theory, this might seem very beneficial for women. However, from the introduction of the policy to the time of the case, there had only been a 7% increase in the number of female employees, and it was not clear whether this was caused by the policy.

Emphasising women's differences and adjusting for them may actually have done more harm than good in this case, therefore, especially if the idea that childcare is a women's issue was perpetuated."

220. What does the word 'perpetuated' mean here?
   A. Caused to continue
   B. Defeated altogether
   C. Partially dealt with
   D. Made stronger
   E. Made more widespread

221. What does the writer think about the 7% increase?
   A. That it means the policy was a success
   B. That it justified the cost of subsidised childcare
   C. That it does not necessarily show that the policy made a difference
   D. That most people didn't want it
   E. That it is a significant figure

222. What is the negative outcome of the policy of subsidising childcare for women only?
   A. Men may be resentful and angry
   B. It may be expensive
   C. Women may go back into the workplace
   D. It may reinforce the idea that women are responsible for childcare
   E. The policy is random in its operation

223. What was the aim of the policy of subsidising childcare for women only?
   A. To support women because they are poorer than men
   B. To help them continue working after childbirth
   C. To force them to continue working after childbirth
   D. To stop men taking advantage of free childcare
   E. To give women as many life advantages as men

224. Which of these ideas can be inferred from the Passage?
   A. Highlighting gender differences may not help gender equality
   B. Men will always try to take advantage of schemes aimed at women
   C. Highlighting gender differences always help gender equality
   D. Gender neutrality is a bad thing
   E. It is impossible to find a fair way of dealing with gender differences

Passage 44 - An Extract from a Piece on Policing:

In 1829, when Sir Robert Peel was Home Secretary, the first Metropolitan Police Act was passed and the Metropolitan Police Force was established. Previously, three different groups had strived to protect London; the Bow Street Patrols, the police force constables who were under the control of the magistrates, and the River Police. However, overall, before 1829, the law enforcement had been severely lacking in organisation. As London expanded during the 19th century, the issue of maintaining law and order became more and more pertinent.

The original mandate of Peel's Metropolitan Police placed the greatest emphasis on the prevention of crime. The police sought to prevent the violent crimes which were common in London at that time – including robberies and murders. More petty thefts and public disorder were amongst the less serious crimes which the force also aimed to pre-empt. This was done mainly through visible patrol. During the 19th century, a detective function was added to the job. The two strategies of preventative patrol and criminal investigation continued to form the core of policing for over a century. Recent decades have seen important developments in policing, many of which were prompted by the pressures under which all criminal justice agencies were placed by governments keen to secure value for money. Changes aimed at combating the way the police are viewed by the public have also been important, especially in the wake of recent criticisms of the conduct of officers and accusations of police brutality: new developments in policing are now almost always as much about police legitimation as they are about police effectiveness.

The most significant change occurring in the function and nature of policing is the pluralisation of the system. There has been a dramatic increase in the number of different groups which form part of our law enforcement. The extent of this change has been so great that leading commentators have argued that 'future generations will look back on our era as a time when one system of policing ended and another took its place'. The non-Home Office forces include, on the public side: specialist nationalist forces; police sections of broader public organisations and municipal policing; and on the private side, they include voluntary self-policing or civil policing.

One major change has been the commercial security sector growing and taking over some role traditionally filled by the Home Office police. For those who can afford it, provision of security will be increasingly privatised, either in residential areas or in the 'mass private property' sector where more and more middle-class leisure and work takes place. In this sense, the police are changing in response to a changing world. The growth of the non-Home Office sector, in particular, commercial and municipal policing is a compensatory response to the financial crisis of the state. It also has to do with the growth of mass private property – shopping centres, office plazas and so forth. These give rise to considerable security issues because they are open to the public. These developments don't quite fit with the traditional view of police on public streets – and so private policing takes over.

225. Which of the following is merely an assertion?
    A. New developments in policing are almost always as much about police legitimation as they are about police effectiveness
    B. The most significant change occurring in the function and nature of policing is the pluralisation of the system
    C. These developments don't quite fit with the traditional view of police on public streets – and so private policing takes over
    D. The original mandate of Peel's Metropolitan Police placed the greatest emphasis on the prevention of crime
    E. The police are changing in response to a changing world

226. What reason is given for the major changes in policing in the first paragraph?
    A. The growth of mass private property
    B. Peel's Metropolitan Police had become old-fashioned
    C. Visible patrol wasn't working
    D. Governments being keen to secure value for money
    E. Public pressure to change the structure of the police force

227. What evidence is cited for the claim that "the most significant change occurring in the function and nature of policing is the pluralisation of the system"?
    A. A list of different private and public police forces
    B. The statement of leading commentators
    C. An explanation of what pluralisation means
    D. The fact that voluntary self-policing is happening
    E. The growth of the commercial security sector

228. Which of these is not included in the Passage in support of the statement that commercial security is becoming increasingly important?
    A. The fact that there has been a fiscal crisis in the state
    B. The increase in mass private property
    C. An increased number of private security firms
    D. The security issues generated by large shopping centres and office complexes
    E. New security issues

229. What is the main point of the Passage?
    A. To persuade the reader that we have a problem with policing
    B. To inform the reader of changes taking place within the police
    C. To inform the reader of the dangers of spending time in areas of mass private property
    D. To persuade the reader to join the police
    E. To inform the reader of how changes in the public sector will affect the private sector

Passage 45 – International Law

The international legal system lacks one body which has authority to legislate for all states. Some states are not members of the United Nations, and even those which are, are only bound by that which they have agreed to be bound to. Essentially, for most states, co-operation with international law is a matter of political goodwill, rather than one of legal or physical compulsion. This would seem to suggest that there cannot be any kind of successful international legislative process: but the commentators seem all to agree that violations of international law are rare.

Because there is no independent body to legislate for all states, it can be difficult to establish what exactly constitutes international law. However, there is a consensus that various sources, however—principally treaties between states—are authoritative statements of international law. International law involves four sources of law: international conventions; international custom; general principles of law and judicial teachings. These are set out in Article 38(1) of the Statute of the International Court of Justice 1945. An example of custom is the practice relating to ambassadors. For thousands of years, countries have given protection to ambassadors. As far back as the ancient Greek and Roman world, ambassadors from another country were not harmed whilst on their diplomatic missions, even if the countries they represented were at war with the country they were located in or travelling through. Throughout history, many countries have also publicly stated that they believe that ambassadors should be given this sort of protection. Therefore, today, if a country harmed an ambassador it would constitute a violation of customary international law. Treaties are the most common source today; they are similar to contracts between countries; promises between States are exchanged, put into formal writing, and signed. States may query the interpretation or implementation of a treaty, but the written provisions of a treaty are considered to be binding. Treaties can address any number of topics, such as trade relations, like the North American Free Trade Agreement, or control of nuclear weapons, such as the Nuclear Non-Proliferation Treaty. Treaties may be multilateral or bilateral - although more treaties now are bilateral and, thus, bind only the two states which sign them.

The fact that the international legislative process works reasonably well is often met with surprise. This is perhaps because breaches of international law are so well-publicised, or because many people imagine that international law only governs war: the area where most breaches of the law occur. Steve Smith argues that the fact that "the law is normally observed... receives limited attention because most people are more interested in the occasions on which it is broken. And yet these occasions are very rare." It is important to recognise that in the day-to-day business of states, the great majority of treaties are observed. Such treaties include rules on international postage and telephone calls: areas which function without issue all the time. This shows that the legislative process does work reasonably well: the majority of states do obey the majority of the law.

HSPSAA: SECTION A — QUESTIONS

230. What is the paradox highlighted in the Passage?
    A. States are only bound by that which they have agreed to but some states are not members of the UN
    B. There is no one body which can authoritatively legislate for all states but violations of international law are rare
    C. International law involves four sources but one is more common than others
    D. People are surprised that the international legislative process works well but they are not interested in the law
    E. Most violations of international law concern war

231. What can we infer about how the nature of treaties has changed?
    A. More of them are now bilateral; in the past more were multilateral
    B. They have become a lot more popular
    C. They used to be contained in a completely different statute
    D. They have become far less useful since World War Two
    E. More treaties are observed nowadays than in the past

232. What is the central argument of the piece?
    A. International law is not very useful
    B. Most people are only interested in breaches of international law
    C. International telephone calls function without issue
    D. The international legislative process actually works well
    E. People do not believe that international law works

233. Which of these is not presented as a reason for why people are surprised to hear that the international legislative process functions well?
    A. Breaches of international law are heavily publicised
    B. Some people think international law is all about war
    C. International law does not have a good PR system
    D. People are most interested in the breaches of international law
    E. People do not focus on the areas of life in which international law functions well

234. What point are the rules on international postage and telephone calls used to illustrate?
    A. That the great majority of treaties are observed
    B. That the great majority of treaties are not observed
    C. That people are most interested in the breaches of international law
    D. That treaties are the most common source of international law
    E. That treaties relating to postage and telephone calls are amongst the most successful

Passage 46 – The Nature of law

For many years, academics have debated and written on the topic of whether law is, by nature, coercive. It is important to find an answer to the question of whether or not law is coercive because, as the Utilitarians argued, we need to stop those who make law from abusing their power. If, in making law, the legislature in-fact coerces people into certain behaviours, this is much more important, because their power is much greater. This situation can be contrasted with one in which every man is like Austin's 'puzzled man' – who wishes to follow the law voluntarily, if he can only find out what it is. If, as it will be argued here, most people choose to follow the law, at least some of the time, because they will experience negative consequences otherwise, then keeping law makers in check is much more important and needs to be taken very seriously and should be at the centre of our focus. Thus, finding an answer to this question is important firstly because it helps us respond appropriately to law makers.

A second reason it is important to find an answer to the question of whether or not law is essentially coercive is that it helps to understand how people respond to the law, and why it is that, most of the time, people are in the habit of obeying it (as Austin states). This is crucial because law should be made for the good of society, and, therefore, for the people who make up that society. If law is coercive, and that is why people obey it, law makers can better choose appropriate sanctions, at least in the criminal law, so that people continue to do so. For instance, if a particular area of law is frequently broken – such as traffic laws or laws relating to fly-tipping – an apt solution might be to increase the penalty for breach of such laws in order to bring about the fear necessary for the coercion effect. If, however, law was not coercive and most people were like the aforementioned 'puzzled man', then appropriate sanctions for breaches might well be different. For example, we might implement lighter sentences – such as community service orders, or even dispense with sanctions altogether. However, it is here argued that a substantial portion of society obeys the law because of fear of sanction and therefore, serious sanctions are needed for a breach of the criminal law. To put it frankly, we do not live in a 'society of angels', and many individuals would readily admit that they would freely break a number of provisions were it not for the hefty penalties attached to breach.

The criminal law is the clearest example of law being like commands (as argued by Austin) issued by the legislature, and despite Hart's criticism of Austin, he too concedes this. The criminal law tells people how they are expected to behave and that sanctions will be imposed if they breach these standards of behaviour. This is totally coercive in nature.

HSPSAA: SECTION A — QUESTIONS

235. What does the author think is the most important reason to find an answer to the question of whether or not law is coercive?
    A. It helps to understand how people respond to the law
    B. We need to stop those who make law from abusing their power
    C. The criminal law tells people how they are expected to behave
    D. There is not enough information in the Passage to know
    E. To verify Austin's theory

236. What point do Hart and Austin agree on?
    A. The criminal law is the clearest example of law being like commands
    B. Most people choose to follow the law because they will experience negative consequences otherwise
    C. The criminal law has a lot of sanctions
    D. Most people do obey the law
    E. Serious sanctions are needed for breach of the criminal law

237. Which of these statements is closest to what the Utilitarians argued?
    A. People who make law enjoy using sanctions
    B. It's important to ensure those who make law don't abuse the power they have
    C. Lawmakers are all very puzzled
    D. Law is only coercive when it makes people feel puzzled
    E. All of the above

238. What is 'coercive' used to mean in the Passage?
    A. The law is used to make people puzzled
    B. The law is used to make people do things
    C. The law is used to make people happy
    D. The law is used to make people commit crime
    E. The law is used to show people what to do

239. Why does the author think that major sanctions are needed for breaches of the criminal law?
    A. People obey the law a lot of the time
    B. People only obey the law because they fear sanctions
    C. People do not fear sanctions enough and criminal law should scare them
    D. The author does not think this at all
    E. None of the above

Passage 47 – Multinational Companies

New management structures in multinational companies are big news for those wanting to make a career move. Increasingly, consultancies are advising such companies to hire from within their own firms rather than bring in new people from outside. The logic behind this appears to be that long-term employees will have had time to come up with reliable new ideas rather than high-risk ones which are more likely if one hires from outside the company. For instance, the Fast Company Group have written an article warning against hiring 'tons of people quickly'. The idea seems to be that focusing on long-standing employees - employees with 'shared interest, preferences and priorities' - will be a better strategy for building up a successful company. The dominant criteria for hiring, according to this consultancy, should be whether the new individual fits with the character, ethos, and ideas of the firm.

It's unfortunate, however, that this means there will be so much less innovation in such companies. Sahara's London office, for example, has only hired three people from outside the company at management level in the last two years. In the two years prior to that, it hired fifteen. The big changes in approach – like introducing drones for delivery – that they have been working on recently almost all came from those who did not start their working lives at Sahara. It's concerning, therefore, to those of us who enjoy the big changes and crazy new business ideas, that there will be so much less cross-stimulation of ideas in big businesses.

The statistics for other large firms are similarly bleak. A recent survey revealed that many had either slowed down their hiring or were planning on doing so in the coming months.

If multinational companies are going to be making safer choices as a result of their new structures and hiring policies, there is one way in which we might all benefit significantly: we're much less likely to go crashing into another financial crisis. The crash was, of course, caused by lots of risky decisions being made by lots of banks. Examples include the granting of mortgages to sub-prime candidates, both in the field of residential estates and in that of commercial estates. Other risky decisions included the loans made to financial markets (up to 32% of the money created by the big banks at that time). Avoiding a repeat of that could mean that we all avoid a great deal of misery.

240. What is the viewpoint of the author about the new structures overall?
    A. Very against them – only presents negative arguments
    B. Very in favour of them – only presents positive arguments
    C. Neutral – presents both positive and negative arguments
    D. She does not understand them
    E. She believes that they are risky

241. Which of the following is an argument in favour of the new management structures?
    A. We're less likely to experience a financial crisis
    B. We might get more drones for delivery services
    C. There will be less cross-stimulation in business
    D. Fewer people will be hired by new companies
    E. Unemployment will reduce

242. What can be gathered from the statistics about Sahara's recent hiring policy?
    A. They are worried about the financial crisis
    B. They have been listening to the advice of consultancies
    C. They don't want to use drones after all
    D. They have run out of money for new staff
    E. They do not want new ideas

243. Which idea does not appear in the text?
    A. The recession
    B. New delivery methods
    C. Entry level staff
    D. Consultancy firms
    E. Reliable ideas

244. What can be inferred from what the author says about the financial crisis?
    A. It caused a lot of misery
    B. It was caused by drones
    C. It was because of consultancies
    D. It wasn't actually all that bad
    E. None of the above

Passage 48 – Women and the law

There is an enduring belief that female offenders are protected from the full rigours of the law.

However, there is a significant amount of evidence that women actually suffer more in the criminal justice system than men do, however. 40% of the women sentenced in the Crown Court are now being given custodial sentences. This is in contrast to the figure from eight years ago when it was less than a quarter. This is not because, according to the Home Office, female offending has become more serious or more violent. Indeed, there is little reason to suggest that this is the case. It may be, instead, a result of the 'enduring belief' that female offenders are treated too leniently by the criminal justice system. The justice system often attempts to respond to allegations of discrimination by changing its practices – it seems that, in this case, false reports or beliefs have influenced the treatment of women by the judiciary over the years.

Moreover, female offenders, especially those sent to prison, are best viewed as an especially disadvantaged group: 70% have an addiction, double the proportion for men. A higher proportion of women in prison have suffered abuse or neglect as children and a higher proportion self-harm or commit suicide in prison. Indeed, the Prisoners' Reform Trust recently reported that 'Women in prison are highly likely to be victims as well as offenders. More than half (53%) report having experienced emotional, physical or sexual abuse as a child.' Indeed, the Corston report of 2007 identified a myriad of problems with the treatment of more vulnerable female offenders by the prison system – one being the frequency of strip searches and the absence of adequate sanitation. Furthermore, prison itself is harder for women because they tend to be held further from home (because there are fewer women's prisons). This means that women in prisons often feel more isolated from family and friends and, as a result, less able to cope with the harshness of prison life than their male counterparts. One should not underestimate the impact of the geographical location where imprisonment is concerned. It should also be noted that women also more likely to lose their children to care – perhaps because a third of women in prison are lone parents. This can be extremely detrimental to their mental health – especially where the child is the only family they have and they are serving a long prison sentence and potentially face a battle for custody of the child when they eventually leave prison.

There have also been significant failures in programmes designed for women. When women are the subject of "special penal treatment", the result is often the development of "benevolently repressive regimes" which emphasise dependency and traditional femininity, and most crucially, fail to aid rehabilitation. Such programmes tend to be structured around assumed characteristics and needs of women, rather than evidence. Thus, it is argued, women may actually suffer more at the hands of the criminal justice system than men do. There is no place to argue they are treated too leniently.

245. What is the main argument of the Passage?
    A. Female offenders are protected from the full rigours of the law
    B. Arguments that women are treated too leniently are wrong
    C. Female offending has become more serious
    D. Prison is easier for women
    E. Men are treated harshly by the criminal justice system

246. Which of these is not given as evidence about how women are treated in the criminal justice system?
    A. Statistics on losing children to care
    B. Statistics on addiction
    C. Statistics on the types of crimes committed by women
    D. Statistics on how many women are sent to prison
    E. Information about the location of prisons for women

247. What is the reason for the 'enduring belief' that women are treated more leniently in the criminal justice system?
    A. A lot of women have addiction problems
    B. Women tend to be held further from home
    C. Women do not commit a lot of crime
    D. We do not have enough evidence to say
    E. None of the above

248. What can we infer from the information about programmes designed for women?
    A. They do not help women very much
    B. They make women less likely to lose their children to care
    C. They mean women are treated more leniently
    D. They help women to change
    E. They aid rehabilitation

249. What proportion of men in prison have an addiction problem?
    A. 35%
    B. 20%
    C. 70%
    D. We do not have enough information to say
    E. 30%

Passage 49 - Prisons

Prisons in the UK are failing. The reality is that the use of imprisonment is less a reflection of crime rates than an outcome of a country's political, economic, and institutional conditions. Neo-liberal nations, including the USA and the UK, imprison at much higher rates than countries where there is a more egalitarian culture, with more of a welfare state. We are over-burdening the taxpayer by throwing people into prison and paying to keep them there, rather than allowing them to undertake rehabilitation schemes within the community.

There is little evidence that prisons are effective in terms of deterrence or reform at a general level, although certain programs and certain individuals sometimes show positive effects. Despite the positive effects on the minority of prisoners, the high rates of re-offending overall are, according to Clark, stark evidence of the failure of the system. Clarke told BBC Radio 4's Today programme that the prison system was failing to deter a 'criminal underclass' who revert back to committing "more crime" as soon as they come out of prison because underlying problems such as drug abuse and mental illness issues were not being tackled by the prison system. Another issue was the lack of support for those able to change their ways who were striving (unsuccessfully) to obtain some form of legal employment. The prison has, in fact, been found to have an overall negative effect – destabilising family ties, disrupting employment opportunities on a long-term basis, stigmatising, and otherwise deskilling its population.

29% of the prison population are serving sentences of over 4 years but often such prisoners are not dangerous at all. Rather, they have committed lots of property-related offences. The public are not benefitted from keeping these people in prison. In relation to these types of prisoners, Clarke said 'What has been happening is there has been a huge increase in the number of people in prison, which is not only bad value for money, but even more importantly, I don't think that is the right way to keep on protecting people ... some of my critics think you should put more and more people in prison for longer and longer and longer. I personally don't think that is the best way of protecting society. It seems that a thoughtless Victorian-style 'bang em' up' mentality has prevailed in the UK.'

Moreover, it goes without saying that prison is a truly bleak experience for many. This means that some prisoners who might be reformed on the outside become too miserable or depressed to engage with the programmes being offered to them in prison. In England and Wales in 1995, the government introduced an incentives and earned privileges (IEP) scheme. Prisoners on 'basic' – the lowest tier of the IEP scheme – are subject to quite an austere regime. Their in-cell TV is removed, they have reduced opportunities for mixing with other prisoners and they are forced to wear prison uniform. Making people miserable is not the way to bring about reform. We can never hope to cultivate something positive from such negative conditions.

250. What is the main argument of the passage?
    A. Some individuals benefit from prison
    B. Prisons in the UK are better than the US
    C. Prisons in the UK are not working well
    D. Prisons make people sad
    E. We should not punish people

251. What can we infer from the fact that prison may destabilise family ties and disrupt employment opportunities?
    A. Prison may actually make rehabilitation harder
    B. Some people do well in prison
    C. Prison makes rehabilitation easy
    D. The public are benefitted by keeping lots of people in prison
    E. Prisons always reduce social mobility

252. What does the author think about the IEP scheme?
    A. That it makes people happy and thereby hinders rehabilitation
    B. That it makes people sad and thereby hinders rehabilitation
    C. That it makes people sad and thereby helps rehabilitation
    D. That it makes people happy and thereby helps rehabilitation
    E. It makes people sad and thereby aptly punishes them

253. What is an unstated assumption of the passage?
    A. Making people miserable is not the way to bring about reform
    B. Prisons have a positive effect
    C. Prisons have a negative effect
    D. Rehabilitation should be a goal of the prison system
    E. Everyone deserves to be able to maintain their family ties

254. Which of these is not offered as a criticism of keeping too many people in prison?
    A. It may cause fights within prisons
    B. It costs the taxpayer a lot of money
    C. Prison is not helping to rehabilitate many people
    D. Keeping non-dangerous people in prison does not benefit the public
    E. All of the above

Passage 50 – Sleep

Sleeping badly? We all are these days. The regularity with which I hear complaints from friends and colleagues that try as they might, they just cannot get to sleep, leads me to think we have something of a non-sleeping epidemic at the moment. Recently, the Guardian reported that up to 51% of British people struggle to get to sleep – and women are three times more likely than men to suffer from this problem. I'm not saying we're *all* insomniacs for the purposes of medical science – I'm no doctor – but certainly I've noticed something of a pattern, and I'm not alone in that. Professor Colin Espie of Glasgow University said that "Insomnia affects people's quality of life during the day, not just their sleep at night," he said. "Indeed, the survey data show significant effects across different aspects of personal functioning. Living with poor sleep and its consequences is not only very common, but it is in all likelihood degrading Britain's health. This is not a trivial matter. It's time for the NHS to pay attention to the scientific evidence that persistent poor sleep elevates the risk of developing new illnesses. This has been shown in disorders such as diabetes, but also very convincingly in depression." In light of the severity of this problem, and as someone who does rather well with sleep, I've devised some top tips for getting more kip...

Firstly, don't eat immediately before going to bed. You will feel too full and heavy to drift off into the land of nod. Eating too close to bedtime can also cause reflux problems which will either wake you up at night or leave you with a very sore chest the morning after.

Secondly, always have water with you in your bedroom – it's refreshing. It'll stop you from getting up within 15 minutes of trying to sleep just because you've become parched. Another benefit is that when you inevitably feel dehydrated in the morning, water is there with you already! Be careful, though, you might knock it over.

Thirdly – and this is important - keep your room cool. It's amazing to me that so many people have their bedrooms heated up to the very last moment before they attempt to sleep. This will only serve to keep you awake! A mild drop in temperature has been found to induce sleep. Heller says, "If you are in a cooler [rather than too-warm] room, it is easier for that to happen." But if the room becomes uncomfortably hot, you are more likely to wake up.'

Fourthly, make sure your room is very dark. If that's not possible, consider investing in a sleeping mask. It'll help you to sleep if you have fewer visual distractions.

Fifth and finally, consider doing some light exercise before bed. Outdoing some stretches can help you get into a nice relaxed state before you get into bed.

I hope this helps you all sleep much better. Leave your comments below with tips and tricks which work for you!

255. Which of these is not offered as a benefit of having water in your bedroom?
    A. It will refresh you
    B. It's useful when you wake up
    C. You might knock it over
    D. You won't become thirsty
    E. It will stop you from having to get up

256. Which of these is a direct contradiction?
    A. We are all sleeping badly these days but the author is not a doctor
    B. We are all sleeping badly these days but the author does well with sleep
    C. We're not all insomniacs but some people are
    D. The author is not a doctor but has tips for sleeping better
    E. None of the above

257. Which of these is an example of hyperbole?
    A. "Sleeping badly? We all are these days"
    B. "I'm no doctor – but certainly I've noticed something of a pattern"
    C. "I'm not saying we're all insomniacs for the purposes of medical science"
    D. "Always have water with you in your bedroom – it's refreshing"
    E. "Stretching out can help you get into a nice relaxed state"

258. Which does the author think is the best piece of advice?
    A. The first piece
    B. The third piece
    C. The fourth piece
    D. We don't have enough information to say
    E. The fifth piece

259. What might we infer about the author's occupation?
    A. She is a doctor
    B. She is a nurse
    C. She is a blog writer
    D. She sells water
    E. She is a sleep therapist

Passage 51 - Statehood

An extract from a passage on statehood:

Recently, debate has swirled around whether Palestine ought to be recognised as a state. This issue ought to be settled in a fair and neutral manner - by reference to the traditional criteria for statehood. Clearly, if the Palestinian entity fails to satisfy the traditional legal criteria for statehood, it cannot be recognised as a sovereign state. Eligibility for recognition does not depend on whether an entity wishes to satisfy the criteria for statehood, but on whether it meets those standards as a matter of fact. It is a well-established principle that unless an entity can show that, in practice, it meets the four criteria of statehood, recognition of statement must be withheld. As Kelsen has stated, 'a state violates international law and, thus, infringes upon the rights of other states if it recognises as a state a community which does not fulfil the requirements of international law.' Similarly, Lauterpacht has argued that the recognition of an entity which is not legally a state: '...is a wrong...because it constitutes an abuse of the power of recognition. It acknowledges as an independent state a community which is not, in law, independent and which does not, therefore, fulfil the essential conditions of statehood. It is, accordingly, a recognition which an international tribunal would declare not only to constitute a wrong but probably also to be in itself invalid.'

The four criteria for statehood contained in Article 1 of the 1933 Montevideo Convention are: a territory; a permanent population; a government which exercises authority and has the right to do so; and the capacity to enter into legal relations. It is submitted that all four are useful and are relatively complete as a set, meaning that the criteria do not need to be re-written.

There is no limit on the minimum territorial area necessary and a state may exist even when there are other claims to its territory – as Israel did in 1948. It is self-evident that we expect states to be territorial entities and it is clear that this is an appropriate criterion for statehood. States are required to have a population with a reasonable prospect of sustaining itself: because Western Sahara does not have this, it has not become a state. States are necessarily legal entities made up of people: it is evident that this is an appropriate criterion for a state.

The 'government' requirement has two elements: the actual exercise of authority, and the right to do so. This may not necessarily be control without outside help: when Republic of the Congo (now Democratic Republic of Congo) became a state, it needed UN assistance for control. The government need not be 'legitimate' or 'democratic' – it just needs to be in effective control. This is a necessary criterion because, without it, other states would not be able to interact with the state in question. Capacity to enter into relations with other states is essentially 'independence' from any other state. Taiwan is not a state because it lacks independence from China. The two main elements here are the separate existence of an entity with reasonably coherent frontiers and the fact that the entity is not subject to the authority of any other state or group of states. This is a necessary criterion for statehood because it permits the state to interact with other states and be an actor on the world stage: ensuring the principle of equality of states.

HSPSAA: SECTION A — QUESTIONS

260. What is the passage arguing?
    A. That the current criteria for determining statehood are inappropriate
    B. That Taiwan deserves independence
    C. That the current criteria for determining statehood are appropriate
    D. That government is not a good criterion for determining statehood
    E. That Western Sahara should be a state

261. Why is Taiwan not a state?
    A. It lacks a government
    B. It lacks a permanent population
    C. It isn't very important
    D. It lacks the capacity to enter into legal relations
    E. It lacks boundaries

262. What does the author think about the fact that government need not be 'legitimate' or 'democratic'?
    A. She thinks it's immoral
    B. She thinks it's a really good thing because it's neutral
    C. She thinks it's unfair on Taiwan
    D. She does not offer a viewpoint
    E. None of the above

263. Which of the following is an argument given in favour of the permanent population requirement?
    A. It is necessary that states are entities made up of people
    B. There wouldn't be a government without a population
    C. There wouldn't be an army without a population
    D. Western Sahara is not a state
    E. There needs to be a population over which to exercise control

264. Which criterion lacks any real argument in favour of its existence?
    A. Permanent population
    B. Territory
    C. Government
    D. Capacity to enter into legal relations
    E. All of the above

Passage 52- Sex Education

Recently, the Educational Select Committee has been calling for sex education to be made compulsory in schools. This may well be necessary, however, more pressing, in my view, is the argument that sex education in schools has got to change. The current system leaves children totally confused and unequipped for dealing with relationships. The whole system ought to be built around teaching healthy and happy relationships, with the biology section firmly as a secondary point to that. A report has warned that some children are able to name body parts but yet do not properly understand what was meant by giving consent. Admittedly, the proportion of young people citing school lessons as their main source of information about sexual matters has increased; however, according to the National Survey of Sexual Attitudes and Lifestyles from 2010-12, 61 percent of children still get their information elsewhere.

This means that as it is, children are going to the internet or their peers to glean more information about sexual relationships and this is leading to unstable adolescents. MPs were told it is now "normal" for 14-year-olds to pose in bras for social media photos and that around one in three 15-year-olds had sent someone a naked photo of themselves. Change must come in order to address problems such as teen pregnancy, STIs, sexual exploitation, and cyberbullying. Concurring with this view, Graham Stewart said, 'It's important that school leaders and governors take PSHE seriously and improve their provision by investing in training for teachers and putting PSHE [personal, social, health and economic education] lessons on the school timetable. Statutory status will help ensure all of this happens.' The Tory MP added that 'young people have a right to information that will keep them healthy and safe' and said that changes to the system could help children 'live happy and healthy lives'.

I propose that we change the curriculum so that the first few lessons are based on different kinds of relationships and how to have them in a healthy way. If it's really necessary, we could even start with learning about happy friendships. After that, we could proceed on to romantic relationships and marriage and co-habitation. Teachers should explain conflict resolution, compromise, and communication to children, as well as parenthood. All these things are more useful to young children than talking about sperm and eggs. Moreover, children would not be traumatised because they are forced to learn, instead of things entirely inappropriate for them to know.

I admit that children do need to learn about the biology of sex – but this should not be pushed as the most important element of their lessons. The classes themselves would be better labelled 'relationship education' than 'sex education' anyway because that is what the lessons should focus on. The truth, of course, is that even adults struggle with issues like compromise and communication. Children would benefit enormously from learning about these things: and it would create adults who were much better prepared for the world of love and relationships.

265. What is the main argument of the passage?
    A. We should teach children communication skills
    B. We should change how sex education is taught
    C. We should rename sex education classes
    D. We should stop children going on the internet
    E. We should ban the teaching of sex education

266. What concession does the author make in the second paragraph?
    A. She admits children do need to learn about biology
    B. She agrees we could start classes by learning about friendship
    C. She says we should teach children about marriage
    D. She says we should change the curriculum
    E. She admits that it would be impossible to avoid teaching sex education

267. Which of these arguments is not made in favour of a new teaching approach?
    A. Children would enjoy such classes more
    B. They would mean children were more able to have healthy relationships
    C. The classes would be more useful to children
    D. Children would not be traumatised
    E. Children would be more prepared for love

268. What does the author regard as the relationship between teaching about relationships and about the biology of sex?
    A. We shouldn't teach biology at all; only relationships
    B. Teaching biology is more important
    C. Teaching relationships is more important
    D. We shouldn't teach relationships at all; only biology
    E. None of the above

269. What does the author think is leading to unstable adolescents?
    A. Too many sex education classes
    B. The fact that children go to the wrong sources for sex education
    C. Children do not have happy friendships
    D. Children do not know how to communicate
    E. Children being traumatised and confused by hearing about sex

Passage 53 – Life at work

The UK workforce has undoubtedly become more diverse as society itself has changed and become more diverse. For instance, recent years have seen an increase in the numbers of women at work, the numbers of single parents; reports of UK demographics have also revealed that we have a much larger ageing population than before. Domestic and family responsibilities have also shifted over the years and in response, legislation has evolved and changed to offer both men and women the opportunity to request flexible working which better suits modern conditions and families.

The need to provide parents with more flexible working patterns was first identified following the issue of the Government's Green Paper – "Work and Parents: Competitiveness and Choice". The Government then set up the Work and Parents Taskforce to consider the issue of working parents and flexible working. They submitted their final report – "About Time: Flexible Working" at the end of 2001. Since then, the report has been updated to extend the recommendation for a right to request flexible working to all employees.

It is also promising that many businesses have started to recognise that there are myriad benefits in allowing their staff to have flexible working hours. Such arrangements may include working flexi-time, job shares, and part-time work. This is especially useful for new parents, who want to return to work but not do as much as they had previously. It may also be used by those who want to phase into retirement but not stop working too abruptly, or by those struggling with low-level health problems.

One of the major benefits from the perspectives of businesses is that their employees become much more productive. This may be for several reasons. Firstly, their employees may simply be grateful to the business for allowing them to plan their lives as they wish. It could also be that staff working fewer hours have more energy to give to the business, more progressive companies believe that by allowing workers time off to deal with personal issues and childcare, there is less likelihood of employees having to resort to calling in sick. Alternatively, they may have greater job satisfaction because they are happier in their jobs, meaning they give more to their jobs. Some have suggested that employees become more productive simply because they feel if they do not, flexible working hours will be taken away from them. This is unlikely, however, because businesses which offer flexi-time have largely invested in the scheme wholesale.

Flexible working hours are especially useful for those who have just had children. Given that the government has recently made movements towards allowing shared parental leave, businesses which are allowing a flexible return for their employees are essentially ahead of the curve. It may soon be that all businesses are required to have this policy – no bad thing, if you consider how many fathers wish to be more involved with the early weeks of their children's lives. Businesses might also consider introducing nurseries if they wish to accommodate new parents further.

270. What does the author think about the possibility of all businesses having to offer flexible returns to work for new parents?
- A. She thinks it's positive
- B. She thinks it's negative
- C. She is neutral
- D. There is not enough information to say
- E. She thinks it has pros and cons

271. Which group does the author think benefit most from flexible working?
- A. Ill people
- B. Old people
- C. People who have just had children
- D. There is not enough information to say
- E. Disabled people

272. Which reason does the author think is unlikely to explain why employees become much more productive when working flexi-time?
- A. Employees may be grateful
- B. They may have greater job satisfaction
- C. They may have more energy
- D. They may feel flexi-time will be taken away if they don't work hard
- E. They may feel more determined

273. What benefit can we be certain that businesses gain from offering flexi-time?
- A. They are ahead of the curve
- B. Their staff is more productive
- C. Their employees have more energy
- D. They make more money
- E. Their employees feel indebted to them

274. What is the purpose of the piece?
- A. To inform the reader of the new trend of flexi-time
- B. To persuade the government to make flexi-time compulsory
- C. To persuade new parents to take flexi-time
- D. To persuade people not to retire abruptly
- E. To persuade trade unions to campaign for flexi-time

Passage 54 – The Economy

The global downturn has resulted in soaring rates of unemployment and dramatic cuts to wages. This has brought about a stark decline in living standards across the country and has even, according to one commentator this week, brought about a decline in cardiovascular health. Given the severity of the crisis, it is no wonder that commentators are now putting pressure on the government in the hope of spurring them on to more effective action.

Some commentators have been arguing this week that due to continuing global economic uncertainty, it would be appropriate for governments to invest much more seriously in large-scale infrastructure projects. These might include the construction of new homes, development of the railway and road systems, or work on major bridges. It is well-known that such projects do a great deal to stimulate the economy because the projects employ a lot of people in the building. More significant, however, is that they employ even more people in the planning and sales of such projects. Moreover, a lot of people will spend money in response to these new projects – for example, buying flats, further helping to stimulate the economy. One wonders, then, why the government is choosing not to invest much further. Economic recovery will not happen by itself.

Environmental groups have expressed concern at the pressure being put on the government to invest in infrastructure, saying that the carbon footprint of such projects is huge. It is true that the building of new roads alone has a significant impact on noise pollution, water pollution, habitat destruction, and local air pollution. An increased number of cars on the roads also has the potential to affect climate change. However, it seems that the time to worry about climate change is not right now. Of course, environmental groups are concerned for people's welfare, but they must realise that people are becoming poorer and suffering due to the economic downturn *right now* and that ought to be our top priority at the moment. Climate change is more of a long-term issue and after we have averted the current economic crisis, we will have the opportunity and the resources to turn our attention towards it.

The proposals have also faced criticism from people living in greenbelt areas. They are worried that land near their homes will inevitably be built on and ruin their views. This is a possibility and it would be foolish to deny it. However, theirs is a selfish attitude to take. The best way to stimulate the economy has to be big infrastructure projects, and people living in the greenbelt need to make sacrifices like the rest of us have had to.

House building companies have, to everyone's surprise, been sitting on the fence about this issue. They are of course keen to take on new contracts but have expressed concern about how fast they might be expected to roll out new projects. This is unacceptable – such companies ought to be leading the way in attempting to save the UK from a double dip recession.

275. What does the author think about the relationship between the number of people employed to build large-scale infrastructure projects and the number of people involved in planning and selling those projects?
    A. She thinks they are equally important
    B. She thinks the number employed to build is more important
    C. She thinks the number employed in planning and selling is more important
    D. There is not enough information to say
    E. She doesn't outline any relationship between the two

276. What is the unstated assumption in the first paragraph?
    A. A lot of people will be employed thanks to big infrastructure projects
    B. The government ought to help with stimulating the economy
    C. The economic recovery will not happen without help
    D. It's good for people to live in flats
    E. There is currently global uncertainty

277. Which of the groups in the passage does the author agree with?
    A. The commentators arguing for infrastructure investment
    B. Environmental groups arguing against it
    C. House building companies which are unsure
    D. People living in green areas arguing against it
    E. People living in green areas arguing for it

278. What effect does the author think infrastructure projects would have on the economy?
    A. It will annoy people in greenbelt areas
    B. It will mean more money is going into the economy and lead to growth
    C. It will not impact the economy
    D. It will cause pressure on house building companies
    E. It will reduce the price of houses

279. Which group does the author think are not considering other people?
    A. The commentators arguing for infrastructure investment
    B. Environmental groups arguing against it
    C. House building companies which are unsure
    D. People living in green areas arguing against it
    E. The government

Passage 55 - Tourism

Tourism is seriously big business in this country. The website, visitengland.com, has presented research this week on where and how the UK makes an income from tourism. Cardiff had more visitors than the rest of Wales combined, with Bristol and Manchester also proving popular with international visitors. The World Tourism rankings can also offer insight as to the impact of tourism on economies in the world; the rankings are compiled by the United Nations World Tourism Organisation (UNWTO) as part of their *World Tourism Barometer* publication. This publication is released three times throughout the year. In the publication, UN regions are ranked by three factors: the number of international visitor arrivals, by the revenue generated by inbound tourism, and by the expenditures of outbound travellers. In 2014, there were over 51 million international tourist arrivals to the Middle East, an increase of 5.0% over 2013. In 2014, there were over 582 million international tourist arrivals to Europe, an increase of 3.0% over 2013. We also discovered that London is the world's most popular tourist destination!

The most profitable tourist attraction in London is Madame Tussauds, bizarrely enough. People queued on average two hours last summer to get into a museum which is essentially just wax models of celebrities. And yet, it made £5 million of profit in 2015. It is astonishing that Madame Tussauds received three times as many visitors as the Science Museum last year – but apparently that is what the people want. There really is no accounting for taste.

It is a concern, however, that some councils have responded to this news by announcing plans to divert more money into advertising their cities to tourists. Given that vital services are being cut due to lack of local authority funding, councils should not be investing in tourism. This is because it is such a high-risk industry. Holidays are luxuries, rather than necessities. During recessions or times of economic downturn, families cut back their spending on holidays. This can mean that the tourism industry suffers the most when a crash or any sort of crisis occurs. Political relations between different nations can also have an impact on the level of tourism that one nation receives. The potential income to be obtained through tourism is also very seasonal. Much of the UK, London notwithstanding, receives virtually no tourism in the winter months. Families wishing to take their children abroad also tend to only travel during the long school holidays.

280. Which city in the UK receives the most visitors?
    A. Bristol
    B. Manchester
    C. London
    D. Cardiff
    E. The passage does not say

281. What point is the author making in the third paragraph?
    A. London gets tourists in winter
    B. Councils are making a risky move
    C. Councils are making a good move
    D. Everywhere gets tourists in winter
    E. Even London receives no tourism in winter

282. Which idea is not discussed in the passage?
    A. Tourists going to the beach
    B. The recession
    C. Tourists going to museums
    D. A report on tourism
    E. Investment in tourism

283. Which of the following ideas is supported by the passage?
    A. Other countries would benefit from copying the UK's approach
    B. London is a very nice place to live
    C. London is the most fun place to visit in the UK
    D. Madame Tussauds is not as interesting or enriching as people think
    E. Madame Tussauds is a good place to visit

284. What does the author mean by saying that the income from tourism is 'very seasonal'?
    A. That there is income all year round
    B. That no money can be made outside summer
    C. That the income depends on the seasons
    D. That people spend more money in winter
    E. No income is made in winter

Passage 56 – The drinks industry

The most profitable drinks industry in the USA is the soft drinks industry, with brands like Coca-Cola raking in most of their sales revenue there; whereas in Europe, it's the alcohol industry. This has caused some worries for Europe; Alcohol-related harm is a major public health concern in the EU as it is accountable for over 7% of all ill health and early deaths. Even moderate alcohol consumption has been found to increase the long-term risk of certain heart conditions, liver diseases, and cancers, and frequent consumption of large amounts can, of course, lead to dependence.

Young people are particularly at risk of short-term effects of drunkenness, which include accidents and violence, with alcohol-related deaths accounting for around 25% of all deaths in young men aged between 15 and 29. This revelation has also received a great deal of attention on social media, with American teens tweeting to call Europeans 'alcoholics'. However, although Europe must, undoubtedly, decrease its consumption of alcohol, the real reason for the difference between the European and American statistics is simply the high sugar taxes imposed on much of Europe and the high alcohol taxes imposed in the US. Tax, it seems, makes all the difference.

There is more sugar in American fizzy drinks than their European equivalents. In fact, there is even less in Asian markets. American senators have had very little joy in trying to tackle this problem because drinks companies provide financial support to so many of those in politics in the US. In the UK, at least, we cannot imagine what that would be like. But the truth is, the American politicians have their hands tied on this issue. In the UK and EU more broadly, sugar is also becoming more unpopular with consumers. Brands are seeking to offer more appealing sweeteners in soft drinks, with a growing media focus on the health hazards of "hidden" sugar in soft drinks. Firms are, therefore, increasingly investing in 'reduced sugar' options. A new set of pocket squashes was, for example, created by brands such as Robinsons Squash'd and Oasis Mighty Drops in 2014, with these products all containing no added sugar. However, consumers remain concerned about artificial sweeteners too.

American teenagers are not allowed to consume alcohol until they are 21 years old – an idea which many Europeans find truly bizarre. The French and Italians, in particular, allow young people to start drinking at a very young age as long as they are accompanied by their parents. The French – very meritoriously – take children with them to dinner parties and slowly allow them to start drinking alcohol in a sensible way. The British are yet to catch on to this. As a result, the Americans have a significant problem with the drinking habits of young people. They've attempted to tackle this by slapping a heavy tax on alcohol – but this appears to have made little difference to those in their twenties. The Europeans have taken the same approach with fizzy drinks, which has been somewhat more effective.

285. To what does the author attribute the difference between the USA and Europe in terms of drinks industries?
    A. Sugar levels
    B. Tax
    C. The fact Europeans are alcoholics
    D. She does not attribute it to anything
    E. Branding

286. Which market has the most sugar in their fizzy drinks?
    A. We do not know
    B. European market
    C. American market
    D. Asian market
    E. None of the above

287. What does the author mean when she says that "American politicians have their hands tied"?
    A. They find it difficult to tackle the sugar levels in fizzy drinks
    B. They cannot make alcohol more popular
    C. They cannot communicate with UK politicians on this issue
    D. They cannot get Asian markets to put more sugar in their drinks
    E. Legislation prevents them from tackling the issue of sugar consumption

288. With regards to alcohol, which country's approach does the author commend?
    A. The USA
    B. The UK
    C. The Italians
    D. The French
    E. The Chinese

289. What impact has the tax on alcohol in the USA had on the drinking habits of young people?
    A. They have stopped drinking entirely
    B. They drink a lot more as a rebellion
    C. It has reduced their drinking significantly
    D. It has not had much effect at all
    E. It has increased their consumption of cheaper brands of alcohol

Passage 57 – Age Imbalance

There are statistics which suggest that in many of the world's least developed countries, close to half the population are under the age of 20. Such countries have not experienced the same decrease in birth rates that we have seen in the more developed West. One reason may be that less developed countries depend on farming for food and wealth. More children mean more potential farm workers, and more food for everyone (and more money). In less developed countries, generally, children are less likely to survive into adulthood (disease, etc.). So having more children is a way of ensuring that a parent has, at least, some children to take care of them in their old age. Lastly, people may not always have access to birth control in less developed countries. So although here in the UK we can drive down to the pharmacy for condoms, people in rural India don't have that option. Consequently, the demographics here in the West are quite different. In fact, in the UK, more than 20% of the population are over the age of 75 – a proportion which in itself is not sustainable. 10 million people in the UK are over 65 years old. The latest projections are for 5½ million more elderly people in 20 years' time and the number will have nearly doubled to around 19 million by 2050. Within this total, the number of very old people grows even faster. There are currently three million people aged more than 80 years and this is projected to almost double by 2030 and reach eight million by 2050. France finds itself in a similar position.

In countries such as Japan, the percentage of the population aged over 75 is set to hit almost 30%. This is concerning because governments are likely to struggle to pay for their ageing populations. Much of today's public spending on benefits is focused on elderly people. 65% of Department for Work and Pensions benefit expenditure goes to those over working age, equivalent to £100 billion in 2010/11 or one-seventh of public expenditure. According to a parliament publication, 'continuing to provide state benefits and pensions at today's average would mean additional spending of £10 billion a year for every additional one million people over working age.' As a direct result of this issue, those in the workforce will have to retire much later. It may also be that pensions are cut, along with social care. There is serious concern that the ageing population could lead to a reduction in government support for care homes.

Most alarmingly, in countries such as Niger, there will simply not be enough money to fund education for all these young people. It is widely accepted that education is the most efficient route for development and for Niger, which routinely finds itself in the bottom 10% of the world's countries on development indexes, education of its youth could make a huge difference. But the surge in births means this simply will not be possible. Other issues preventing development may include the relative lack of healthcare and climate change.

290. Which consequence can we be sure will result from Japan's ageing population?
    A. A cut in government support for care homes
    B. A cut to pensions
    C. A cut to social care
    D. People working for more of their lives
    E. None of the above

291. What reason does the author give for the difference between the birth rates between the developed West and developing countries?
    A. Differing employment opportunities
    B. She does not give a reason
    C. In developing countries, children are a financial asset
    D. In developed countries, people are too career-focused to have children
    E. Lack of money for contraception

292. Which country is the author most concerned for?
    A. Niger
    B. The UK
    C. Japan
    D. France
    E. Nigeria

293. What is the unstated assumption in the last paragraph?
    A. Education leads to development
    B. Development is a good thing in itself
    C. Niger is very undeveloped
    D. The West should help Niger
    E. Climate change is more important than healthcare

294. What can we infer from the second paragraph about an ageing population?
    A. They work hard
    B. Families of elderly people are not looking after them properly
    C. Governments only care about elderly people
    D. They are very expensive
    E. They are able to care for grandchildren

Passage 58 – Jobs for graduates

Joining a tech start-up is the number one trendy move for top graduates across the UK and the US today. Graduates nowadays are gravitating towards app development and other technology markets. Indeed, these industries are welcoming graduates with open arms; opportunities in search engine optimisation and in pay per click advertising. However, many graduates do not properly think through the options and opt for these roles all too quickly. It's depressing to see young people just go and do something because it seems 'cool' rather than because it's actually of any use. They swan around thinking they are so on trend and yet most of them produce nothing of value whatsoever. Further – a lot of their jobs are pretty dull in practice.

More interesting, in my view, is a career in the arts – for instance, a career as an art gallery curator. This job involves the managing of collections of paintings and objects. Curators also undertake art research, identifying and cataloguing paintings and other items. Moreover, they interact with the public, answering visitors' queries and giving talks about the art collections they manage. The job also involves organising displays and negotiation funding for the sale or loan of paintings to the art gallery. An alternative job in the arts is that of a museum curator. These curators manage collections of objects of historical or scientific interest. They ensure that these objects are stored in the right conditions, give talks to groups, and liaise with staff in other museums. They also have to have good finance management skills as they are given the responsibility of managing museum budgets. One unfortunate consequence of the recession has been the cutting of government provision to the arts. Regardless, it is an exciting career path for those who have the strength of character to overcome the difficulties the area is currently facing. The opportunity to create and to help others to do the same has to be one the most exciting things anyone could do in their twenties.

Jobs in finance may seem like good ideas for graduates but jobs in publishing actually offer more opportunities for the truly talented. This is because publishers are much more rigorous in their hiring procedures – and rightly so – and as such, get a much better crop of graduates. One type of job in publishing is that of the commissioning editor. These individuals commission or buy new authors, book titles, or ideas for publication. You'll choose books or media products that you think will sell well. You'll also monitor the performance of published titles. If you love reading and you're able to combine that with market research and spot market trends, then this could be the role for you. Content creation is another option for those who enjoy writing; firms are crying out for graduates to produce content which will enable them to promote their businesses. Graduates hoping to produce or edit content will do well in this fast-growing industry. The point here is that although I'm sure you've been told that jobs in the industries that graduates typically go into have a lot to offer, you should not close your mind to other options. Think a little bigger!

295. What is the attitude of the author towards those who join start-ups?
    A. She looks down on them
    B. She admires them
    C. She thinks they are selfish
    D. She doesn't understand their motivations
    E. She is accepting of them

296. What is the unstated assumption in the passage?
    A. The best jobs are well paid
    B. The best jobs are in tech
    C. The best jobs are interesting
    D. The best jobs are charitable
    E. All of the above

297. Which pair of jobs does the author draw a direct contrast between?
    A. Jobs in finance and jobs in publishing
    B. Jobs in finance and jobs in the arts
    C. Jobs in the arts and jobs in publishing
    D. Jobs in the publishing and jobs in technology
    E. Jobs in technology and jobs in government

298. What view does the author take on hiring procedures in publishing firms?
    A. She does not give a view
    B. She thinks they're not as good as hiring procedures in finance
    C. She thinks they're too hard
    D. She thinks they're the right approach
    E. She thinks that they are unfair

299. What is the aim of the article?
    A. To recruit people into publishing
    B. To recruit people into the arts
    C. To get students to consider less traditional career paths
    D. To get students to work hard at university
    E. To argue that careers in arts are the best

Passage 59- The Theory of Social Revolutions – Brooks Adams

Were all other evidence lacking, the inference that radical changes are at hand might be deduced from the past. In the experience of the English-speaking race, about once in every three generations a social convulsion has occurred; and probably such catastrophes must continue to occur in order that laws and institutions may be adapted to physical growth. Human society is a living organism, working mechanically, like any other organism. It has members, a circulation, a nervous system, and a sort of skin or envelope, consisting of its laws and institutions. This skin, or envelope, however, does not expand automatically, as it would had Providence intended humanity to be peaceful, but is only fitted to new conditions by those painful and conscious efforts which we call revolutions. Usually, these revolutions are warlike, but sometimes they are benign, as was the revolution over which General Washington, our first great "Progressive," presided, when the rotting Confederation, under his guidance, was converted into a relatively excellent administrative system by the adoption of the Constitution.

Taken for all in all, I conceive General Washington to have been the greatest man of the eighteenth century, but to me, his greatness chiefly consists in that balance of mind which enabled him to recognise when an old order had passed away, and to perceive how a new order could be best introduced. Washington was, in his way, a large capitalist, but he was much more. He was not only a wealthy planter, but he was an engineer, a traveller, to an extent a manufacturer, a politician, and a soldier, and he saw that, as a conservative, he must be "Progressive" and raise the law to a power high enough to constrain all these thirteen refractory units. For Washington understood that peace does not consist in talking platitudes at conferences, but in organising a sovereignty strong enough to coerce its subjects.

The problem of constructing such a sovereignty was the problem which Washington solved, temporarily at least, without violence. He prevailed not only because of an intelligence and elevation of character which enabled him to comprehend, and to persuade others, that, to attain a common end, all must make sacrifices, but also because he was supported by a body of the most remarkable men whom America has ever produced. Men who, though doubtless in a numerical minority, taking the country as a whole, by sheer weight of ability and energy, achieved their purpose.

Yet, even Washington and his adherents could not alter the limitations of the human mind. He could postpone, but he could not avert the impact of conflicting social forces. In 1789, he compromised, but he did not determine the question of sovereignty. He eluded an impending conflict by introducing courts as political arbitrators, and the expedient worked more or less well until the tension reached a certain point. Then it broke down, and the question of sovereignty had to be settled in America, as elsewhere, on the field of battle.

300. What is meant by the phrase 'social convulsion'?
    A. A catastrophe
    B. An attack
    C. A period of change
    D. Development of human society
    E. A revolution

301. Which of the following ideas is the skin metaphor used to illustrate?
    A. Human beings are comparable to skin
    B. Human society grows over time
    C. Progression is inevitable
    D. There are now too many laws
    E. Change does not come about peacefully and organically

302. Which of the following would most weaken the author's argument in relation to General Washington?
    A. Washington's supporters went on to achieve great things independently
    B. Many intelligent men opposed Washington
    C. Washington was known as a genius
    D. Most of Washington's supporters had little experience or charisma
    E. Washington's supporters produced ingenious solutions

303. Which of the following is not used to characterise Washington?
    A. Successful
    B. Sacrificial
    C. Persuasive
    D. Traveller
    E. Energetic

304. Why, according to the author, was Washington unable to prevent a revolution?
    A. He was too disorganised
    B. He was able only to postpone it
    C. Because it is impossible for the human mind to devise a means of doing so
    D. He didn't face the problem head-on
    E. He commanded the support of only a minority

Passage 60 - Culture and anarchy - Matthew Arnold

The whole scope of the essay is to recommend culture as the great help out of our present difficulties; culture being a pursuit of our total perfection by means of getting to know, on all the matters which most concern us, the best which has been thought and said in the world, and, through this knowledge, turning a stream of fresh and free thought upon our stock notions and habits, which we now follow staunchly but mechanically, vainly imagining that there is a virtue in following them staunchly which makes up for the mischief of following them mechanically. This, and this alone, is the scope of the following essay.

I say again here, what I have said in the pages which follow, that from the faults and weaknesses of bookmen a notion of something bookish, pedantic, and futile, has got itself more or less connected with the word culture, and that it is a pity we cannot use a word more perfectly free from all shadow of reproach. And yet, futile as are many bookmen, and helpless as books and reading often prove for bringing nearer to perfection those who use them, one must, I think, be struck more and more the longer one lives to find how much, in our present society, a man's life of each day depends for its solidity and value on whether he reads during that day. More and more, he who examines himself will find the difference it makes to him, at the end of any given day, whether or not he has pursued his avocations throughout it without reading at all.

This, however, is a matter for each man's private conscience and experience. If a man without books or reading, or reading nothing but his letters and the newspapers, gets nevertheless a fresh and free play of the best thoughts upon his stock notions and habits, he has got culture. He has got that for which we prize and recommend culture; he has got that which at the present moment we seek culture that it may give us. This inward operation is the very life and essence of culture, as we conceive it.

Nevertheless, it is not easy so to frame one's discourse concerning the operation of culture, as to avoid giving frequent occasion to a misunderstanding whereby the essential inwardness of the operation is lost sight of. We are supposed, when we criticise by the help of culture some imperfect doing or other, to have in our eye some well-known rival plan of doing, which we want to serve and recommend. Thus, for instance, because I have freely pointed out the dangers and inconveniences to which our literature is exposed in the absence of any centre of taste and authority like the French Academy, it is constantly said that I want to introduce here in England an institution like the French Academy.

I have indeed expressly declared that I wanted no such thing; but let us notice how it is just our worship of machinery, and of external doing, which leads to this charge being brought; and how the inwardness of culture makes us seize, for watching and cure, the faults to which our want of an academy inclines us, and yet prevents us from trusting to an arm of flesh, as the Puritans say – from blindly flying to this outward machinery of an academy, in order to help ourselves. For the very same culture and free inward play of thought which shows us how the Corinthian style, or the whimsies about the One Primeval Language, are generated and strengthened in the absence of an academy, shows us, too, how little any academy, such as we should be likely to get, would cure them.

305. What is the main argument of the passage?
    A. Culture should be pursued because it will give us fresh perspective
    B. Reading makes a big difference to the value of one's day
    C. We do not need an academy
    D. We worship machinery
    E. It doesn't matter how you obtain culture, so long as you obtain it

306. The author mentions the 'charge' brought against him to illustrate what idea?
    A. That culture is inward
    B. That an academy is desirable
    C. That an academy is futile
    D. That we only care about external actions
    E. That his critics do not understand him

307. What is meant by the phrase 'inward operation'?
    A. One's inner thoughts
    B. Emotions
    C. That culture manifests its effects only in our thoughts
    D. That culture is powerful
    E. That culture leads to secret change

308. Why, according to the author, would an academy be unhelpful?
    A. It is outward in its operation
    B. It is inward in its operation
    C. It is puritan
    D. It would be too large
    E. We are all already cultured enough without one

309. What is meant by the phrase 'a matter for each man's private conscience and experience'?
    A. It should be up to the individual to choose how to get culture
    B. Culture is subjective
    C. Culture is objective
    D. People feel guilty without culture
    E. All of the above

Passage 61 - Laughter: An Essay on the Meaning of Comic

Henri Bergson, member of the Institute Professor at the College de France

What does laughter mean? What is the basal element in the laughable? What common ground can we find between the grimace of a merry-andrew, a play upon words, an equivocal situation in a burlesque, and a scene of high comedy? The greatest of thinkers, from Aristotle downwards, have tackled this little problem, which has a knack of baffling every effort, of slipping away and escaping only to bob up again, a pert challenge flung at philosophic speculation. Our excuse for attacking the problem in our turn must lie in the fact that we shall not aim at imprisoning the comic spirit within a definition. We regard it, above all, as a living thing. We shall confine ourselves to watching it grow and expand. Passing by imperceptible gradations from one form to another, it will be seen to achieve the strangest metamorphoses. We shall disdain nothing we have seen.

And maybe we may also find that we have made an acquaintance that is useful. For the comic spirit has a logic of its own, even in its wildest eccentricities. It has a method in its madness. It dreams, I admit, but it conjures up, in its dreams, visions that are at once accepted and understood by the whole of a social group. Can it then fail to throw light for us on the way that human imagination works, and more particularly social, collective, and popular imagination? Begotten of real life and akin to art, should it not also have something of its own to tell us about art and life?

At the outset, we shall put forward three observations which we look upon as fundamental. The first point to which attention should be called is that the comic does not exist outside the pale of what is strictly human. A landscape may be beautiful, charming and sublime, or insignificant and ugly; it will never be laughable.

Here I would point out, as a symptom equally worthy of notice, the absence of feeling which usually accompanies laughter. Indifference is its natural environment, for laughter has no greater foe than emotion. I do not mean that we could not laugh at a person who inspires us with pity, for instance, or even with affection, but in such a case we must, for the moment, put our affection out of court and impose silence upon our pity. It is enough for us to stop our ears to the sound of music, in a room where dancing is going on, for the dancers at once to appear ridiculous. How many human actions would stand a similar test? Should we not see many of them suddenly pass from grave to gay, on isolating them from the accompanying music of sentiment? To produce the whole of its effect, then, the comic demands something like a momentary anaesthesia of the heart. Its appeal is to intelligence, pure and simple.

This intelligence, however, must always remain in touch with other intelligences. And here is the third fact to which attention should be drawn. Our laughter is always the laughter of a group. It may, perchance, have happened to you, when seated in a railway carriage or at table d'hôte, to hear travellers relating to one another stories which must have been comic to them, for they laughed heartily. Had you been one of their company, you would have laughed like them; but, as you were not, you had no desire whatever to do so.

To understand laughter, we must put it back into its natural environment, which is society, and above all must we determine the utility of its function, which is a social one. Laughter must answer to certain requirements of life in common. It must have a social signification.

310. The writer uses the word 'basal' to mean:
    A. Essential
    B. Notable
    C. Undeveloped
    D. Elusive
    E. Significant

311. What is the central motivation for the writer's exploration of the topic of laughter?
    A. To avoid imprisoning the concept within a definition
    B. To watch it achieve 'strange metamorphoses'
    C. To throw light on human functioning and behaviour
    D. To demonstrate that laughter has 'a method in its madness'
    E. The fact that other great thinkers have failed to reach a conclusion

312. What is the conclusion of the fourth paragraph?
    A. We can only laugh at those we pity by momentarily ignoring that sentiment
    B. Indifference is laughter's natural environment
    C. It is noteworthy that absence of feeling accompanies laughter
    D. If we stop our ears to the sound of the accompanying music, the dancers immediately appear ridiculous
    E. Music determines the sentiments of dancers

313. Which of the following is a metaphor used by the author?
    A. The accompanying music of sentiment
    B. Its appeal is to intelligence
    C. Akin to art
    D. Pass from grave to gay
    E. The comic does not exist outside the pale of what is strictly human

314. Which one of the following is not used to characterise laughter?
    A. It is the laughter of a group
    B. Social
    C. Sentimental
    D. Illuminating
    E. A living thing

Passage 62 - The God-Idea of the Ancients

Eliza Burt Gamble

Nowhere is the influence of sex more plainly manifested than in the formulation of religious conceptions and creeds. With the rise of male power and dominion, and the corresponding repression of the natural female instincts, the principles that originally constituted the God-idea gradually gave place to a Deity better suited to the peculiar bias that had been given to the male organism. An anthropomorphic God, like that of the Jews, whose chief attributes are power and virile could have had its origin only under a system of masculine rule.

Religion is especially liable to reflect the vagaries and weaknesses of human nature; and, as the forms and habits of thought connected with worship take a firmer hold on the mental constitution than do those belonging to any other department of human experience, religious conceptions should be subjected to frequent and careful examination in order to perceive, if possible, the extent to which we are holding on to ideas which are unsuited to existing conditions.

In an age when every branch of inquiry is being subjected to reasonable criticism, it would seem that the origin and growth of religion should be investigated from beneath the surface and that all the facts bearing upon it should be brought forward as a contribution to our fund of general information. As well might we hope to gain a complete knowledge of human history by studying only the present aspect of society, as to expect to reach reasonable conclusions respecting the prevailing God-idea by investigating the various creeds and dogmas of existing faiths.

Doubtless, the worship of a female energy prevailed under the matriarchal system and was practised at a time when women were the recognised heads of families and when they were regarded as the more important factors in human society. After women began to leave their homes at marriage, and after property, especially land, had fallen under the supervision and control of men, the latter, as they manipulated all the necessaries of life and the means of supplying them, began to regard themselves as superior beings, and later, to claim that as a factor in reproduction, or creation, the male was the more important. With this change, the ideas of a Deity also began to undergo a modification. The dual principle necessary to creation, and which had hitherto been worshipped as an indivisible unity, began gradually to separate into its individual elements, the male representing spirit, the dominant moving or forming force in the creation processes. A little observation and reflection will show us that during this change in the ideas relative to a creative principle, or God, descent and the rights of succession which had hitherto been reckoned through the mother were changed from the female to the male line, the father having in the meantime become the only recognised parent.

315. What assumption does the author make in the first paragraph?
    A. There is no God
    B. The Jewish God does not exist
    C. The Jewish ideas of God did not come about through divine revelation
    D. The Jewish God is a product of patriarchy
    E. In a more equal society, we would have a gender neutral conception of God

316. Why does the author believe that religious conceptions are in special need of being subjected to careful examination?
    A. Religious views and rites have a very strong hold on the mental constitution
    B. In order to determine whether we are holding on to ideas that are unsuited to existing conditions
    C. They have a huge impact on the structure of society
    D. They afford insight into our fund of information about society
    E. They can influence the way in which women are perceived

317. What comes closest to the author's view of the relationship between religion and society?
    A. Religion determines the structure of society
    B. Religion and society evolve together
    C. There is no relationship between the two
    D. The structure of society determines our religious views
    E. Different societies have different conceptions of religion

318. Which of the following is merely an assertion?
    A. Religious conceptions should be subjected to frequent and careful examination
    B. Religion is liable to reflect the vagaries and weaknesses of human nature
    C. The origin and growth of religion should be investigated
    D. Nowhere is the influence of sex more plainly manifested than in the formulation of religious conceptions and creeds
    E. An anthropomorphic god like that of the Jews could have had its origin only under a system of masculine rule

319. What is stated to be the origin of contemporary attributions of might to a Deity?
    A. The valuing by men of male qualities over female qualities
    B. The weaknesses of human nature
    C. The repression of the female instincts
    D. The rise of male dominance
    E. (a) The value by men of male qualities over female qualities AND (d) The rise of male dominance

Passage 63 - The Nature of Goodness

George Herbert Palmer

In undertaking the following discussion, I foresee two grave difficulties. My reader may well feel that goodness is already the most familiar of all the thoughts we employ, and yet he may at the same time suspect that there is something about it perplexingly abstruse and remote. Familiar it certainly is. It attends all our wishes, acts, and projects as nothing else does so that no estimate of its influence can be excessive. When we take a walk, read a book, make a dress, hire a servant, visit a friend, attend a concert, choose a wife, cast a vote, enter into business, we always do it in the hope of attaining something good. The clue of goodness is accordingly a veritable guide of life. On it depend actions far more minute than those just mentioned. We never raise a hand, for example, unless with a view to improve in some respect our condition. Motionless we should remain forever, did we not believe that by placing the hand elsewhere we might obtain something that we do not now possess. Consequently, we employ the word or some synonym of it during pretty much every waking hour of our lives.

But while thus familiar and influential when mixed with action, and just because of that very fact, the notion of goodness is bewilderingly abstruse and remote. People, in general, do not observe this curious circumstance. Since they are so frequently encountering goodness, both laymen and scholars are apt to assume that it is altogether clear and requires no explanation. But the very reverse is the truth. Familiarity obscures. It breeds instincts and not understanding. So inwoven has goodness become with the very web of life that it is hard to disentangle. We cannot easily detach it from encompassing circumstance, look at it nakedly, and say what in itself it really is. Never appearing in practical affairs except as an element, and always intimately associated with something else, we are puzzled how to break up that intimacy and give to goodness independent meaning. It is as if oxygen were never found alone, but only in connection with hydrogen, carbon, or some other of the eighty elements which compose our globe. We might feel its wide influence, but we should have difficulty in describing what the thing itself was. Just so if any chance a dozen persons should be called on to say what they mean by goodness, probably not one could offer a definition that he would be willing to hold to for fifteen minutes.

It is true; this strange state of things is not peculiar to goodness. Other familiar conceptions show a similar tendency, and just about in proportion, too, to their importance. Those that count for most in our lives are least easy to understand. What, for example, do we mean by love?

For ordinary purposes probably it is well not to seek to understand it. Acquaintance with the structure of the eye does not help seeing. To determine beforehand just how polite we should be would not facilitate human intercourse. And possibly a completed scheme of goodness would rather confuse than ease our daily actions. Science does not readily connect with life. For most of us all the time, and for all of us most of the time, instinct is the better prompter. But if we mean to be ethical students and to examine conduct scientifically, we must evidently at the outset come face to face with the meaning of goodness. This word being the ethical writer's chief tool, both he and his readers must learn its construction before they proceed to use it.

320. Which of the following qualities is not attributed to goodness?
    A. A motivator of action
    B. All-pervasive
    C. In woven
    D. Curious
    E. Independent

321. Why, according to the author, is the nature of goodness so difficult to grasp?
    A. Because it is a very familiar concept
    B. Because humans have difficulty in describing concepts
    C. Because we cannot employ scientific means to work out real-life ideas
    D. Because things which mean the most to our lives are the most difficult to understand
    E. Because we have difficulty in describing what it is, though we feel its wide influence

322. Which comes closest to what is meant by the phrase *'familiarity obscures"*?
    A. Familiarity with a concept prevents us from exploring its true meaning
    B. The familiarity of a concept prevents us from detaching it from the circumstances in which we find it and giving it independent meaning.
    C. Widespread concepts do not have independent meanings
    D. It is difficult to understand familiar concepts because they are of great significance to our lives
    E. We relate to familiar concepts by instinct and not through rational thought

323. Why does the author use the statement *'acquaintance with the structure of the eye does not help seeing"*?
    A. To show that science has little application in everyday life
    B. To show that certain forms of knowledge can hinder us in day to day life
    C. To show that there is no point in studying the concept of goodness in depth
    D. To demonstrate that knowledge of a topic does not assist in the practical application of that topic to everyday life
    E. None of the above

324. What is the main conclusion of the final paragraph?
    A. An understanding of the concept of goodness is crucial for ethical students
    B. We need to understand goodness in order to become better people
    C. A completed scheme of goodness would confuse everyday life
    D. Scientists need not preoccupy themselves with matters of everyday life
    E. The word *'goodness'* is the ethical writer's chief tool

Passage 64 - Marriage and Love

Eliza Burt Gamble

The popular notion about marriage and love is that they are synonymous, that they spring from the same motives, and cover the same human needs. Like most popular notions, this also rests not on actual facts, but on superstition.

Marriage and love have nothing in common; they are as far apart as the poles; they are, in fact, antagonistic to each other. No doubt some marriages have been the result of love. Not, however, because love could assert itself only in marriage; much rather is it because few people can completely outgrow a convention. There are today large numbers of men and women to whom marriage is naught but a farce, but who submit to it for the sake of public opinion. At any rate, while it is true that some marriages are based on love, and while it is equally true that in some cases love continues in married life, I maintain that it does so regardless of marriage, and not because of it.

On the other hand, it is utterly false that love results from marriage. On rare occasions, one does hear of a miraculous case of a married couple falling in love after marriage, but on close examination, it will be found that it is a mere adjustment to the inevitable. Certainly growing used to each other is far away from the spontaneity, the intensity, and beauty of love, without which the intimacy of marriage must prove degrading to both the woman and the man.

That marriage is a failure none but the very stupid will deny. One has but to glance over the statistics of divorce to realise how bitter a failure marriage really is. Nor will the stereotyped Philistine argument that the laxity of divorce laws and the growing looseness of woman account for the fact that: first, every twelfth marriage ends in divorce; second, that since 1870, divorces have increased from 28 to 73 for every hundred thousand population; third, that adultery, since 1867, as ground for divorce, has increased 270.8 percent; fourth, that desertion increased 369.8 percent.

Henrik Ibsen, the hater of all social shams, was probably the first to realise this great truth. Nora leaves her husband, not—as the stupid critic would have it—because she is tired of her responsibilities or feels the need of woman's rights, but because she has come to know that for eight years she had lived with a stranger and borne him children. The moral lesson instilled in the girl is not whether the man has aroused her love, but rather is it, "How much?" The important and only God of practical American life: Can the man make a living? Can he support a wife? That is the only thing that justifies marriage. Gradually this saturates every thought of the girl; her dreams are not of moonlight and kisses, of laughter and tears; she dreams of shopping tours and bargain counters. Can there be anything more humiliating, more degrading than a life-long proximity between two strangers? No need for the woman to know anything of the man, save his income. As to the knowledge of the woman—what is there to know except that she has a pleasing appearance?

But the child, how is it to be protected, if not for marriage? After all, is not that the most important consideration? The sham, the hypocrisy of it! Marriage, protecting the child, yet thousands of children destitute and homeless. So long as love begets life no child is deserted, or hungry, or famished for the want of affection. I know this to be true. I know women who became mothers in freedom by the men they loved. Few children in wedlock enjoy the care, the protection, the devotion free motherhood is capable of bestowing.

325. In the final paragraph, what is meant by the phrase '*in freedom*'?
    A. Being unmarried
    B. Freedom from the dictates of society
    C. Freedom from social stigma
    D. Freedom from male presence
    E. Economic freedom

326. What does the author imply in the fifth paragraph is ultimately responsible for unsuccessful marriages?
    A. Use of a flawed criteria for determining who to marry
    B. Marrying a person unsuited to you
    C. A feeling of estrangement from one's spouse
    D. The women's rights movement
    E. Women's need for greater freedom

327. What, according to the author, is the relationship between marriage and love?
    A. Marriage always springs from love
    B. Marriage stifles love
    C. There is no relationship between the two
    D. After a long time, marriage can bring about love
    E. Marriages break down when the love is lost

328. What assumption is made by the author in the final paragraph?
    A. The parents of the destitute children are married
    B. That children of married couples are happier than those of unmarried couples
    C. That unmarried couples are able to love children more than married couples
    D. That society is doing nothing to help children
    E. That the underlying rationale for marriage is the protection of children

329. What is the main conclusion in the passage?
    A. Marriage cannot protect children
    B. Marriage has been unable to bring about love
    C. Most marriages will end in divorce
    D. Abolishing the institution of marriage is the best way to protect children
    E. The institution of marriage is a failure

Passage 65 - Minorities versus Majorities

Emma Goldman

If I were to give a summary of the tendency of our times, I would say, Quantity. The multitude, the mass spirit, dominates everywhere, destroying quality. Our entire life—production, politics, and education—rests on quantity, on numbers. The worker who once took pride in the thoroughness and quality of his work has been replaced by brainless, incompetent automatons who turn out enormous quantities of things, valueless to themselves, and generally injurious to the rest of mankind. Thus, quantity, instead of adding to life's comforts and peace, has merely increased man's burden.

In politics, naught but quantity counts. In proportion to its increase, however, principles, ideals, justice, and uprightness are completely swamped by the array of numbers. In the struggle for supremacy, the various political parties outdo each other in trickery, deceit, cunning, and shady machinations, confident that the one who succeeds is sure to be hailed by the majority as the victor. That is the only God—success. As to what expense, what terrible cost to character, is of no moment. We have not far to go in search of proof to verify this sad fact. Never before did the corruption, the complete rottenness of our government stand so thoroughly exposed. Yet when the crimes of that party became so brazen that even the blind could see them, it needed but to muster up its minions, and its supremacy was assured.

The oft-repeated slogan of our time is, among all politicians, the Socialists included, that ours is an era of individualism, of the minority. Only those who do not probe beneath the surface might be led to entertain this view. Have not the few accumulated the wealth of the world? Are they not the masters, the absolute kings of the situation? Their success, however, is due not to individualism, but to the inertia, the cravenness, the utter submission of the mass. The latter wants but to be dominated, to be led, to be coerced. As to individualism, at no time in human history did it have less chance of expression, less opportunity to assert itself in a normal, healthy manner.

Need I say that in art we are confronted with the same sad facts? One has but to inspect our parks and thoroughfares to realize the hideousness and vulgarity of the art manufacture. Certainly, none but a majority taste would tolerate such an outrage on art. False in conception and barbarous in execution, the statuary that infests American cities has as much relation to true art, as a totem to a Michael Angelo. Yet that is the only art that succeeds. The true artistic genius, who will not cater to accepted notions, who exercises originality, and strives to be true to life, leads an obscure and wretched existence. His work may someday become the fad of the mob, but not until his heart's blood had been exhausted; not until the pathfinder has ceased to be, and a throng of an idealess and visionless mob has done to death the heritage of the master.
I know so well that as a compact mass, the majority has never stood for justice or equality. It has suppressed the human voice, subdued the human spirit, and chained the human body. In other words, the living, vital truth of social and economic well-being will become a reality only through the zeal, courage, the non-compromising determination of intelligent minorities, and not through the mass.

330. What is the conclusion of the first paragraph?
    A. Quantity is prioritised over and has destroyed quality
    B. Workers who took pride in their work have been replaced by brainless automatons
    C. Goods produced nowadays are generally injurious to us
    D. Politics now focuses on quantity
    E. We must focus on quality in order to improve wellbeing

331. Which of the following is a metaphor employed by the author?
    A. False in conception and barbarous in execution
    B. Success is the only god
    C. The mob
    D. Its supremacy was assured
    E. Suppressed the human voice

332. Which of the following would most weaken the argument in the fourth paragraph?
    A. The head of the city council has sole responsibility for commissioning statues and works of arts to be erected in public places
    B. Artistic geniuses are all acknowledged upon their deaths
    C. Many artistic geniuses have been acknowledged just immediately prior to their deaths
    D. Most people enjoy abstract art
    E. The statues and works of art in public places are reviewed every five years

333. Which of the following lines most strongly supports/advances the author's rejection of the '*oft-repeated slogan*' in the third paragraph?
    A. Have not the few accumulated the wealth of the world?
    B. Only those who do not probe beneath the surface might be led to entertain this view
    C. Their success, however, is due not to individualism, but to the inertia, the cravenness, the utter submission of the mass
    D. As to individualism, at no time in human history did it have less chance of expression
    E. None of the above

334. In the second paragraph, what, according to the writer, is the relationship between morals/character in politics and democracy?
    A. Democracy allows those with poor morals to thrive
    B. Democracy encourages trickery
    C. Democracy helps to root out politicians of poor moral character
    D. There is no relationship
    E. Democracy destroys the morals of political parties

Passage 66 - What is a novel?

F. Marion Crawford

"What is a novel?" A novel is a marketable commodity, of the class collectively termed "luxuries," as not contributing directly to the support of life or the maintenance of health. The novel, therefore, is an intellectual artistic luxury in that it can be of no use to a man when he is at work, but may conduce to peace of mind and delectation during his hours of idleness.

Probably, no one denies that the first object of the novel is to amuse and interest the reader. But it is often said that the novel should instruct as well as afford amusement, and the "novel-with-a-purpose" is the realisation of this idea. The purpose-novel, then, proposes to serve two masters, besides procuring a reasonable amount of bread and butter for its writer and publisher. It proposes to escape from my definition of the novel in general and make itself an "intellectual moral lesson" instead of an "intellectual artistic luxury." It constitutes a violation of the unwritten contract tacitly existing between writer and reader. A man buys what purports to be a work of fiction, a romance, a novel, a story of adventure, pays his money, takes his book home, prepares to enjoy it at his ease and discovers that he has paid a dollar for somebody's views on socialism, religion, or the divorce laws.

Such books are generally carefully suited with an attractive title. The binding is as frivolous as can be desired. The bookseller says it is "a work of great power," and there is probably a sentimental dedication on the flyleaf to a number of initials to which a romantic appearance is given by the introduction of a stray "St." and a few hyphens. The buyer is possibly a conservative person, of lukewarm religious convictions, whose life is made "barren by marriage, or death, or division"—and who takes no sort of interest in the laws relating to divorce, in the invention of a new religion, or the position of the labour question. He has simply paid money, on the ordinary tacit contract between furnisher and purchaser, and he has been swindled, to use a very plain term for which a substitute does not occur to me. Or say that a man buys a seat in one of the regular theatres. He enters, takes his place, preparing to be amused, and the curtain goes up. The stage is set as a church, there is a pulpit before the prompter's box, and the Right Reverend the Bishop of the Diocese is on the point of delivering a sermon. The man would be legally justified in demanding his money at the door, I fancy, and would probably do so, though he might admit that the Bishop was the most learned and edifying of preachers. In ordinary cases, the purpose-novel is a simple fraud, besides being a failure in nine hundred and ninety-nine cases out of a thousand.

What we call a novel may educate the taste and cultivate the intelligence; under the hand of genius it may purify the heart and fortify the mind; but it has no right to tell us what its writer thinks about the relations of labour and capital, nor to set up what the author conceives to be a nice, original, easy scheme of salvation, any more than it has a right to take for its theme the relative merits of the "broomstick-car" and the "storage system," temperance, vivisection, or the "Ideal Man" of Confucius. Lessons, lectures, discussions, sermons, and didactics generally belong to institutions set apart for especial purposes and carefully avoided, after a certain age, by the majority of those who wish to be amused. The purpose-novel is an odious attempt to lecture people who hate lectures, to preach at people who prefer their own church, and to teach people who think they know enough already. It is an ambush, a lying-in-wait for the unsuspecting public, a violation of the social contract—and as such, it ought to be either mercilessly crushed or forced by law to bind itself in black and label itself "Purpose" in very big letters.

335. Which of the following is merely an assertion?
    A. The purpose-novel, then, proposes to serve two masters
    B. The purpose-novel is an odious attempt to lecture people
    C. The man would be legally justified in demanding his money at the door
    D. Probably, no one denies that the first object of the novel is to amuse and interest the reader
    E. The purpose-novel constitutes a violation of the unwritten contract tacitly existing between writer and reader

336. Which comes closest to the point being made by the bishop example in paragraph three?
    A. People shouldn't be tricked into reading a book, regardless of how otherwise beneficial that book is
    B. Purpose-novels aim to preach at people
    C. Purpose-novels often concern subjects in which the reader has no interest
    D. The purpose-novel is a failure in nine hundred and ninety-nine cases out of a thousand.
    E. A contract to purchase a novel is the same as any other contract

337. What is meant by the phrase *'the purpose-novel purports to serve two masters"*?
    A. The purpose-novel aims to educate and provide an income for the author
    B. The purpose-novel aims to entertain and to provide an income for the author
    C. The purpose-novel aims to entertain and to educate the reader
    D. The purpose-novel aims to provide income for the writer and for the publisher
    E. The purpose-novel aims to lecture on religion and society

338. Which of the following topics is the author likely to view as inappropriate for a novel?
    A. Romance
    B. Comedy
    C. Politics
    D. Sibling bickering
    E. Love triangles

339. Which of the following would most strengthen the author's argument?
    A. A recent survey found that most people pick a novel on the basis of its title alone
    B. A few purpose-novels are known to have been very entertaining
    C. Research has shown that fewer and fewer people are reading nowadays
    D. Works of non-fiction are highly in demand nowadays
    E. Religious and political books are often bestsellers

Passage 67 - We the Media

Dan Gillmor

We freeze some moments in time. Every culture has its frozen moments, events so important and personal that they transcend the normal flow of news.

Americans of a certain age, for example, know precisely where they were and what they were doing when they learned that President Franklin D. Roosevelt died. Another generation has absolute clarity of John F. Kennedy's assassination. And no one who was older than a baby on September 11, 2001, will ever forget hearing about, or seeing, airplanes exploding into skyscrapers.

In 1945, people gathered around radios for the immediate news and stayed with the radio to hear more about their fallen leader and about the man who took his place. Newspapers printed extra editions and filled their columns with detail for days and weeks afterward. Magazines stepped back from the breaking news and offered perspective.

September 11, 2001, followed a similarly grim pattern. We watched—again and again—the awful events. Consumers of news learned about the attacks, thanks to the television networks that showed the horror so graphically. Then we learned some of the how's and why's as print publications and thoughtful broadcasters worked to bring depth to events that defied mere words. Journalists did some of their finest work and made me proud to be one of them.

But something else, something profound, was happening this time around: news was being produced by regular people who had something to say and show, and not solely by the "official" news organizations that had traditionally decided how the first draft of history would look. This time, the first draft of history was being written in part, by the former audience. It was possible—it was inevitable—because of new publishing tools available on the Internet.

Another kind of reporting emerged during those appalling hours and days. Via emails, mailing lists, chat groups, personal web journals—all nonstandard news sources—we received valuable context that the major American media couldn't, or wouldn't, provide.

We were witnessing—and in many cases were part of—the future of news.

In the 20th century, making the news was almost entirely the province of journalists; the people we covered, or "news-makers"; and the legions of public relations and marketing people who manipulated everyone. The economics of publishing and broadcasting created large, arrogant institutions—call it Big Media, though even small-town newspapers and broadcasters exhibit some of the phenomenon's worst symptoms.

Big Media, in any event, treated the news as a lecture. We told you what the news was. You bought it, or you didn't. You might write us a letter; we might print it. (If we were television and you complained, we ignored you entirely unless the complaint arrived on a libel lawyer's letterhead.) Or you cancelled your subscription or stopped watching our shows. It was a world that bred complacency and arrogance on our part. It was a gravy train while it lasted, but it was unsustainable.

Tomorrow's news reporting and production will be more of a conversation or a seminar. The lines will blur between producers and consumers, changing the role of both in ways we're only beginning to grasp now. The communication network itself will be a medium for everyone's voice, not just the few who can afford to buy multimillion-dollar printing presses, launch satellites, or win the government's permission to squat on the public's airwaves.

This evolution—from journalism as a lecture to journalism as a conversation or seminar—will force the various communities of interest to adapt. Everyone, from journalists to the people we cover to our sources and the former audience, must change their ways. The alternative is just more of the same.

We can't afford more of the same. We can't afford to treat the news solely as a commodity, largely controlled by big institutions. We can't afford, as a society, to limit our choices. We can't even afford it financially because Wall Street's demands on Big Media are dumbing down the product itself. There are three major constituencies in a world where anyone can make the news. Once largely distinct, they're now blurring into each other.

HSPSAA: SECTION A — QUESTIONS

340. What is implied by the line: *'no one who was older than a baby on September 11, 2001, will ever forget hearing about, or seeing, airplanes exploding into skyscrapers'*?
    A. No one will ever forget the events of 9/11
    B. 9/11 was a highly televised and widely discussed tragedy
    C. 9/11 was an extremely destructive event
    D. 9/11 is of little significance to American history
    E. Children were badly affected by the events of 9/11

341. Which of the following is an argument against '*Big Media*'?
    A. Under 'Big Media', people were told what the news was
    B. The economics of publishing and broadcasting created 'Big Media'
    C. Big Media provides a well-rounded view of news
    D. The dominance of Big Media allows for media complacency and ignorance in manner in which news is presented
    E. There are other potential sources of news

342. What, according to the author, first triggered the change in the identity of the publishers of news?
    A. 9/11
    B. The financial unsustainability of Big Media
    C. Society's refusal to continue to treat media as a lecture
    D. The blurring of the lines between producers and consumers
    E. The availability of new publishing tools on the internet

343. What is stated to be the future effect of the evolution to journalism as a conversation?
    A. Big Media will be entirely eradicated
    B. Different interest groups will be forced to adapt
    C. News reporting will become more of a conversation
    D. The way in which our community functions will improve
    E. There will be no effect/change

344. What purpose does the repetition of '*we can't afford*' in the final paragraph serve?
    A. It makes clearer the author's argument
    B. It is employed as a device to convince the reader of the truth of the author's propositions
    C. It reinforces the idea that change is necessary
    D. It reinforces the idea that we can no longer support Big Media financially
    E. It suggests that the progression of broadcasting is no longer under our control

Passage 68 - Foreword for Authorama

Jonathan Dunn

Throughout history, all literature was in the public domain, but, in the United States, "intellectual property" is traded as if it were some sort of tangible commodity. This is especially shameful when one considers that the public domain is precisely what drives the advancement of society. As the technology to promulgate and store information increases, so too does the ability to use that information as a framework for future advances. It is unfortunate that as the physical obstacles are overcome, legal ones are created to replace them.

Intellectual property rights simply do not exist outside of man's legislation, and this type of law is, in my opinion, akin to protectionism. Let me explain: on one hand we constantly endeavour to improve transportation and the moving of goods. But as the obstacles to trade are eliminated, we find that trade is increased. In order to "protect" our labour, taxes or tariffs are placed on the products that are thus exchanged. It is essentially the same as building a highway between two cities in order to make travel less expensive and then charging a toll that entirely replaces the expense saved by the highway. In the end, it brings no increase in efficiency. The parallel is that while we have advanced methods of storing and promulgating information, we replace any advantage gained in that respect with legislation that restricts the flow of information (such as our oppressive copyright laws). On the one hand, the laws of nature no longer inhibit us from accumulating knowledge, but on the other hand, the laws of men make it more difficult than ever.

Until the digital revolution, intellectual property was rarely separated from its physical manifestation. By that, I mean that if you wanted to read a book, you bought the physical product and the price of the intellectual property was hidden within the price of its materials. But when the medium and the actual content became separated, suddenly the issue of intellectual property came into being. But how can a product be sold without a transfer of something? If I purchase an e-book, it costs the publisher nothing to sell one to someone else because, from the one original copy, an infinite amount of copies can be grafted. It costs something to produce the original e-book, perhaps, but I am merely buying a copy of it. First, we had a fiat currency, which the government can conjure up at whim and promulgate for profit, and now we also have a fiat product with which publishers can do the same.

The only argument against the public domain is the protection of the writers and artists and programmers who create the work in the first place. It should be noted, however, that in many cases they are not even the ones who own the copyrights. A poverty-stricken musician could, perhaps, argue that he needed copyrights to survive, but how can a corporation of people who did not produce the work in the beginning argue the same? "But", one says, "the artist sold the copyright to the corporation by his own will, and that is how he supports himself." Perhaps, but that is assuming that a piece of intellectual property – in essence, a thought – can be traded as if it were a physical entity as if there were no difference between it and a piece of land or a car. Yet, by its very definition, it is something that is not tangible, something that has no value outside of its communication with a human brain.

The basic question is this: is a thought a piece of property, is an entity that exists beyond its physical manifestation the same as one which only is its physical manifestation? If I buy a chair, I am paying for the materials and the labour that went into the individual chair. But if I buy an e-book or mp3, what am I paying for? There is no cost for materials and the same labour that went into making what I bought also went into what everyone else bought. If that were the measure of its price, e-books would cost an insignificant amount.

I will conclude by saying that it is shameful that there are so many children (and adults) around the world who have received an insufficient education for no other reason than that they couldn't afford it when all the knowledge of the world could be given away freely in a digital format. Knowledge is power, as they say, and right now knowledge is kept from the people through the oppression of copyright laws and the forces that maintain them.

345. Which of the following is not stated as an argument in favour of the public domain?
    A. The public domain drives the advancement of society
    B. Man-made laws make it more difficult than ever to accumulate information
    C. The abolition of copyright laws would enable the education of children
    D. Intellectual property is, by definition, something that is not tangible
    E. The abolition of copyright laws would empower the people

346. What is the main premise of the author's argument against the trading (for value) of intangible property?
    A. Thought cannot be viewed as something physical
    B. No costs or extra labour are incurred in the marginal production of such property
    C. Making intangible property widely available would advance the free flow of knowledge
    D. E-books are currently too expensive
    E. The wide availability of intangible property would remedy the problem of insufficient education

347. What point is made by the *'protectionism'* example in the second paragraph?
    A. Restrictive laws tend to be inefficient
    B. Copyright laws offset the advantages we have gained in the storing and accumulating information
    C. Eliminating obstacles to trade is a useful means of increasing trade
    D. Society cannot advance if protectionist attitudes prevail
    E. The effects of protectionist behaviour are oppressive

348. Which of the following is merely an assertion?
    A. Intellectual property laws are akin to protectionism
    B. It is shameful that there are so many children (and adults) around the world who have received an insufficient education for no other reason than that they couldn't afford it
    C. The public domain is precisely what drives the advancement of society
    D. Intellectual property [should not] be traded as if it were a physical entity
    E. Knowledge is power

349. Which of the following is a logical conclusion of the argument in paragraphs four and five?
    A. People should not be able to rent property for money
    B. Aeroplane tickets should be free
    C. Music CDs should be free
    D. Recipe books should be free
    E. None of the above

Passage 69 - History

Ralph Waldo Emerson

There is one mind common to all individual men. Every man is an inlet to the same and to all of the same. He that is once admitted to the right of reason is made a freeman of the whole estate. What Plato has thought, he may think; what a saint has felt, he may feel; what at any time has befallen any man, he can understand. Who hath access to this universal mind is a party to all that is or can be done, for this is the only and sovereign agent. Of the works of this mind, history is the record. Its genius is illustrated by the entire series of days. Man is explicable by nothing less than all his history. Without hurry, without rest, the human spirit goes forth from the beginning to embody every faculty, every thought, and every emotion, which belongs to it, in appropriate events. But the thought is always prior to the fact; all the facts of history pre-exist in the mind as laws. Each law, in turn, is made by circumstances predominant and the limits of nature give power to but one at a time. A man is the whole encyclopaedia of facts. The creation of a thousand forests is in one acorn, and Egypt, Greece, Rome, Gaul, Britain, America, lie folded already in the first man. Epoch after epoch, camp, kingdom, empire, republic, democracy, is merely the application of his manifold spirit to the manifold world.

This human mind wrote history, and thus must read it. The Sphinx must solve her own riddle. If the whole of history is in one man, it is all to be explained from individual experience. There is a relation between the hours of our life and the centuries of time. Of the universal mind, each individual man is one more incarnation. All its properties consist in him. Each new fact in his private experience flashes a light on what great bodies of men have done, and the crises of his life refer to national crises. Every revolution was first a thought in one man's mind, and when the same thought occurs to another man, it is the key to that era. Every reform was once a private opinion, and when it shall be a private opinion again it will solve the problem of the age.

The fact narrated must correspond to something in me to be credible or intelligible. We, as we read, must become Greeks, Romans, Turks, priest and king, martyr and executioner; must fasten these images to some reality in our secret experience, or we shall learn nothing rightly. What befell Asdrubal or Caesar Borgia is as much an illustration of the mind's powers and depravations as what has befallen us. Each new law and political movement have meaning for you. This throws our actions into perspective; and as crabs, goats, scorpions, the balance and the waterpot lose their meanness when hung as signs in the zodiac, so I can see my own vices without heat in the distant persons of Solomon, Alcibiades, and Catiline.

All that Shakespeare says of the king, yonder slip of a boy that reads in the corner feels to be true of himself. We sympathise in the great moments of history, in the great discoveries, the great resistances, the great prosperities of men;—because there, law was enacted, the sea was searched, the land was found, or the blow was struck, for us, as we ourselves in that place would have done or applauded.

We have the same interest in condition and character. We honour the rich because they have externally the freedom, power, and grace that we feel to be proper to man, proper to us. So all that is said of the wise man by Stoic or Oriental or modern essayist, describes to each reader his own idea, describes his unattained but attainable self.

350. What, according to the author, is the main benefit of studying history?
    A. It allows us to learn about the lives of prominent historical figures
    B. It enables reform
    C. It has a meaning for us because it enables us to learn more about ourselves
    D. It is a puzzle which is interesting to solve
    E. It allows us to see what great men have done

351. What is meant by the statement: *'there is one mind common to all of mankind'*?
    A. People tend to 'follow the crowd'
    B. All humans have shared characteristics and values
    C. We all remember historical facts and are affected by them
    D. We can see our own flaws in the actions of others
    E. Our biological makeup is largely identical

352. Which of the following is a metaphor employed by the author?
    A. The blow was struck
    B. Crabs, goats, scorpions, the balance and the waterpot lose their meanness when hung as signs in the zodiac
    C. The Sphinx must solve her own riddle
    D. The whole of history is in one man
    E. A man is the whole encyclopaedia of facts

353. Which of the following best sums up the author's main argument?
    A. We sympathise in the great moments of history
    B. All humans have shared characteristics
    C. We should not judge wrongdoers as we ourselves have the same propensity for wrongdoing
    D. We can learn about and improve ourselves through a study of history
    E. Everyone aspires to have certain characteristics

354. What can be inferred from the author's repeated use of *'we'* in the final paragraph?
    A. Generalised statements can be made about the attitudes and values of all human beings
    B. Everyone deserves human rights
    C. Humans are identical
    D. All of the above
    E. None of the above

Passage 70 - Self-Reliance

Ralph Waldo Emerson

What I must do is all that concerns me, not what the people think. This rule, equally arduous in actual and in intellectual life, may serve for the whole distinction between greatness and meanness. It is harder because you will always find those who think they know what your duty is better than you know it. It is easy in the world to live after the world's opinion; it is easy in solitude to live after our own but the great man is he who in the midst of the crowd keeps with perfect sweetness the independence of solitude.

The objection to conforming to usages that have become dead to you is that it scatters your force. It loses your time and blurs the impression of your character. If you maintain a dead church, contribute to a dead Bible-society, vote with a great party either for the government or against it, spread your table like base housekeepers, —under all these screens I have difficulty to detect the precise man you are: and of course so much force is withdrawn from your proper life. Most men have bound their eyes with one or another handkerchief, and attached themselves to some one of these communities of opinion. This conformity makes them not false in a few particulars, authors of a few lies, but false in all particulars. Their every truth is not quite true. Their two is not the real two, their four not the real four; so that every word they say chagrins us and we know not where to begin to set them right. Meantime nature is not slow to equip us in the prison-uniform of the party to which we adhere. We come to wear one cut of face and figure and acquire by degrees the gentlest asinine expression. There is a mortifying experience in particular, which does not fail to wreak itself also in the general history; I mean "the foolish face of praise," the forced smile which we put on in company where we do not feel at ease in answer to conversation which does not interest us. The muscles, not spontaneously moved but moved by a low usurping wilfulness, grow tight about the outline of the face with the most disagreeable sensation.

For nonconformity, the world whips you with its displeasure. And therefore, a man must know how to estimate a sour face. The by-standers look askance on him in the public street or in the friend's parlour. If this aversion had its origin in contempt and resistance like his own, he might well go home with a sad countenance; but the sour faces of the multitude, like their sweet faces, have no deep cause, but are put on and off as the wind blows and a newspaper directs. Yet is the discontent of the multitude more formidable than that of the senate and the college? It is easy enough for a firm man who knows the world to brook the rage of the cultivated classes. Their rage is decorous and prudent, for they are timid, as being very vulnerable themselves. But when to their feminine rage the indignation of the people is added, when the ignorant and the poor are aroused, when the unintelligent brute force that lies at the bottom of society is made to growl and mow, it needs the habit of magnanimity and religion to treat it godlike as a trifle of no concernment.

The other terror that scares us from self-trust is our consistency; a reverence for our past act or word because the eyes of others have no other data for computing our orbit than our past acts, and we loath to disappoint them.
But why should you keep your head over your shoulder? Why drag about this corpse of your memory, lest you contradict somewhat you have stated in this or that public place? Suppose you should contradict yourself; what then? It seems to be a rule of wisdom never to rely on your memory alone, scarcely even in acts of pure memory, but to bring the past for judgment into the thousand-eyed present, and live ever in a new day.

355. Which of the following is, according to the author, the most difficult?
    A. To live according to one's opinion in solitude
    B. To follow one's own opinion whilst living amongst others
    C. To formulate one's own opinion
    D. To be given sour looks
    E. To conform to the world's expectations

356. What is most challenging about non-conformity according to the author?
    A. Disapproval of masses at bottom of society
    B. Being shunned by the privileged classes
    C. It saps one's life force
    D. It becomes hard for others to tell what sort of person you really are
    E. We end up hurting the feelings of others

357. Which of the following is an argument (by the author) against '*reverence for our past acts*'?
    A. It is difficult, in any case, to maintain consistency with one's past actions
    B. Whether or not we disappoint others is irrelevant
    C. Our priority shouldn't be to please others
    D. Being predictable is foolish
    E. Reflecting on the past is always unhelpful

358. Which of the following conclusions is best supported by the passage above?
    A. We should refuse to follow social conventions
    B. We should always reflect on our behaviour
    C. We should decide for ourselves if a convention is worth following
    D. We should not join religious groups or political parties
    E. It is best to avoid incurring the wrath of the masses

359. To what effect does the author employ the phrase '*corpse of your memory*'?
    A. To show that remembrance of past events is largely unhelpful for life in the present
    B. To encourage the reader to consider whether memories are in fact burdensome
    C. To show that recalling the past is tedious
    D. To show that memories of past events are often unpleasant
    E. To portray memory as the ghost of past events

Passage 71 - Seven Discourses on Art

Joshua Reynolds

The principal advantage of an academy is, that, besides furnishing able men to direct the student, it will be a repository for the great examples of the art. These are the materials on which genius is to work, and without which the strongest intellect may be fruitlessly or deviously employed. By studying these authentic models, that idea of excellence which is the result of the accumulated experience of past ages may be at once acquired, and the tardy and obstructed progress of our predecessors may teach us a shorter and easier way. The student receives at one glance the principles which many artists have spent their whole lives in ascertaining; and, satisfied with their effect, is spared the painful investigation by which they come to be known and fixed. How many men of great natural abilities have been lost to this nation for want of these advantages? They never had an opportunity of seeing those masterly efforts of genius that at once kindle the whole soul, and force it into sudden and irresistible approbation.

Raffaelle, it is true, had not the advantage of studying in an academy; but all Rome, and the works of Michael Angelo in particular, were to him an academy. On the site of the Capella Sistina, he immediately, from a dry, Gothic, and even insipid manner, which attends to the minute accidental discriminations of particular and individual objects, assumed that grand style of painting, which improves partial representation by the general and invariable ideas of nature.

Every seminary of learning may be said to be surrounded with an atmosphere of floating knowledge, where every mind may imbibe somewhat congenial to its own original conceptions. Knowledge, thus obtained, has always something more popular and useful than that which is forced upon the mind by private precepts or solitary meditation. Besides, it is generally found that a youth more easily receives instruction from the companions of his studies, whose minds are nearly on a level with his own, than from those who are much his superiors; and it is from his equals only that he catches the fire of emulation.
Impressed as I am, therefore, with such a favourable opinion of my associates in this undertaking, it would ill become me to dictate to any of them. But as these institutions have so often failed in other nations, and as it is natural to think with regret how much might have been done and how little has been done, I must take leave to offer a few hints, by which those errors may be rectified, and those defects supplied. These, the professors and visitors may reject or adopt as they shall think proper.

I would chiefly recommend that an implicit obedience to the rules of art, as established by the great masters, should be exacted from the <u>young</u> students. That those models, which have passed through the approbation of ages, should be considered by them as perfect and infallible guides as subjects for their imitation, not their criticism.

I am confident that this is the only efficacious method of making a progress in the arts; and that he who sets out with doubting will find life finished before he becomes a master of the rudiments. For it may be laid down as a maxim, that he who begins by presuming on his own sense has ended his studies as soon as he has commenced them. Every opportunity, therefore, should be taken to discountenance that false and vulgar opinion that rules are the fetters of genius. They are fetters only to men of no genius; as that armour, which upon the strong becomes an ornament and a defence, upon the weak and misshapen turns into a load, and cripples the body which it was made to protect.

360. What, according to the author, is the main benefit of having a 'repository for the great examples of the art'?
    A. Students gain insight into useful principles without having to experiment to discover them for themselves
    B. Students need not think for themselves
    C. Students who don't have natural ability are able to thrive nonetheless
    D. Future generations are able to appreciate and enjoy the great examples
    E. To ensure that certain styles of art do not die out

361. What is the main premise of the view that students should not focus on criticising works of great masters?
    A. The works of the great masters are infallible
    B. They will produce work which departs from the style of the great masters
    C. Those who presume to be better than the great masters will not be able to learn anything new
    D. Only students without talent focus on criticism rather than just accepting rules of art
    E. There has already been enough criticism of these works

362. Which of the following, if true, would most weaken the author's argument?
    A. Raffaelle produced his best work before gaining access to the works of Michael Angelo
    B. The works of Michael Angelo are highly valued today
    C. Contemporaries of Raffaelle produced better work than him
    D. Raffaelle was noted for his artistic talent even before gaining access to the works of Michael Angelo
    E. Raffaelle did not esteem the art or architecture of Rome very highly

363. What purpose is served by the 'armour' illustration in the final paragraph?
    A. To show that rules enhance the skills of those who possess artistic abilities, whilst further hindering those who lack those abilities
    B. To show that the abilities of weak students can be improved if they dispense with rules
    C. To show that art rules can protect the talented artist
    D. To show that military life has similarities to art
    E. None of the above

364. What is the underlying assumption of the passage?
    A. Art students wish to improve
    B. The value of a piece of art is objective
    C. Students can learn more from the works of art than they can learn on their own
    D. Students don't want to learn through their own mistakes
    E. Studying the works of the great masters can improve a student's own work

Passage 72 - Discourses on Art: Discourse IV

Joshua Reynolds

Gentlemen, the value and rank of every art is in proportion to the mental labour employed in it, or the mental pleasure produced by it. As this principle is observed or neglected, our profession becomes either a liberal art or a mechanical trade. In the hands of one man it makes the highest pretensions, as it is addressed to the noblest faculties. In those of another, it is reduced to a mere matter of ornament, and the painter has but the humble province of furnishing our apartments with elegance.

This exertion of mind, which is the only circumstance that truly ennobles our art, makes the great distinction between the Roman and Venetian schools. I have formerly observed that perfect form is produced by leaving out particularities, and retaining only general ideas. I shall now endeavour to show that this principle, which I have proved to be metaphysically just, extends itself to every part of the art; that it gives what is called the grand style to invention, to composition, to expression, and even to colouring and drapery.

Invention in painting does not imply the invention of the subject, for that is commonly supplied by the poet or historian. With respect to the choice, no subject can be proper that is not generally interesting. It ought to be either some eminent instance of heroic action or heroic suffering. There must be something either in the action or in the object in which men are universally concerned, and which powerfully strikes upon the public sympathy. Strictly speaking, indeed, no subject can be of universal, hardly can it be of general concern: but there are events and characters so popularly known in those countries where our art is in request, that they may be considered as sufficiently general for all our purposes. Such are the great events of Greek and Roman fable and history, which early education and the usual course of reading have made familiar and interesting to all Europe, without being degraded by the vulgarism of ordinary life in any country. Such, too, are the capital subjects of Scripture history, which, besides their general notoriety, become venerable by their connection with our religion.

As it is required that the subject selected should be a general one, it is no less necessary that it should be kept unembarrassed with whatever may anyway serve to divide the attention of the spectator. Whenever a story is related, every man forms a picture in his mind of the action and the expression of the persons employed. The power of representing this mental picture in canvas is what we call invention in a painter. And as in the conception of this ideal picture, the mind does not enter into the minute peculiarities of the dress, furniture, or scene of action, so when the painter comes to represent it, he contrives those little necessary concomitant circumstances in such a manner that they shall strike the spectator no more than they did himself in his first conception of the story.

365. Which of the following is the author likely to view as being of most value?
    A. A rough sketch by a court artist
    B. A sculpture of a hand
    C. A complicated scene planned for 10 years and painted across the ceiling of a huge cathedral
    D. A blank piece of canvas
    E. A detailed picture of a beach, produced by an artist immediately upon seeing noticing the beach

366. What is implied by the third paragraph?
    A. Works of art which depict merely personal subjective experiences are of lesser value
    B. Art should depict instances of heroism
    C. A piece of art is not valuable if a majority of people do not appreciate it
    D. Artists have little scope for choice of the subject of their paintings
    E. The nature of invention differs for the artist and for the poet

367. Which of the following is not stated to be a requirement of good art?
    A. Of universal concern
    B. Embodying a grand style
    C. The product of mental labour or producing mental pleasure
    D. Generally interesting
    E. Expressing general ideas

368. What is the assumption of the argument in the last paragraph?
    A. People's minds do not focus on tiny details
    B. The recording of reality is not the purpose of art
    C. Spectators are easily distracted by details
    D. Painters wish to be inventors
    E. Every painting tells a story

369. The author uses the phrase '*invention in painting*' to mean/what meaning does the author give to the phrase?
    A. Inspiring poets and writers through one's paintings
    B. Passing across a message through one's paintings
    C. Developing new innovative ways of painting
    D. Representing a mental image using a painting on canvas
    E. Creating an idea in people's minds

Passage 73 - Patriotism: A Menace to Liberty

Emma Goldman

What is patriotism? Is it love of one's birthplace, the place of childhood's recollections and hopes, dreams, and aspirations? Is it the place where, in childlike naivety, we would watch the fleeting clouds and wonder why we, too, could not run so swiftly? The place where we would count the milliard glittering stars, terror-stricken lest each one "an eye should be," piercing the very depths of our little souls? Is it the place where we would listen to the music of the birds, and long to have wings to fly, even as they, to distant lands? Or the place where we would sit at mother's knee, enraptured by wonderful tales of great deeds and conquests? In short, is it love for the spot, every inch representing dear and precious recollections of a happy, joyous, and playful childhood?

If that were patriotism, few American men of today could be called upon to be patriotic, since the place of play has been turned into a factory, mill, and mine, while deafening sounds of machinery have replaced the music of the birds. Nor can we longer hear the tales of great deeds, for the stories our mothers tell today are but those of sorrow, tears, and grief.

What, then, is patriotism? "Patriotism, sir, is the last resort of scoundrels," said Dr. Johnson. Leo Tolstoy, the greatest anti-patriot of our times, defines patriotism as the principle that will justify the training of wholesale murderers; a trade that requires better equipment for the exercise of man-killing than the making of such necessities of life as shoes, clothing, and houses; a trade that guarantees better returns and greater glory than that of the average workingman.

Gustave Herve, another great anti-patriot, justly calls patriotism a superstition—one far more injurious, brutal, and inhumane than religion. The superstition of religion originated in man's inability to explain natural phenomena. That is, when primitive man heard thunder or saw the lightning, he could not account for either, and therefore concluded that back of them must be a force greater than himself. Similarly, he saw a supernatural force in the rain, and in the various other changes in nature. Patriotism, on the other hand, is a superstition artificially created and maintained through a network of lies and falsehoods; a superstition that robs man of his self-respect and dignity, and increases his arrogance and conceit.

Indeed, conceit, arrogance, and egotism are the essentials of patriotism. Let me illustrate. Patriotism assumes that our globe is divided into little spots, each one surrounded by an iron gate. Those who have had the fortune of being born on some particular spot, consider themselves better, nobler, grander, and more intelligent than the living beings inhabiting any other spot. It is, therefore, the duty of everyone living on that chosen spot to fight, kill, and die in the attempt to impose his superiority upon all the others.

The inhabitants of the other spots reason in like manner, of course, with the result that, from early infancy, the mind of the child is poisoned with blood-curdling stories about the Germans, the French, the Italians, Russians, etc. When the child has reached manhood, he is thoroughly saturated with the belief that he is chosen by the Lord himself to defend HIS country against the attack or invasion of any foreigner. It is for that purpose that we are clamouring for a greater army and navy, more battleships and ammunition. It is for that purpose that America has within a short time spent four hundred million dollars. Just think of it—four hundred million dollars taken from the produce of the people. For surely, it is not the rich who contribute to patriotism. They are cosmopolitans, perfectly at home in every land. We in America know well the truth of this. Are not our rich Americans Frenchmen in France, Germans in Germany, or Englishmen in England? And do they not squander with cosmopolitan grace fortunes coined by American factory children and cotton slaves? Yes, theirs is the patriotism that will make it possible to send messages of condolence to a despot like the Russian Tsar, when any mishap befalls him, as President Roosevelt did in the name of HIS people, when Sergius was punished by the Russian revolutionists.

HSPSAA: SECTION A — QUESTIONS

370. How, according to the author, does patriotism differ from the *'superstition of religion'*?
    A. The latter is maintained through lies
    B. The former has the effect of robbing man of his self-respect
    C. The latter is more widespread
    D. The former is artificially created
    E. The former is more widespread

371. Which one of these is not stated by the author to be a feature of patriotism?
    A. It justifies the training of murderers
    B. It is a superstition
    C. Conceit and arrogance are its essentials
    D. It leads one group to try to impose their superiority on another
    E. It poisons children's minds

372. Which of the following is merely an opinion?
    A. America has within a short time spent four hundred million dollars
    B. The rich are cosmopolitans, perfectly at home in every land
    C. We are clamouring for a greater army and navy, more battleships and ammunition
    D. The stories our mothers tell today are of grief
    E. Sergius was punished by the Russian revolutionists

373. Who, according to the last paragraph, bears the principal detriment of patriotism?
    A. Only factory children and cotton slaves
    B. The rich
    C. Children
    D. The people
    E. The army

374. What word best sums up the way in which the rich are portrayed by the author in the final paragraph?
    A. Non-conformist
    B. Inconsiderate
    C. Hypocritical
    D. Stingy
    E. Selfish

Passage 74 - Friendship

Ralph Emerson Waldo

Friendship, like the immortality of the soul, is too good to be believed. The lover, beholding his maiden, half knows that she is not verily that which he worships; and in the golden hour of friendship, we are surprised with shades of suspicion and unbelief. We doubt that we bestow on our hero the virtues in which he shines. Shall we fear to cool our love by mining for the metaphysical foundation of this Elysian temple? Shall I not be as real as the things I see? If I am, I shall not fear to know them for what really they are. Their true essence is not less beautiful than their appearance, though it needs finer organs for its appreciation.

The law of nature is alternation forevermore. Each electrical state super-induces the opposite. The soul environs itself with friends that it may enter into a grander self-acquaintance or solitude; and it goes alone, for a season, that it may exalt its conversation or society. This method betrays itself along the whole history of our personal relations. The instinct of affection revives the hope of union with our mates, and the returning sense of insulation recalls us from the chase. Thus, every man passes his life in the search after friendship, and if he should record his true sentiment, he might write a letter like this, to each new candidate for his love.

> Dear Friend:—
> If I was sure of thee, sure of thy capacity, sure to match my mood with thine, I should never think again of trifling flaws. Thou art very wise; thy moods are quite attainable; and I respect thy genius; it is to me as yet unfathomed; yet dare I presume in thee a perfect match for me? And so thou art to me a delicious torment. Thine ever, or never.

Yet this form of worship, these uneasy pleasures, and fine pains are for curiosity, and not for life. They are not to be indulged. This is to weave cobweb and not cloth. Our friendships hurry to short and poor conclusions because we have made them a texture of wine and dreams, instead of the tough fibre of the human heart. The laws of friendship are great, austere, and eternal, of one web with the laws of nature and of morals. But we have aimed at a swift and petty benefit, to suck a sudden sweetness. We snatch at the slowest fruit in the whole garden of God, which many summers and many winters must ripen. We seek our friend not sacredly but with an adulterate passion which would appropriate him to ourselves.

375. What is meant by '*is too good to be believed*'?
    A. Friendship is a beautiful thing
    B. Friendship is a sham
    C. We are unrealistic in our expectation of friends
    D. We view our friends in an extraordinarily positive light
    E. We are unrealistic in expecting to have perfect friendships

376. Which of the following is a simile employed by the author?
    A. Their true essence is not less beautiful than their appearance
    B. Each electrical state super-induces the opposite
    C. Like the immortality of the soul
    D. This method betrays itself
    E. Thou art to me a delicious torment

377. What is meant by the phrase '*we snatch at the slowest fruit in the whole garden of God*'?
    A. We always want what is forbidden
    B. We are not patient enough to cultivate a deep friendship and want to obtain it instantly
    C. We desire things which seem attractive outwardly
    D. Friendship takes a long time to cultivate
    E. We make poor friendship choices

378. Which of the following are not presented as contrasting pairs?
    A. Swift and petty
    B. Sacredly and passionately
    C. Eternal laws and sudden sweetness
    D. Cobweb and cloth
    E. None of the above

379. What is the main argument of the first paragraph?
    A. Friendship is too good to be believed
    B. We attribute qualities to our friends which they do not possess
    C. Friendship is a sham
    D. We often falsely worship our friends
    E. We should not be afraid to confront and explore our friends' true characteristics

Passage 75- Gifts

Ralph Emerson Waldo

The law of benefits is a difficult channel, which requires careful sailing, or rude boats. It is not the office of a man to receive gifts. How dare you give them? We wish to be self-sustained. We do not quite forgive a forgiver. The hand that feeds us is in some danger of being bitten. We can receive anything from love, for that is a way of receiving it from ourselves (hence the fitness of beautiful, not useful things for a gift); but not from anyone who assumes to bestow. We sometimes hate the meat that we eat, because there seems something of degrading dependence in living by it.

He is a good man, who can receive a gift well. We are either glad or sorry at a gift, and both emotions are unbecoming. Some violence, I think, is done, some degradation borne, when I rejoice or grieve at a gift. I am sorry when my independence is invaded, or when a gift comes from such as do not know my spirit, and so the act is not supported; and if the gift pleases me overmuch, then I should be ashamed that the donor should read my heart, and see that I love his commodity, and not him.

This giving is flat usurpation, and therefore when the beneficiary is ungrateful, as all beneficiaries hate all Timons, not at all considering the value of the gift, but looking back to the greater store it was taken from, I rather sympathise with the beneficiary, than with the anger of my lord, Timon. For, the expectation of gratitude is mean and is continually punished by the total insensibility of the obliged person. It is a great happiness to get off without injury and heart-burning, from one who has had the ill luck to be served by you. It is a very onerous business, this of being served, and the debtor naturally wishes to give you a slap. A golden text for these gentlemen is that which I admire in the Buddhist, who never thanks, and who says, "Do not flatter your benefactors."

The reason of these discords I conceive to be, that there is no commensurability between a man and any gift. You cannot give anything to a magnanimous person. After you have served him, he at once puts you in debt by his magnanimity. The service a man renders his friend is trivial and selfish, compared with the service he knows his friend stood in readiness to yield him, alike before he had begun to serve his friend, and now also. Compared with that good-will I bear my friend, the benefit it is in my power to render him seems small. Besides, our action on each other, good as well as evil, is so incidental and at random, that we can seldom hear the acknowledgments of any person who would thank us for a benefit, without some shame and humiliation. We can rarely strike a direct stroke, but must be content with an oblique one; we seldom have the satisfaction of yielding a direct benefit, which is directly received. But rectitude scatters favours on every side without knowing it and receives with wonder the thanks of all people.

380. In the third paragraph, the author's main argument is that:
    A. It is unkind to expect gratitude
    B. Gift givers should not expect gratitude on the part of receivers
    C. Receivers of gifts are angered by givers
    D. All beneficiaries are like Timon
    E. Receivers of gifts can be violent

381. The writer uses the term '*magnanimous*' to mean:
    A. Easy-going
    B. Wealthy
    C. Meek
    D. Generous
    E. Noble

382. Why, according to the author, are we unworthy of being thanked for conferring a benefit on someone else?
    A. Receiving thanks is shameful
    B. We tend to succeed in conferring benefits only by luck
    C. We are obliged, in any case, to be altruistic
    D. The benefits we confer are insignificant
    E. The benefits are unsolicited

383. What is implied by the line '*He is a good man who can receive a gift well*'?
    A. Most people cannot receive a gift well
    B. Those who cannot receive a gift well are bad men
    C. Good men receive more gifts
    D. The author is able to receive gifts graciously
    E. Graciousness is a quality which is not found in abundance amongst people

384. Why might it be acceptable to receive a gift bestowed out of love?
    A. Such givers mean no harm
    B. Gift-giving is one of the main ways of expressing love
    C. The intention of the giver is not to provide for the recipient
    D. Beneficiaries who feel loved are less likely to be ungrateful
    E. Gifts given out of love are more likely to be beautiful

Passage 76- Prudence

Ralph Emerson Waldo

What right have I to write on Prudence, whereof I have little, and that of the negative sort? My prudence consists in avoiding and going without, not in the inventing of means and methods, not in adroit steering, not in gentle repairing. I have no skill to make money spend well, no genius in my economy, and whoever sees my garden discovers that I must have some other garden. Yet, I love facts and hate lubricity and people without perception. Then I have the same title to write on prudence that I have to write on poetry or holiness. We write from aspiration and antagonism, as well as from experience. We paint those qualities which we do not possess. The poet admires the man of energy and tactics; the merchant breeds his son for the church or the bar; and where a man is not vain and egotistic, you shall find what he has not by his praise.

There are all degrees of proficiency in knowledge of the world. It is sufficient to our present purpose to indicate three. One class lives to the utility of the symbol, esteeming health and wealth a final good. Another class live above this mark of the beauty of the symbol, as the poet and artist and the naturalist and man of science. A third class live above the beauty of the symbol to the beauty of the thing signified; these are wise men. The first class have common sense; the second, taste; and the third, spiritual perception. Once in a long time, a man traverses the whole scale, and sees and enjoys the symbol solidly, then also has a clear eye for its beauty, and lastly, whilst he pitches his tent on this sacred volcanic isle of nature, does not offer to build houses and barns thereon reverencing the splendour of the God which he sees bursting through each chink and cranny.

The world is filled with the proverbs and acts and winkings of a base prudence, which is a devotion to matter, as if we possessed no other faculties than the palate, the nose, the touch, the eye, and ear; a prudence which adores the Rule of Three, which never subscribes, which gives never, which seldom lends, and asks but one question of any project—Will it bake bread? This is a disease like a thickening of the skin until the vital organs are destroyed. But culture, revealing the high origin of the apparent world and aiming at the perfection of the man as the end, degrades everything else, as health and bodily life, into means. It sees prudence not to be a several faculty, but a name for wisdom and virtue conversing with the body and its wants. Cultivated men always feel and speak so as if a great fortune, the achievement of a civil or social measure, great personal influence, a graceful and commanding address, had their value as proofs of the energy of the spirit. (But this is not so).

385. In which of the following does the writer employ irony?
    A. I have little prudence
    B. I have no skill to make money spend well
    C. We paint those qualities which we do not possess
    D. The world is filled with the proverbs
    E. None of the above

386. What purpose is served by the illustration: *'the merchant breeds his son for the church or the bar'*?
    A. It shows that we esteem qualities which we ourselves do not possess
    B. People want their children to have different life experiences to them
    C. Parents often restrict their children's freedom of choice
    D. It shows that there are very few career options for those of certain backgrounds
    E. It suggests that the most prudent career choices lie in the church or the bar

387. What does it mean to: *'live above the beauty of the symbol to the beauty of the thing signified'*?
    A. To seek to find beauty in everything
    B. To be wise
    C. To appreciate nature
    D. To be sensual
    E. To focus on the spiritual significance of physical things

388. Which of the following best summarises the author's main argument?
    A. There are different forms of prudence
    B. Those who have the least prudence aspire to it the most
    C. Prudence involves being spiritual
    D. We don't need to know how to use money economically in order to be prudent
    E. Prudence is difficult to obtain

389. Which of the following words does the author use to signify disapproval?
    A. Disease
    B. The palate
    C. Several
    D. Commanding
    E. Apparent

Passage 77 - Russia's part in the war

C. M. Shumsky-Solomonov

In discussing Russia's role in the past World War, it is customary to cite the losses sustained by the Russian Army, losses numbering many millions. There is no doubt that Russia's sacrifices were great, and it is just as true that her losses were greater than those sustained by any of the other Allies. Nevertheless, these sacrifices are by far not the only standard of measurement of Russia's participation in this gigantic struggle. Russia's role must be gauged, first of all, by the efforts made by the Russian Army to blast the German war plans during the first years of the War, when neither America, nor Italy, nor Romania were among the belligerents, and the British Army was still in the process of formation.

[Secondly], and this is the main thing, the role played by the Russian Army must be considered also in this respect that the strenuous campaign waged by Russia, with her 180 millions of inhabitants, for three years against Germany, Austro-Hungary and Turkey, sapped the resources of the enemy and thereby made possible the delivery of the final blow. This weakening of the powers of the enemy by Russia was already bound at various stages of the War to facilitate correspondingly the various operations of the Allies. Therefore, at the end of the War three years of effort on the part of Russia, which had devoured the enemy's forces, were destined to enable the Allies to finally to crush the enemy. The final catastrophe of the Central Powers was the direct consequence of the offensive of the Allies in 1918, but Russia made possible this collapse to a considerable degree, having effected, in common with the others, the weakening of Germany, and having consumed during the three years of strenuous fighting countless reserves, forces and resources of the Central Powers.
Could Germany have won the war? A careful analysis of this question brings home the conviction that Germany was very close to victory, and that it required unusual straining of efforts on the part of France and Russia to prevent Germany from "winning out."

The plan of the old Field Marshal, Moltke, was far from worthless. It is a fact that it took from six weeks to two months to mobilise the armed forces of Russia, during which period Russia was unprepared for action. The population of Germany was 70 million and that of Austria-Hungary 52 million, a total of 122 million persons. During these two months of forced inaction, those 122 million of Teutons were faced only by 40 million Frenchmen, for Russia was not yet ready. A threefold superiority in numbers, in addition to an equal degree of military skill, technical equipment, and culture, was bound to crush lone France.

The outcome was different. The concentrated attack upon France failed because of the fact that of the 104 German divisions and the 50 Austrian divisions, only about 92 or 94 divisions were on the scene of action in France. The Russian Army, unprepared for action for another 40 days, nevertheless rushed into East Prussia in an impulse of self-sacrifice and received, in addition, the full strength of the blow from the Austro-Hungarian Army. This generous move on the part of Russia destroyed the Moltke plan and his basic idea "the concentration of *all forces* against France", as a part of the German force had been diverted from that front. The plan collapsed, and the only actual chance that the Germans had of winning a victory was lost with it. Later, when Russia was prepared, when the English Army began to grow and Italy, Romania and America had abandoned their neutrality, Germany's chances for a final victory vanished.

It is the recognition of these facts that should prompt every impartial historian of the War to admit that the self-sacrifice of the unprepared Russian Army during the first days of the War played an enormous role in the only period when Germany had victory almost within her grasp. It is to be regretted that the extraordinary conditions that developed in Russia towards the end of the War are obscuring the true historic role of Russia in the sanguine World struggle. It is just as easy—from an examination of the maps of the first three years of the War, maps which speak only of two principal fronts, the French and the Russian, and no other—to grasp the significance of the gigantic role played in this War by great Russia and the millions of sacrifices she consecrated to the common cause of the Allies. Sadly enough, this only correct criterion of Russia's historic role in the War is becoming more and more obscured from the public opinion of the world.

390. What is the main conclusion in the first paragraph?
    A. Russia's sacrifices were great
    B. The losses sustained by the Russian Army should not be the primary means of gauging their role in the war
    C. Russia made victory possible for the allies
    D. The Russian army's losses numbered millions
    E. Russia's losses were greater than those of the other allies

391. What is the main premise of the argument that Russia had a significant role in the defeat of Germany?
    A. Russia's efforts ensured that the German army was significantly weakened
    A. Russia delivered the final blow to Germany
    B. Russia received the full strength of the blow from the Austro-Hungarian army
    C. Russia rushed into the war although they were unprepared
    D. The Russian army was the only army large enough to confront Germany

392. Which one of the following statements does the least to support the argument that Russia had a significant role in the defeat of Germany?
    A. Maps of the first three years of the War speak only of two principal fronts, the French and the Russian, and no other
    B. Russia destroyed the Moltke plan
    C. Russia weakened the powers of the enemy
    D. The Russian army acted in an impulse of self-sacrifice
    E. The concentrated attack upon France failed because of the fact that of the 104 German divisions and the 50 Austrian divisions, only about 92 or 94 divisions were on the scene of action in France

393. Which of the following, if true, would most significantly weaken the author's argument?
    A. Very few Germans died during conflict with Russia
    B. The Russian army lost more men than the German army
    C. The other allies lost more men than the Russian army
    D. The efforts of the other allied nations were essential to the defeat of Germany
    E. France played a minimal role in the attaining of victory

394. What is implied by the phrase *'It is the recognition of these facts that should prompt every impartial historian of the War to admit...'*
    A. Historians ought to base their views on those facts
    B. Historians are all aware of the facts
    C. The facts alone are very compelling
    D. Only biased historians fail to concede the significance of Russia's role in the war
    E. Many historians have an anti-Russian bias

Passage 78 - Goethe's Theory of Colour: Translator's Preface

Charles Lock Eastlake

English writers who have spoken of Goethe's "Doctrine of Colours," have generally confined their remarks to those parts of the work in which he has undertaken to account for the colours of the prismatic spectrum, and of refraction altogether, on principles different from the received theory of Newton. The less questionable merits of the treatise consisting of a well-arranged mass of observations and experiments, many of which are important and interesting, have thus been in a great measure overlooked. The translator, aware of the opposition which the theoretical views alluded to have met with, intended at first to make a selection of such of the experiments as seem more directly applicable to the theory and practice of painting. Finding, however, that the alterations this would have involved would have been incompatible with a clear and connected view of the author's statements, he preferred giving the theory itself, reflecting, at the same time, that some scientific readers may be curious to hear the author speak for himself even on the points at issue.

In reviewing the history and progress of his opinions and research, Goethe tells us that he first submitted his views to the public in two short essays entitled "Contributions to Optics." Among the circumstances which he supposes were unfavourable to him on that occasion, he mentions the choice of his title, observing that by a reference to optics he must have appeared to make pretensions to a knowledge of mathematics, a science with which he admits he was very imperfectly acquainted. Another cause to which he attributes the severe treatment he experienced was in having ventured so openly to question the truth of the established theory: but this last provocation could not be owing to mere inadvertence on his part; indeed, the larger work, in which he alludes to these circumstances, is still more remarkable for the violence of his objections to the Newtonian doctrine.

There can be no doubt, however, that much of the opposition Goethe met with was to be attributed to the manner as well as to the substance of his statements. Had he contented himself with merely detailing his experiments and showing their application to the laws of chromatic harmony, leaving it to others to reconcile them as they could with the pre-established system, or even to doubt in consequence, the truth of some of the Newtonian conclusions, he would have enjoyed the credit he deserved for the accuracy and the utility of his investigations. As it was, the uncompromising expression of his convictions only exposed him to the resentment or silent neglect of a great portion of the scientific world, so that for a time he could not even obtain a fair hearing for the less objectionable or rather highly valuable communications contained in his book. A specimen of his manner of alluding to the Newtonian theory will be seen in the preface.

It was quite natural that this spirit should call forth a somewhat vindictive feeling and with it not a little uncandid as well as unsparing criticism. "The Doctrine of Colours" met with this reception in Germany long before it was noticed in England, where a milder and fairer treatment could hardly be expected especially at a time when, owing perhaps to the limited intercourse with the continent, German literature was far less popular than it is at present. This last fact, it is true, can be of little importance in the present instance, for although the change of opinion with regard to the genius of an enlightened nation must be acknowledged to be beneficial, it is to be hoped there is no fashion in science, and the translator begs to state once for all, that in advocating the neglected merits of the "Doctrine of Colours," he is far from undertaking to defend its imputed errors. Sufficient time has, however, now elapsed since the publication of this work (in 1810) to allow a calmer and more candid examination of its claims. In this more pleasing task, Germany has again for some time led the way, and many scientific investigators have followed up the hints and observations of Goethe with a due acknowledgment of the acuteness of his views.

395. Why did the writer decide against selecting only certain parts of Goethe's views for showcasing?
   A. In order to maintain honesty
   B. Goethe himself preferred to state his views in their entirety
   C. The views are more convincing in their entirety
   D. It would have obscured the clarity of the author's statements
   E. All of Goethe's views are useful to the practice of painting

396. Which of the following was not stated by Goethe to be a reason for the unfavourable treatment of his work?
   A. His uncompromising expression of his convictions
   B. His choice of title
   C. The fact that he openly ventured to question the truth of the established theory
   D. His lack of mathematical knowledge
   E. None of the above

397. Which of the following, if true, would most strengthen the author's main argument?
   A. Goethe's work met the most success in France
   B. Goethe's contemporaries, who published similar theories in more tentative language, were hailed as geniuses
   C. Most of Goethe's contemporaries were conservative in their approach to science
   D. All of Goethe's work was expressed in uncompromising terms
   E. Most of Goethe's work was unaccepted by the scientific community

398. The author uses the phrase *'fashion in science'* to mean:
   A. Popularity contests in the world of scientists
   B. Changes in scientific opinion that are not based on reason
   C. Periodic changes in scientific opinion
   D. The way in which things are done in the scientific community
   E. Competition amongst scientists

399. Which of the following does the author use to convey his approval?
   A. Popular
   B. Due
   C. Imputed
   D. Milder
   E. Sufficient

Passage 79 - Town Life in the Fifteenth Century

JR Green

There is nothing in England today with which we can compare the life of a fully enfranchised borough of the fifteenth century. The town of those earlier days in fact governed itself after the fashion of a little principality. Within the bounds which the mayor and citizens defined with perpetual insistence in their formal perambulation year after year it carried on its isolated self-dependent life.

The inhabitants defended their own territory, built and maintained their walls and towers, armed their own soldiers, trained them for service, and held reviews of their forces at appointed times. They elected their own rulers and officials in whatever way they themselves chose to adopt, and distributed among officers and councillors just such powers of legislation and administration as seemed good in their eyes. They drew up formal constitutions for the government of the community, and as time brought new problems and responsibilities, more were made, re-made and revised; again their ordinances with restless and fertile ingenuity, till they had made of their constitution a various medley of fundamental doctrines and general precepts and particular rules, somewhat after the fashion of an American state of modern times.

In all concerns of trade, they exercised the widest powers, and bargained and negotiated and made laws as nations do on a grander scale today. They could covenant and confederate, buy and sell, deal and traffic after their own will; they could draw up formal treaties with other boroughs, and could admit them to or shut them out from all the privileges of their commerce; they might pass laws of protection or try experiments in free trade. Often, their authority stretched out over a wide district and surrounding villages gathered to their markets and obeyed their laws; it might even happen in the case of a staple town that their officers controlled the main foreign trade of whole provinces.

Four hundred years later, the very remembrance of this free and vigorous life was utterly blotted out. When Commissioners were sent in 1835 to enquire into the position of the English boroughs, there was not one community where the ancient traditions still lived. There were Mayors, and Town Councils, and Burgesses; but the burgesses were for the most part deprived of any share whatever in the election of their municipal officers while these officers themselves had lost all the nobler characteristics of their former authority. Too often the very limits of the old "liberties" of the town were forgotten; or if the ancient landmarks were remembered at all it was only because they defined bounds within which the inhabitants had the right of voting for a member of Parliament; and in cases where the old boundaries now subsisted for no other reason, it was wholly forgotten that they might ever have had some other origin.

There were, it is true, exceptions to this common apathy and towns like Lynn might still maintain some true municipal life while others like Bristol might yet show a good fighting temper which counted for much in the political struggles of the early nineteenth century. But the ordinary provincial burghers had lost, or forgotten, or been robbed of the heritage bequeathed by their predecessors of the fifteenth century. With the loss of their municipal independence went the loss of their political authority; and the four hundred or so of members whom they sent to Parliament took a very different position there from that once held by their ancestors. In the Middle Ages, the knights of the shire were the mere nominees of the wealthy or noble class, returned to Parliament by the power of the lord's retainers, while the burgesses of the towns preserved a braver and freer tradition. At the time of the Reform Bill, on the other hand, a vast majority of the town members sat among the Commons as dependents and servants of the landed aristocracy, whose mission it was to make the will of their patrons prevail, and who in their corrupt or timid subjection simply handed back to the wealthier class the supreme political power which artisans and shopkeepers and "mean people" of the medieval boroughs had threatened to share with them.

400. Which of the following is stated to be the ultimate reason for the prevailing apathy towards political freedom in towns?
    A. The loss of independent political authority
    B. The manipulation of the voting system
    C. The Reform Bill
    D. Servitude to the landed aristocracy
    E. The loss of municipal independence

401. What is meant by the phrase '*little principality*'?
    A. A small region
    B. A politically independent state
    C. Local government
    D. A tribe
    E. An army

402. In what way was former town life '*free and vigorous*'?
    A. The reform bill had not yet been passed
    B. The citizens could define the bounds of the town
    C. The towns could bargain and negotiate trade laws
    D. They had established peace treaties with other towns for their protection
    E. They could impose their rule on other towns

403. Which of the following, if true, would most weaken the author's argument?
    A. The emergence of political apathy in towns preceded the loss of their municipal independence
    B. Some knights during the Middle Ages were not subject to the control of the lords
    C. Some towns still maintain vigorous municipal life
    D. Some town inhabitants would like to return to the way things were in times past
    E. The reform bill had little impact on the political status of towns

404. Which is the best explanation for why the author uses quotation marks in the final line?
    A. He wishes to challenge those who use the term
    B. In order to use a term commonly used without himself endorsing it
    C. Because he is quoting another person/other persons
    D. To emphasise the difference between the mean people and the landed aristocracy
    E. All of the above

Passage 80 - Counter-Terrorism Laws and Human Rights

Melody Ihuoma

During the 1960s and 70s, terrorism was a contemporary subject due to the conflict between the UK government and the IRA. 'The Troubles' (the name given to the violence) originated in the 1920s and eventually resulted in bombings on the streets of Northern Ireland and occasionally in England. The government felt that in order to prevent mayhem their actions needed to be swift and decisive. Thus, a series of temporary measures were initiated; policemen and soldiers all over Ulster were given the right to stop, question, search and arrest members of the public.

In 2000, the Terrorism Act 2000 was passed as a definitive measure following twenty years of temporary measures. Policemen were given wider stop and search powers and enabled to detain suspects for up to 48 hours without charge. The Act was met with strong criticism as it outlawed certain Islamic fundamentalist groups and this was seen as a portrayal of Islam as a religion that fuels terrorism. This, in turn, made it likely that discrimination would occur in the form of the disproportionate stopping and searching of Asians who were thought to 'look Muslim'.

Although, prior to the September 2001 attacks on Washington D.C, government legislation in the UK had attempted to prevent the occurrence of terrorism; the counter-terrorism strategies had focused a lot of attention on the punishment of terrorists and the criminalisation of new offences following their occurrence. However, the Anti-Terrorism Crime and Security Act 2001 (ATCSA) marked a more firm move towards the 'management of anticipatory risk' (Piazza, Walsh, 2010) which was to characterise the counter-terrorism legislation of the 21st century.

In December 2001, the setting aside of Article 5 of the Human Rights Act (by the Terrorism Act 2000) was found to be incompatible with the Human Rights Act (HRA). Lord Bingham led the House of Lords in the judgement that the law aimed to combat the threat posed to the UK by foreign nationals yet ignored the threat posed by British citizens and was thereby, 'ipso facto discriminatory'. This ruling is a clear indication that counter-terrorism laws have a tendency to cause certain groups of people to suffer the infringement of their human rights more so than others.

Criticism of this piece of legislation also came from the Human Rights Watch. In March 2003, the group stated that the September 2001 attacks resulted in legislation within the UK which undermined fundamental human rights and that the UK was the only member of the Council of Europe to have departed from the ECHR whilst passing counter-terrorism laws.

405. How do the counter-terrorism laws passed after 9/11 differ to their predecessors?
    A. They punish terrorists more harshly
    B. They focus more on preventing the occurrence of terrorist attacks
    C. They were more definitive measures
    D. They were more discriminatory against certain groups of people
    E. They were driven by fear

406. What is implied by the fact that the UK was the only council member to depart from the ECHR?
    A. A departure may not have been necessary for the protection of the UK
    B. Other nations were under pressure to stay within the terms of the ECHR
    C. The ECHR is too rigid
    D. The threat of terrorism to the UK was higher than to the other council members
    E. The British government cares less about human rights

407. Which of the following are not presented as contrasting pairs in the passage?
    A. Temporary and definitive measures
    B. Punishment and management of risk
    C. The UK and other members of the council of Europe
    D. UK foreign nationals and British citizens
    E. The Terrorism Act 2000 and the Human Rights Act

408. Which of the following, if true, would most weaken the author's argument in paragraph 4.
    A. Minority groups such as the Chinese have not been unfairly affected by terrorism legislation
    B. Many parts of the 2000 Act were compatible with the HRA
    C. A disproportionately large number of foreign nationals are stopped and searched
    D. The 2000 Act is the only piece of terrorism legislation that has been found to be incompatible with the HRA
    E. Foreign nationals in the UK receive many benefits

409. Which one of the following is stated as a possible cause of draconian counter-terrorism legislation?
    A. The need to combat the threat posed by foreign nations
    B. The government felt that in order to prevent mayhem their actions needed to be swift and decisive
    C. The side-lining of the HRA
    D. The portrayal of Islam as a religion which fuels terrorism
    E. Giving policeman in Ulster the right to stop, search, and arrest members of the public

Section 2

The ultimate goal of any essay is to convey an argument to the reader. In order to do that, the essay needs to be as clear as possible, follow a logical structure, and develop a coherent argument. In the exam, you will have 60 minutes to write the essay.

The key to creating a solid essay in the exam is to develop a good, persuasive argument in clear written English. It is **not** about writing as much as you can – indeed, some of the best essays are the shortest; and a rambling essay can attract low marks.

Ultimately, the examiners are testing your **ability to argue** and **not** particularly on your knowledge. That being said, having a good general knowledge will help you create good arguments and will stand you well for the exam. Crucially, it means that you'll be comfortable answering the questions in the exam.

Structuring your Essay

The structure of an essay consists of 3 parts:
1. Introduction
2. Main Body
3. Conclusion

This is a well-known structure and while it is not necessary to give headings or to say that you're writing your introduction, keeping your essay in this format will be more clear and understandable.

A well-known saying is that: In your introduction, say what you're going to say; in the main body, you say it and in your conclusion, say what you've already said by bringing it all together.

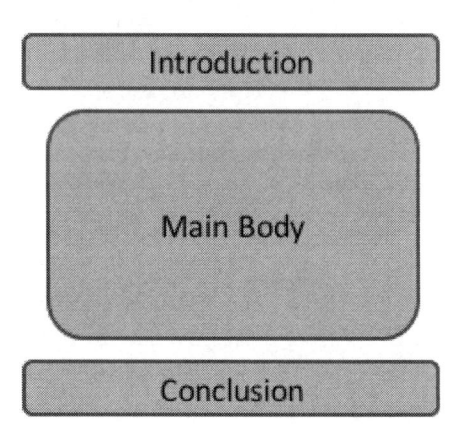

The Exam Approach

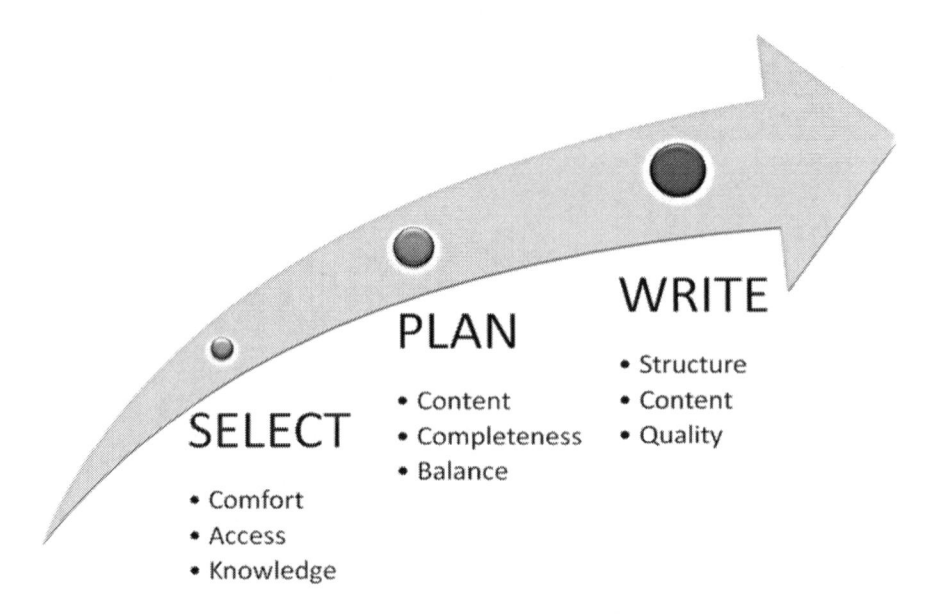

SELECT
- Comfort
- Access
- Knowledge

PLAN
- Content
- Completeness
- Balance

WRITE
- Structure
- Content
- Quality

Most students think that the "writing" component is most important. This is simply not true.

The vast **majority of problems are caused by a lack of planning and essay selection** – usually, because students just want to get writing as they are worried about finishing on time. 45 minutes is long enough to be able to plan your essay well and *still* have time to write it, so don't feel pressured to immediately start writing.

Step 1: Selecting

You will be given a choice of 8 essays to choose from and crucially, you will have no idea of what it could be beforehand. Selecting your essay is crucial- make sure you're comfortable with the topic and ensure you understand the actual question- it sounds silly but about 25% of essays that we mark score poorly because they don't actually answer the question!

Take five minutes to read all the questions. Whilst one essay might originally seem the easiest, if you haven't thought through it, you might quickly find yourself running out of ideas. Likewise, a seemingly difficult essay might actually offer you a good opportunity to make interesting points.

Use this time to carefully select which question you will answer by gauging how accessible and comfortable you are with it given your background knowledge.

It's surprisingly easy to change a question into something similar, but with a different meaning. Thus, you may end up answering a completely different essay title. Once you've decided which question you're going to do, read it very carefully a few times to make sure you fully understand it. Answer all aspects of the question. Keep reading it as you answer to ensure you stay on track!

Step 2: Planning

Why should I plan my essay?
There are multiple reasons you should plan your essay for the first 5 minutes of Section B:
- As you don't have much space to write, make the most of it by writing a very well-organised essay.
- It allows you to get all your thoughts ready before you put pen to paper.
- You'll write faster once you have a plan.
- You run the risk of missing the point of the essay or only answering part of it if you don't plan adequately.

How much time should I plan for?
There is no set period of time that should be dedicated to planning, and everyone will dedicate a different length of time to the planning process. You should spend as long planning your essay as you require, but it is essential that you leave enough time to write the essay. As a rough guide, it is **worth spending about 5-10 minutes to plan** and the remaining time on writing the essay. However, this is not a strict rule, and you are advised to tailor your time management to suit your individual style.

How should I go about the planning process?
There are a variety of methods that can be employed in order to plan essays (e.g. bullet-points, mind-maps etc). If you don't already know what works best, it's a good idea to experiment with different methods.

Generally, the first step is to gather ideas relevant to the question, which will form the basic arguments around which the essay is to be built. You can then begin to structure your essay, including the way that points will be linked. At this stage, it is worth considering the balance of your argument, and confirming that you have considered arguments from both sides of the debate. Once this general structure has been established, it is useful to consider any examples or real world information that may help to support your arguments. Finally, you can begin to assess the plan as a whole and establish what your conclusion will be based on your arguments.

How do I plan my essay?
Different methods work best for different students, but some are as follows:
- A mind-map
- Bullet-points
- A side by side list of PROS and CONS

Step 3: Writing

Introduction

The introduction should explain the statement and define any key terms. Here, you can say what you're going to say and suggest (either affirmatively or tentatively) a response or answer to the question.

It is important not to spend too long on an introduction as that would use up too much time unnecessarily, which could be better spent on other parts of the essay.

Main Body

The main body is where you discuss your arguments, consider counter arguments or consider the pros and cons of a particular statement or policy position.

In particular, while you may have numerous ideas, it is generally better to spend more time developing and evaluating fewer points, rather than listing as many points as possible and not going into much depth on each point.

Just like in GCSE English, using the Point-Evidence-Evaluation technique can help ensure you develop and deploy your ideas more fully.

In particular, using relevant examples where you can will help bolster your argument and provide for a more persuasive essay. However, it is crucial that real world examples are only used if they fit in with your argument – otherwise, it adds nothing and will not gain you marks.

How do I go about making a convincing point?

Each idea that you propose should be supported and justified in order to build a convincing overall argument. A point can be solidified through a basic Point → Evidence → Evaluation process. By following this process, you can be assured each sentence within a paragraph builds upon the last and that all the ideas presented are well solidified.

How do I achieve a logical flow between ideas?

One of the most effective ways of displaying a good understanding of the question is to keep a logical flow throughout your essay. This means linking points effectively between paragraphs and creating a congruent train of thought for the examiner as the argument develops. A good way to generate this flow of ideas is to provide ongoing comparisons of arguments and discussing whether points support or dispute one another.

Conclusion

The conclusion provides an opportunity to emphasise the **overall sentiment of your essay** which readers can then take away. It should summarise what has been discussed during the main body and give a definitive answer to the question. It's not necessary to restate your points but this is where you can weigh up the advantages and disadvantages and explain why you've attached more weight to an advantage or disadvantage.

Some students use the conclusion to **introduce a new idea that hasn't been discussed**. This can be an interesting addition to an essay and can help make you stand out. However, it is by no means, a necessity. In fact, a well-organised, 'standard' conclusion is likely to be more effective than an adventurous but poorly executed one.

Crucially, it is important to give a judgement in the conclusion, or a decisive response to the question posed, based on the arguments you've advanced in the main body. For example, do you agree with the statement?

Worked Example

"Abortion should only be permitted in certain circumstances" Discuss.

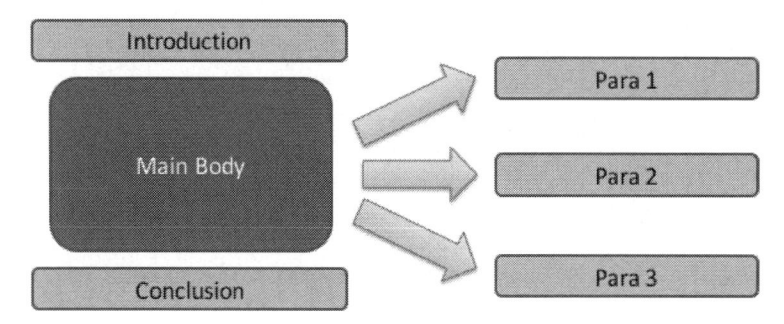

Introduction
In the introduction, it would be useful to present a brief outline of what you're going to discuss. After planning the essay (discussed below), you will know what you're going to talk about in the main body and can give a very brief outline in the introduction.

It is also important to define any key terms in the question here. It is quite clear that 'abortion' could be usefully defined ('the termination of a pregnancy').

If you wish, you can also highlight the key themes that will run through the essay.

Main Body
A key issue is what you write in the main body.

In the planning stage, jot down the ideas that first come to your head. For this question, you should think of possible circumstances where abortion should be permitted and possible circumstances in which it shouldn't be permitted.

Possible circumstances to consider abortion:
- *When the mother just wants to give up the foetus*
- *In the event of a medical issue*
- *Disability of the child*
- *Sexual Assault*
- *When the mother is too young*

Five possible lines of inquiry are listed here but there won't be time in 60 minutes to consider all of them in enough detail. In the exam, it's much better to focus on quality rather than quantity. Accordingly, choose the areas where you have the most knowledge or where you feel like you can make an original contribution and shine.

It is then necessary to choose a structure, and one possible structure is to devote each paragraph to a 'circumstance' and in order to cover fewer points, but in more detail, three circumstances will be considered. In each paragraph, the pros and cons should be considered to produce a balanced essay.

Structure of Main Body:
Paragraph 1: Abortion when the mother wants to give up foetus
Paragraph 2: Disability of the child
Paragraph 3: Medical issue

Detailed Plan of Main Body
- *Abortion when the mother wants to give up foetus*
    1. **For Allowing Abortion**
        a. Some may argue that the mother should be able to give up the foetus should she want to.
        b. This is based on her freedom to plan her life as she chooses.
        c. Forcing the mother to have a child may not be in the child's best interests – would the child be cared for?
    2. **Against Allowing Abortion**
        a. The foetus has a right to life.
        b. The mother already made her choice during consummation and exercised her freedom to choose then.
    3. Therefore, abortion should not be permitted in this circumstance as the right to life should take greater precedence. The mother should be encouraged to think carefully about having a child before consummation.

Disability of the child
    4. **For Allowing Abortion**
        a. The child would have a poor quality of life.
        b. Would be more expensive to bring up a child with a disability.
    5. **Against Allowing Abortion**
        a. Again, against the child's right to life.
        b. Hard to tell what the child's quality of life would be if there's a known disability.
        c. Even if the child will be disabled, disabled people play an important role in society.
        d. The rights of a foetus shouldn't be different depending on a disability.
    6. Arguably, the right to life of the foetus should prevail here. It would, in any case, be discriminatory to lower the rights of an abnormal foetus when compared to that of a healthy foetus. It's against the law to discriminate against disabled humans and surely the same should be the case for a disabled foetus.

Medical Issue
    7. **For Allowing Abortion**
        a. Health risk to the mother.
    8. **Against Allowing Abortion**
        a. Right to life of the foetus.
    9. On balance, the right to life of a living person should take precedence in this circumstance.

This is a detailed plan and your plan in the exam does not need to be this detailed, but it should still cover the main points. Once a plan is written, you can get straight into writing the essay.

Note carefully how alternative points of view are <u>always</u> considered in the detailed plan above. Ultimately, your goal is to write a persuasive and balanced essay. When you consider alternative points of view, it strengthens your main argument. This is because it shows that you have thought about the different sides of the issue.

In the detailed plan above, point (c) is an intermediate (or interim) conclusion at the end of each paragraph. This is simply a statement which concludes a *paragraph*. It is generally desirable to include tentative conclusions where possible here as it makes it easier for the reader to understand your essay.

Conclusion
In the conclusion, the arguments advanced in the main body are brought together. In this question, the interim conclusions on each circumstance went into a lot of depth, so just a basic summary suffices for the main conclusion. An example could be as follows:

"On balance, abortion should only be permitted in certain circumstances. The right to life of the foetus demands that abortion is not allowed at the behest of the mother alone. However, there are certain situations when abortion should be permitted, such as when there is a health risk to the mother as her rights must be considered alongside that of the foetus."

Common Mistakes

1) Ignoring the other side of the argument
Although you're normally required to support one side of the debate, it is important to **consider arguments against your judgement** in order to get the higher marks. A good way to do this is to propose an argument that might be used against you, and then to argue why it doesn't hold true or seem relevant. You may use the format: *"some may say that...but this doesn't seem to be important because..."* in order to dispel opposition arguments whilst still displaying that you have considered them. For example, *"some may say that fox hunting shouldn't be banned because it is a tradition. However, witch hunting was also once a tradition – we must move on with the times"*.

2) Answering the topic/Answering only part of the question
One of the most common mistakes is to only answer a part of the question whilst ignoring the rest of it as it's inaccessible.

3) Long Introductions
Some students can start rambling and make introductions too long and unfocused. Although background information about the topic can be useful, it is normally not necessary. Instead, the **emphasis should be placed on responding to the question**. Some students also just **rephrase the question** rather than actually explaining it. The examiner knows what the question is, and repeating it in the introduction is simply a waste of space.

4) Not including a Conclusion
An essay that lacks a conclusion is incomplete and can signal that the answer has not been considered carefully or that your organisation skills are lacking. **The conclusion should be a distinct paragraph** in its own right and not just a couple of rushed lines at the end of the essay.

5) Sitting on the Fence
Students sometimes don't reach a clear conclusion. You need to **ensure that you give a decisive answer to the question** and clearly explain how you've reached this judgement. Essays that do not come to a clear conclusion generally have a smaller impact and score lower.

General Advice

- ✓ Always answer the question clearly – this is the key thing examiners look for in an essay.
- ✓ Analyse each argument made, justifying or dismissing with logical reasoning.
- ✓ Keep an eye on the time/space available – an incomplete essay may be taken as a sign of a candidate with poor organisational skills.
- ✓ Use pre-existing knowledge when possible – examples and real world data can be a great way to strengthen an argument- but don't make up statistics!
- ✓ Present ideas in a neat, logical fashion (easier for an examiner to absorb).
- ✓ Complete some practice papers in advance in order to best establish your personal approach to the paper (particularly timings, how you plan etc.).
- ✓ Attempt to answer a question that you don't fully understand, or ignore part of a question.
- ✓ Rush or attempt to use too many arguments – it is much better to have fewer, more substantial points.
- ✓ Attempt to be too clever or present false knowledge to support an argument – a tutor may call out incorrect facts etc.
- ✓ Panic if you don't know the answer the examiner wants – there is no right answer, the essay is not a test of knowledge but a chance to display reasoning skill.
- ✓ Leave an essay unfinished – if time/space is short, wrap up the essay early in order to provide a conclusive response to the question.

HSPSAA: SECTION B ESSAYS

Annotated Essays

Example Essay 1

"There is a time and place for censorship of the internet" Discuss with particular reference to the right of freedom of expression.

Internet is the main source of connection for people all around the world. It's where we get the latest news and information worldwide effectively and effortlessly. The lack of barrier in this internet world gives easy access to information that we might not want to see and might cause us offence. This essay is about the act of censorship, which filters offensive information of the internet, given there's a time and a place we can do so in this modern era. There's "a place" suggests there's enough room which needs to be censored and there's "a time" suggest it's the time to act on censorship.

Firstly, censorship is necessary to a certain extent as due to freedom of expression, we might be access to information that we found offended by, such as pornography. These might affect viewers mentally and easily cause depression, and affect minds especially the early teens.
However, an age limit could be set on a pornography website and refuse access to such images. It's taking an active role, to click into those websites. Setting age limits can prevent youngsters receiving non-educational information and affect their youth development. Freedom of expression is also offended as some might treat pornography as a form of art. It's very difficult to monitor whether the viewer is really above the age limit.

Also, definition of Art is very blurry, which as an excuse for people to share it through the internet. Parental education is also a key. Instead of setting limits to the children, we should given them advice on what they should go on, and guide them to make the right decision on choosing suitable materials. In this way, not only the children's development is protected, it also trains them to give the right judgements and develop logical thinking.

Another place for censorship is political/religious offensive comments and materials. Religious behaviours should be protected due to the freedom of expression in society and political views in order to keep harmony. However, in order to achieve this, censorship is not necessary, as it would block the minds and thoughts and might be a chance for the government to brain-wash the citizens with the 'right kind' of political behaviour, which might ironically break harmony in society, and slow down its development.

Examiner's Comments:

Introduction: The introduction rambles on too long – it could have been much shorter and concise. It was also not clear. It's not necessary to say "This essay is about the act of censorship" – this is obvious. It was good to define censorship in the introduction (when the student said 'filters offensive information') although the rest of the introduction was not clear and did not make sense. Accordingly, the student would have lost marks here and wasted time. The student did not address the entire question either – it would have been good to point out how freedom of expression will come into play as well. The introduction only really needs to be 3 or 4 lines.

Main Body: In the main body, the student makes some wild assertions, such as the point regarding depression. The first sentence in the main body doesn't make much sense either. The main issue with the essay is that the student's points are not linked together logically: the essay consists of a large number of separate assertions. The point made about 'art' is not very clear either.

Conclusion: Lastly, the candidate finishes with no conclusion. The final paragraph did not draw together all the relevant information, which is bad practice. Even if a candidate is running out of time, writing a solid conclusion will gain many more marks than not writing one. Indeed, a lack of conclusion would likely lose marks.

Example Essay 2

"There is a time and place for censorship of the internet" Discuss with particular reference to the right of freedom of expression.

Censorship of the internet is not a new concept, nor does it seem like one that will ever cease. I believe that there are a multitude of reasons for its presence and hence in this essay I will argue for the statement provided.

Firstly, censorship of the internet has the capability to protect certain groups. For example, a widely accepted and often promoted form of this is the blocking of certain websites by parents and schools. In this case, the group being protected are children. We accept the fact that children should not be exposed to 'mature' content such as violence and sexual activity and by blocking certain sites, children are free to surf the internet safely. This seemingly innocent form of censorship hardly poses much threat to the right to freedom of expression as no party is being prevented from having their views heard. If this form of censorship was deemed illegal, it may paradoxically push such parties to tone down their content by pressures from parental organisations and child safety bodies in order to create a child friendly internet, which ultimately would be restrictive to free expression.

Secondly, the restriction of content that is deemed extremist or might incite acts of terrorism, whilst going against the right to freedom of expression, could be necessary to uphold the security of a nation. Thus, taking a utilitarian perspective to this issue, as the safety of the nation takes on a greater value than the right to freedom of expression. Although it may seem like a cold approach, it is justified for the well-being of a greater number of individuals and thus, society generally. Truly, the recruitment of ISIS supports is a disturbing example of the necessity of censorship of extremist views and preventative measures must be taken to ensure that the young and susceptible are not taken in by the terrorist propaganda. Accordingly, there must be a point where we deem the safety of a nation as more imperative than the freedom of expression of certain individuals.

Lastly, the freedom of expression is easily abused in the cyber world. The animosity that the internet provides gives the users a sense of invisibility where they see themselves as above the law. Abusive remarks are made without consideration of their consequence or lack of this providing an environment for cyber bullying to grow.

Censorship is not necessarily tyrannical but is a practice that must co-exist with any form of content creation and like all else, there is a time and place for it.

Examiner's Comments:

Introduction: The introduction is very concise, which is good. However, it would have been even better if the student considered freedom of expression in the introduction.

Main Body: This is a good attempt at the question and relates directly to the question. The candidate refers to the relationship between censorship and freedom of expression throughout the main body. She points out when freedom of expression is hindered by censorship and when censorship is justified. Given that it relates to the question throughout, it would yield many more marks than Example 1 (even though both are of a similar length).

However, the candidate did not consider whether censorship might be bad in the first place: why can't the government just censor what they want to? The essay would have been stronger if this were considered (even briefly). It would have been worthwhile to bring in the countervailing principle of 'freedom of expression' at some point in the essay. This would be a reason why the government should *not* be able to censor any information. The penultimate paragraph doesn't add much to the essay though – is censorship acceptable in this situation? Is this the place for censorship? Or should people be expected to put up with other people's views? Other than this paragraph, the rest of the essay is very good.

Conclusion: The conclusion is quite short. While there is nothing inherently wrong with the conclusion being concise, it must answer the question. The candidate's conclusion did not refer to freedom of expression and so she has not fully addressed the question.

Example Essay 3

"There is a time and place for censorship of the internet" Discuss with particular reference to the right of freedom of expression".

In today's day and age it's extremely easy for anyone to access explicit or dangerous content on the internet. There have been talks of censorship on the internet, but is it necessary? One would argue that the censorship of the internet is against our freedom of expression, which is why in this essay I will come with an answer in response to the statement 'There is a time and place for censorship of the internet'.

In our current education system there is a heavy emphasis put on the usage of the internet to aid our learning. However, once children learn how to use the internet, the whole world is just one click away. Children could be easily exposed to indecent images, which is why some say the government should censor the internet for the safety of children. Possible solutions could be only allowing websites with adult material to be accessible at late-night, reducing the chances of indecent exposure to children. Accordingly, in this instance, censorship is justified.

Similarly, one could easily research the internet to find information about illegal activities such as drug or bomb making. This means that the internet could be used as a tool to threaten national security, hence why the internet should have tough censorship in order to prevent criminals from accessing dangerous material, for the benefit of everyone's safety.

On the other hand, blocking certain websites strictly goes against our right of freedom of expression and instead of blocking certain dangerous websites, the government should have a more efficient surveillance strategy in order to track people who are accessing such dangerous websites. This would ensure that our right of freedom of expression isn't breached and at the same time, criminal activity would be prevented.

Furthermore, with regards to the access of sexually explicit websites, more work should be some in order to educate children not to access such websites. Good parent is a better alternative to preventing children accessing such websites, rather than blocking sites which goes against our right of freedom of expression.

In conclusion, there is no time and place for censorship as it goes against our right to freedom of expression. Other alternatives such as internet surveillance would be more effective as it ensures the safety of the general public and at the same time our freedom of expression is not breached.

Examiner's Comments:

Introduction: This is a very good introduction. It highlights the conflict between censorship and freedom of expression, which is a good place to point it out. In the final sentence, though, the student wastes time in saying "which is why in this essay I will come with an answer in response to the statement...." – this is obvious and there's little point in saying it. It just wastes time and prevents one using the time for writing something more useful. Other than this, the introduction is very good and concise.

Main Body: The student considers two main instances of censorship in the main body (indecent images and dangerous websites) and suggests that censorship could be used, but suggests alternatives would be more effective. This is quite a persuasive essay because the student has considered alternative points of view, which makes the essay balanced.

Conclusion: The conclusion is very clear and brings the arguments advanced in the essay to a final judgement. The candidate directly addresses the question and refers to the whole part of the question by considering freedom of expression (unlike in Example Essay 2). On the whole, this is a very impressive essay.

Example Essay 4

"The UK should codify its Constitution" Discuss.

The present constitution of the UK includes sources such as statute law and case law made by the judges. To codify the constitution, the state should come up with one single document that explains and describes the power of the Royal family, the government, the parliament and all the citizens. This essay will critically examine the possibility of codifying the UK's constitution.

Firstly, a codified constitution can make it clear and accessible to the citizens. With a written constitution, the citizens can trace back the rights and obligations of them and also have a better understanding of the relationship between them and the government. This may motivate the UK people to be active in partaking in politics because they can feel that they have a say through voting or other political actions. [This sentence isn't clear – how would codifying the constitution make people feel they can have a say?] It is beneficial for the development of society. [Should use a connective within this – i.e. "It is thus beneficial for...." – as this would make it flow]

Secondly, it helps limit the power of the government. Since the government is formed by the winning party of the election of the House of Commons, the party which is in charge of the government has the strength to implement the policies that they are fond of, even if it opposes the public will. A written constitution which clarifies the duty and the power of a government that when the government does not go in accordance with the public opinion, the constitution will help prevent it from doing so.

However, it is actually unique that the parliament is supreme of all. The parliament should have the ability to change the law or add new rules according to the demand of the public, neither any other organisations nor rules should have a bigger say than parliament, which is elected by the people. If the Constitution is codified, there will be a constitutional court like USA does with judges who are not elected to interpret the law. It actually weakens our democracy.

Furthermore, an uncodified constitution is more flexible. For the UK, getting enough support and votes in the Parliament is the only factor to change the content of a law or add a new act. It only takes a minimal period of time to adopt a new policy which benefits the country. This is totally opposite to the rigid process of changing regulations and rules in a country with a codified constitution such as France, which takes a very long time to pass through all stages to get consent from difference levels. A flexible system helps a country react to international changes faster and diminishes the losses it can possibly come up with.

In addition, the UK does not have a revolution in history to set up the Constitution. Unlike other countries with written constitutions, the UK did not have any revolution (such as in France and the US) to overthrow the old system and set up a democracy. It gradually changes from authoritarian rule of monarch to a state with constitutional monarch. The past has shown that the country actually works well with this system while the democracy of the country does not disappear. It always ranks top 10 in the world, a place where many developing countries would like to learn.

To conclude, it is unnecessary for the UK to set up a codified constitution because the existing system alas makes the country work well. No one can ensure what effects the written one will bring to the UK.

Examiner's Comments:
This is a relatively long essay for 45 minutes, but one which is not that good. It uses a lot of knowledge, but not to good effect.

Introduction: This is concise in just explaining the role of a codified constitution. The issue is that it does not define what a codified constitution is. Having a written constitution is more than just having the constitution written in a single document: It is one which is harder to repeal than other laws.

This is not a big concern to the essay though as the Section B essay is more a test of your persuasive and written skills, rather than your essay. It would also be worth pointing out that an unwritten constitution (like the UK's) is flexible, which means that a government can just change it if it wants. Whereas a written constitution (like in the US) binds the government and Parliament and a special majority is required to alter it. Highlighting such policy tensions can be beneficial in the introduction to essay questions.

Main Body:
Everything you say in the essay must make sense. It is pointless writing the first thing which comes to your mind if it doesn't make sense as this would paint a poor picture with admissions tutors and lead to rejection. In the second paragraph, it is not clear how the sentence "*This may motivate the UK people to be active in partaking in politics because they can feel that they have a say through voting or other political actions*" relates to the question. It isn't clear that people feel they can have a say through voting by virtue of having a written constitution, and the student does not explain it. The sentence does not actually make sense.

The third paragraph is not entirely clear either – surely a government would reflect the public will. It would be more coherent to suggest that the government can infringe on minority rights.

At the beginning of the fourth paragraph, the candidate starts with the sentence: "*However, it is actually unique that the parliament is supreme of all.*" This particular point is not elaborated on further and it does not add to the essay. So what if Britain's system is unique? Does this mean it's bad? It is important to be clear in essays, to make the reader's job (of understanding what you mean) as easy as possible. The candidate also incorrectly uses the connective 'However' – this connection is used to indicate a contrasting point but the student's points before and after the connective do not contrast! This goes to show that it is important to think before writing and ensure you express yourself clearly.

The candidate has clearly deployed significant knowledge but has not used it well to advance an argument and the essay has been confusing at many points. It is important to think and plan what you're going to write before writing it; planning before writing can significantly help the quality of writing. This essay would have likely led to rejections by admissions tutors.

A crucial suggestion would be to think whether you are addressing the question while answering it.

Conclusion: The conclusion is sufficient as it directly answers the question.

Example Essay 5

"The UK should codify its Constitution" Discuss.

Currently, the UK has an uncodified constitution. This means that there is no single legal document defining and storing all of the laws and regulations in the UK. The UK constitution comprises of many different areas. The ambiguity of the UK constitution has created debate within government itself as well as outside of government.

One main reason as to why the constitution should be codified is due to it being ambiguous. Certain laws become ignored as it may be presumed not legislative despite it being a tradition, or an 'unproven rule'. Theresa May, the Home Secretary, violated one of the constitutional conventions, where she publicly blamed and identified one of the civil servants for a mishap in passport checking in Paris. It is known in government that the head of authority is to take responsibility of everything, whether it is or not their fault. Due to there not being a codified constitution, Theresa May was able slip from it. Therefore, having a codified constitution can ensure full responsibility to government.

Furthermore, a codified constitution provides security to the citizens, they would know that government is bounded by a tight set of rules which has little of no loopholes and can easily be accountable for any mistakes. This reduces confusion among the public as well, as there is a clear definition between right and wrong. A legal and authoritative constitution disregards any form of unfair or unequal treatment within the hierarchy.

However, looking at it from a different perspective, the constitution has been within the UK for a long time and has been fine with no major problems. Codifying the constitution may stir major changes and cause unpopularity among those in power. So if it isn't broken, why change it? The constitution's long standing in the UK and is also a form of historical standing which has become an admiration of many countries. It also symbolises trust in government by the people. The constitution holds more than just rights and rules, but also a devoting history in the country. As long as it has been here, there have been no issues with it.

In addition, an uncodified constitution is said to be flexible and up to date. This is because it can easily be changed and corrected if flawed. The bills of rights in the US takes a lengthy and long process to be altered. However, in the UK, adding or removing the law requires not a great amount of time. The flexibility of the constitution is a greatly appreciated characteristic of it, making it unique.

In conclusion, the constitution is fine as it is and does not require change. It is the government's own responsibility to maintain professionalism within parliament and not the laws. There is still the stance of democracy among the people to hold those of government accountable if there is any distasteful occurrence.

Examiner's Comments:

Introduction: The introduction started on the right approach, which was to explain what is meant by a codified constitution. However, the student gave an incorrect definition. It's not correct that all of a country's laws would be in a constitution.

Main Body: Each of the middle four paragraphs in the main body discuss interesting and relevant points in a lucid and concise way. The candidate presents arguments for and then arguments against, then comes to a final conclusion. To improve the essay, it would have been worth trying to evaluate and weigh up the pros and cons a bit more. For example, considering the final point in the fifth paragraph more would have been better – such as, "the flexibility has received criticisms for governments being able to make significant constitutional change, but it has crucially allowed the UK's constitution to adapt to changes in society, which may not have otherwise been possible". A further relevant point would be that the Human Rights Act may help reach a balance.

Conclusion: The first sentence is fine. It is not clear how the rest of the paragraph addresses the question. It would have been clearer to the reader if the candidate said: "The government is more accountable under an uncodified constitution".

Example Essay 6

"The UK should codify its Constitution" Discuss.

A codified constitution is a formal document where the country's main constitutional laws are set out, which defines the rules governing the political system, the distribution of powers between the different branches of government and the rights and responsibilities of citizens. A particular feature of a codified constitution is that it has a special status over other laws, such that it is harder to amend or repeal. The UK's constitution is not codified but is found in statute, case law and conventions. This essay considers whether a codified constitution would be beneficial.

Constitutional law in the UK is ambiguous and unclear. Accordingly, it tends to lead to greater disputes and uncertainty regarding the true constitutional position. For example, much of the constitution is currently in the form of constitutional conventions, which are non-legal norms. An example of such a rule is the one whereby the Queen always gives assent to bills of Parliament passed by the House of Commons and the House of Lords. While this is widely accepted and understood without controversy, other conventions are unclear. For example, the Salisbury convention requires that the House of Lords shall not oppose any government legislation that is promised in its manifesto. In regard to the recent Tax Credit cuts, the government argued that the public voted for its policies of spending cuts and that the Convention applied. However the opposition sides in the House of Lords argued that the convention did not apply because the government did not promise that specific spending cut. Given that this convention was not in a written constitution meant that it was both unclear and that there was no recourse to a court to resolve the issue. Accordingly, a codified constitution would bring clarity in such areas.

Nonetheless, an uncodified constitution does have its advantages. In particular, an uncodified constitution is easier to alter when compared to a codified one. In the UK, the constitution can just be altered like any other law. Whereas in countries with a codified constitution, it is either not possible to change the constitution or it requires an even larger majority of the legislative assembly (such as 2/3 lawmakers consenting). An advantage of the UK's system is thus that the constitution is flexible and adaptable to the changing nature of society. For example, in 1998, the government could easily establish devolution through the creation of a Scottish Parliament and Welsh Assembly in response to changing public attitudes. However, it is likely that the UK government could have done this even with a codified constitution given that it had direct public support for the devolved assemblies through referendums.

There is indeed a concern though that a codified constitution is inflexible: for example, the US constitution came into force centuries ago and thus, reflected the attitudes of that time. It provided the right for citizens to bear arms and for militias to operate. Nonetheless, this does not have to be an issue for the UK. Firstly, fewer constitutional matters can be placed in the codified constitution (in most countries, including the US, the entire constitutional law is not embodied in the written constitutional document). Secondly, it can require a reasonable, but not impossible, majority to amend the constitution.

The most important reason of all for having a codified constitution though is that it can guarantee fundamental rights of the British people. The UK currently has the Human Rights Act, but that can easily be revoked, just like any other law. Arguably, the time has come to give the public human rights in a codified constitution.

In conclusion, it would be beneficial to have a codified constitution.

Examiner's Comments:

Introduction: The introduction was very good – it defined the key term ('codified constitution') and what the significance of that would be.

Main Body: The essay started well and brings in lots of real world examples to good effect. It would have been good though for the student to use 'sign-posting' language a bit more. In the third paragraph, it appears that the student is implying that a codified constitution would still allow big changes. Writing an intermediate conclusion at the end of the paragraph, such as "Thus, the UK should not hesitate to codify its constitution".

However, the student runs out of time and in the smallest paragraph in the main body, brings in the 'most important reason' to back up his argument. The lack of consideration given to that reason makes it less convincing. Nonetheless, the second and third paragraphs did contain a more thorough discussion.

Conclusion: The conclusion is too short here. It does come to a judgement but does not explicitly weigh up the advantages and disadvantages and say why the advantages outweigh the disadvantages of having a written constitution.

Example Essay 7

"**Developed countries have a higher obligation to tackle climate change than developing countries**" Discuss the extent to which you agree with this statement

Developed countries, such as the UK, Dubai and Japan have economies and political standings which are considered fairly stable. Developing countries strive to achieve the stable GDP, inflation and political welfare of developed countries. Climate change occurs due to excess emission of gas pollutants, melting of ice caps, global warming and in the case of such serious disasters, is it fair to place greater responsibility towards the more developed first and then the second world countries?

Statistically, it is shown that developed countries have been the main pollutants and indirectly, cause global warming. Due to its higher living standards, citizens of these countries have a higher propensity to consume, thus contributing to greater factory industries. As they would also have the best resources and research and development facilities, these countries would be more capable of producing greater findings to tackle climate change. This can also avoid conflicting interests among developing countries whose main focus would still be on growing. The countries may still be facing radical political changes which could affect their views and focus on the country's wellbeing. The Kyoto protocol, a Japanese originated project to reduce air pollution mainly forced on the more developed countries, as knowing it might create economical downfall as many of these countries on oil refinement and exporting of cheap factory produced goods. Under these circumstances, having more developed and stable countries to hold higher obligations towards issues of climate change would not be too wrong.

However, looking at this from a different perspective, climate change issues should not be delegated only to a few countries, but everyone altogether. It should be notably, responsibility of all, as it would require effort and contribution, as well as a mutual understanding form every country. It would also be considered unfair, as some may take this for granted. Countries at war, Iran and Syria, should be held dully responsible for the countless bombing and air strikes which has greatly contributed to global warming. This should be an issue for all. Other than that, developed countries would be blamed for any mistake or distasteful occurrences, which would have been inevitable, by countries where the cause originated from. Therefore, it should be recognised that combating climate change should be the responsibility of all.

Why should these countries make sacrifices to their economical welfare for others? World organisations like NATO, combinations of many different countries, work as a whole, with more developed countries contributing resources and research equipment required. Tackling of climate change should be the responsibility of all, and every country should feel obligated to it.

Examiner's Comments:

Introduction: The introduction is fine as the student defines the key terms within the quotation. It could have been a bit more specific when questioning whether greater responsibility should be placed on developing countries.

Main Body: The points in the second paragraph are interesting and the student deploys her own knowledge to good effect. The final sentence in the second paragraph could usefully be adjusted to say something along the lines of "Given the greater needs of developing companies and greater resources of developed ones, developed countries may have a greater capacity to take on the higher obligation of climate change". In the third paragraph, some good points are made. The point regarding the war in Iraq and Syria makes little sense and significantly reduces the quality of the essay. It is very important to make sure that the points you make follow from each other.

Conclusion: The student does address the question in the conclusion and is very succinct. It is not clear how NATO specifically fits into the essay at all and it would have been better to leave that out.

Example Essay 8

"Developed countries have a higher obligation to tackle climate change than developing countries"
Discuss the extent to which you agree with this statement

Developed countries are the nations with mature economies and modernised environments in their states by the development starting from the 18th century, while developing countries refer to the nations which are investing most of their money into the development for economic growth and are trying to catch up to the developed ones. The recent climate changes are mainly incurred by the industrial and business processes of the economic activities in the world. These led to the emission of greenhouse gases and finally global warming. The obligation that countries should bear for this case is to eliminate the pollution of the world and allow the climate to restore. I will now look into the topic economically, historically and environmentally.

To start with, developed countries should take more responsibilities of damaging the climate because they are the starters of it. Looking back to the history, western countries, especially the UK, experienced Industrial Revolution in the 18th Century. Mass production existed by utilising machines and mining for fuels was one of the main businesses at that time. These activities led to the beginning of pollutants and greenhouse gases. This affected their air quality, such as the dark fog in the UK in the past. The businessmen were so greedy that they wanted to exploit other nations' resources for making profits and invested money for further development of new technologies to enlarge the size of production. These behaviours caused even more pollution to be emitted and started changing the climate and damaging nature. Therefore, they should be the first to respond to global warming.

Furthermore, most of the developed countries caused the huge financial and economic gap between them and the developing ones. This forced the developing nations to further increase their economic activities by ignoring the environmental and climatic impacts. It is no longer news when we hear that a developing state has taken on huge debt from a developing one. With the 'good will' of lending other countries in need money to strengthen their economic power by investment in infrastructure and the like, the developed countries always adopt a high interest rate and the debt seems impossible to return. This makes the poorer ones worse because they risk everything, including neglecting the severe consequence of climate change, to produce their economic goods in the cheapest way, which means without any costs on filtering such pollutants. This is actually not directly caused by the privileged countries.

However, it is argued that the rich nations put efforts to start cutting down the emission such as implementing EU emission quotas and keep investigating in new methods to make the production cycle cleaner. Yet, EU emission quotas are actually a failure that many nations persuaded the EU committees for more quotas and this led to the failure of the plan. In addition, those products from investigations are usually expensive and not many products from companies in developed nation will apply it. It ends up failing because of a lack of effectiveness.

To conclude, it is inevitable that developed countries are recognised as the main cause of today's climatic problems. Thus they have to bear the responsibilities more instead of the developing nations.

Examiner's Comments:

Introduction: The introduction is too long and would thus have taken up valuable time in the exam. Nonetheless, it captures the main themes of the question and sets the scene well for the essay.

Main Body: The second paragraph makes a very good point but waffles a bit much and goes off the point when talking about businessmen being greedy and about the dark fog in the UK – these two points are not relevant to the candidate's line of argument. Accordingly, does not gain marks and weakens the essay.
It would have saved a lot of time if the candidate simply stated the following:
- Developed countries have already emitted enormous amounts such as in the industrial revolution,
- So it would only be fair to expect them to do more to clean up the mess which they caused.

In the third paragraph, the student needs to be clearer as to what she means. The implication is that developing countries are hard done by the developed ones, but the student needs to state this clearly. The student also uses a weak link here. The final sentence of the third paragraph didn't make sense and contradicts the rest of the paragraph. The fourth paragraph does not add anything new to the argument. The candidate describes the failure of the EU quotas but it's not clear how this relates to the question. Surely it doesn't matter (for the purposes of this essay) whether the EU have failed with their emission quotas or not. The essay question is asking whether developed countries have a higher obligation to tackle climate change than developing countries. As the paragraph does not advance an argument as to whether developed countries should or should not take on a higher obligation than developing countries, it wastes time and reduces the quality of one's essay

Conclusion: The conclusion is succinct and follows from the main body.

Example Essay 9

"Developed countries have a higher obligation to tackle climate change than developing countries"
Discuss the extent to which you agree with this statement

Climate change is a global issue that affects all nations and its peoples, and in light of the newly released global sustainability goals, perhaps we should focus on what actions should be taken to effect a change rather arguing who should take responsibility. Hence, I disagree with this statement and will be presenting my argument in this essay.

Firstly, climate change is a global issue and all nations are obligated to combat it. We must abandon the attitude that developing nations are somehow inferior to developed nations simply because of their global position. With this approach in mind, all nations therefore must be taken as accountable for this global crisis that affects us all. Perhaps the view that combatting climate change is an 'obligation' should be abandoned. Improving the condition of our world and fixing our mistakes should be regarded not as a chore, but as a responsibility to future generations. After we have confronted these issues and changed our perceptions, will a global effort truly be effectively carried forward?

Secondly, whilst it is true that developed nations have a greater capacity financially and structurally to enact a change, efforts to improve the infrastructure of a country to make it more green can be done by developing countries. Rather than seeing sustainability as an expensive undertaking, requiring new carbon capturing machines, knowledge of other ways to lessen our carbon footprint should be made clear. These simple methods such as planting more trees than the number being cut down or effective garbage disposable and recycling to minimise burning of garbage. Such inexpensive methods could easily be undertaken by developing countries and eliminating the idea that climate change is a concern of the rich.

Thirdly, to separate countries into two spheres is damaging. This segregation lead to the belief that 'developing nations' are somehow able to 'get away' with releasing high amount of greenhouse gases or deforestation by simply claiming that they don't have the capacity to make such a change. It is not enough for the developed countries to take the initiative; developing nations are equally obligated to combat climate change.

In conclusion, no country should be viewed as having a higher obligation towards alleviating climate change.

Examiner's Comments:

Introduction: The introduction is excellent. The candidate states her main view concisely and proceeds to continue with the main body. The candidate also adopts a unique take on the question, which is even better and will signal green lights in the heads of admissions tutors.

Main Body: The second paragraph raises interesting points but it is not clear how it relates to the question. A running theme throughout the essay is that every country shares a responsibility to be sustainable and reduce climate change. However, counter-arguments are not readily considered, accordingly the essay is not as persuasive as it might be.

In the third paragraph, the student makes the (very good) point about developing countries still being able to plant trees. This could be framed in a different way and incorporate a counter argument. For example:

➢ Climate change affects every country and, thus, every country should have an obligation to tackle climate change
➢ [**Counter Argument**] Some argue though that richer countries have far more resources than developing countries and, thus, can spend money and develop non-renewable energy sources (e.g. solar panels), whereas poorer countries would not have the finances to do this.
➢ [**Rebuttal of the counter argument**] Nonetheless, poorer countries can still do their part by planting trees and should not feel that they're 'off the hook'. Climate change affects everyone and, therefore, every country should do what they can to tackle it.
➢ [An example of a policy might be that each country pays a certain percentage of GDP to tackle climate change – this way, it's proportionate to each country]

Conclusion: The candidate succinctly presents her final response to the question in the conclusion. This could have been elaborated on a little more but is still fine nonetheless.

Example Essay 10

"Abortion should only be permitted in certain circumstances" Discuss.

Abortion means the mother decides to take off her foetus from her body in the form of taking away the possibility that the foetus can grow and finally become a baby which is ready to be born. With the permission of doing so, it means that the mother is taking off her foetus legally and she should bear no response afterwards. In my opinion, several circumstances should be raised and some of them should be given the chance to the mother to take her foetus off while some should not be allowed.

First of all, the victims of sexual assault or sexual abuse should have the right to abort. This mainly concerns their willingness of having the sexual activity and being pregnant. The victims are not willing to be raped by someone she did not fall in love with or someone other than her partner. Therefore, it is even more unlikely that she would further agree to be pregnant. The abuser, firstly, has this conviction of sexually assaulting someone who disagrees with his actions. Because it is a criminal action, the victim should not bear the consequences that the baby will bring such as nurturing the baby with her economic ability, which has a chance that it is insufficient to do so. Therefore, abortion should be permitted here.

Other than the above reason, a mother who has a baby which is inherently with problems should be allowed to abandon the foetus. Having children with inherent deficiency such as Down syndrome is not a choice of the parents: no one is a wrongdoer in this situation. While the parents have to bear the heavy burden to spend a lot of money on the medical caring of the baby, they may need to take care of them for their whole life. For these accidents, the authority should give them a chance to choose whether to keep their children or not. Abortion should be permitted in this circumstance. Almost all countries in the world give this choice to the parents with this problem.

However, babies which accidentally created during the illegal acts should not be permitted to abort, unless there is a medical issue raised. Increasing numbers of teenagers start to have sex at an early age such as 12. When they attempt to do these activities, they do not consider any possibilities may occur in the future and most of them do not care about the consequences. Not allowing them to have an abortion can prevent the teenagers from acting unconsciously, such as by having sex early or having sex without proper protection, even though special cases such as too young to give birth to a baby should be also under the consideration.

Furthermore, parents who want to abandon their children randomly should not be allowed. A wrong message may be given to the society that having foetus is not a real matter and we can abandon it anyway. It may also raise the moral issues such as selecting a perfect foetus in the laboratory to give birth. A random abortion also easily damages women's bodies which may affect their ability to have a baby in the future. This may lead to a decline in the birth rates. It can hamper our imbalance social structure seriously that our future generation has to bear all the welfare we need. Therefore, no permission on random abortions should be given.

To conclude, circumstances whereby the parents or the mother do not have the responsibility of having a baby inappropriately should be permitted to have abortion, whilst the others should not do so.

Examiner's Comments:

Introduction: The introduction attempts a definition of abortion, which is good. The final sentence of the introduction could have been more concise though, for example: "this essay argues that the mother should be allowed to abort in certain circumstances" – this says exactly the same thing but uses fewer words and looks better.

Main Body: The second paragraph makes a valid point but too long is spent on it. It was also quite basic and one-sided. If the student made reference to the countervailing principle based on the rights of the foetus, it would have been a more convincing paragraph (e.g. explicitly suggest that the right of the mother here should outweigh that of the foetus).

At each paragraph, the student relates it back to the question by considering whether abortion should be permitted in that circumstance. However, the essay is mainly one-sided and does not consider the possible right to life of the foetus. The student also does not consider why abortion should not be allowed in all other circumstances in enough detail.

In the penultimate paragraph, assertions, such as abortions easily damaging women's bodies are made, but this is not true if carried out by medical professionals. It is important not to make up facts and only use genuine knowledge.

Conclusion: The conclusion is not specific enough but the candidate does come to a reasoned judgement. Nonetheless, since the main body was generally one-sided, the conclusion does not feel like it is sufficiently balanced.

Example Essay 11

"Abortion should only be permitted in certain circumstances" Discuss.

Abortion is an act of ending the life of an embryo before birth. In my opinion I think abortion should be allowed when parents have a disability to take care of the child or the child itself is predicted to have a disability after he or she is born.

Firstly, if the child is detected to have a disability such as a cancer or similar life threatening disease, parents should have the choice to choose if they want the baby or not as the child may not be able to survive long. It might also bring the child discrimination which is bad for life development. However, it could be argued that every child is a gift from god and abortion is morally wrong. It's against the human right of the child itself. Moreover, through the difficulties in the process of early stage of the child, such as heavy medical treatment and discrimination from the public might train the child to be a stronger and more determined individual. Instead of a disadvantage, it might be a special advantage and experience to the child.

On the other hand, it might be argued that the inability of the parents to educate the child might be a legitimate reason for abortion. If the mother is too young to educate the child and needs huge financial support, she may be unable to care for the child. It might also be case if the parents are in prison.
In my opinion, parents should take up the responsibility of having a baby. If the mother is too young and still needs to continue her studies, the baby could be put into a foster home, who can be taken care of by a specialist. The government can consider giving out loans to these young mothers until they finish their education and have the ability to earn money themselves. If the parents are in prison, they can also send their children to a foster home and ask for permission to see their child frequently to keep the bond within the family.

In conclusion, the only permission for abortion should be when the child has a permanent disability and the parents can get to choose whether or not to give birth to the baby.

It might be inhuman to kill the embryo, but it is also not virtuous for the parents to see the child suffering. However, if the problem comes from the parent itself, the child as individuals should have the right to live, regardless of the fact that care homes might have less support to theme than normal homes, it's still a chance for them to explore the beauty of life.

Examiner's Comments:

Introduction: A clear and crisp definition in the first sentence and a nice introduction. It appears that the student is only considering a few circumstances from the introduction.

Main Body: The second paragraph involves assumptions. What if the child can live long enough, though?

The essay launches straight into specific and niche circumstances and considers remote points, such as the life development of the child. Given the time available, it would be better to stick to the main points.

The essay does not consider in much detail the alternatives and why abortion shouldn't be allowed generally apart from a brief sentence in the second paragraph. Considering the alternatives is important as that leads to a more balanced and persuasive essay and, thus, higher marks!

Conclusion: The initial conclusion is very good and succinct. However, the student also makes an additional point after the conclusion. Sometimes, this works but here it does not fit in. It's normally best to introduce completely new arguments in the main body.

Example Essay 12

"Abortion should only be permitted in certain circumstances" Discuss.

Abortion occurs when a pregnant woman decides to no longer carry her child and in turn kills the foetus. By law, pregnancy must be under a certain age limit. There are three main circumstances I believe abortion should be permitted: where the parent(s) cannot financially support their child, where the parent(s) would raise the child in an unsafe environment and finally, under the circumstance that the health of the mother is at risk. However, the law preventing abortion after a specific number of weeks should still be implemented at each instance.

Firstly, if there is evidence that parent(s) of the child are not financially capable of supporting their child in the future, then an abortion should be permitted. This is because a lack of food, shelter or clothing – seen as basic necessities – should be provided in order to ensure the child remains health. Although it can be argued that the child could be sent to adoption where these necessities can be provided, psychological impact on the family can be forgotten. The emotional connection of a mother to her unborn foetus must be less than her to her newborn, hence for the health of the mother, abortion should be permitted. It is not to be assumed however that there will not be mental consequences of abortion.

Secondly, the environment which a child is raised in has been scientifically linked to the future behaviour of said child. An abusive environment is undoubtedly unsafe for any child, both for their physical and mental wellbeing. This sort of environment can involve similar behaviour in the child which wants to be just like their parents may eventually lead to a life of crime. However, this cannot be said for all children of course. Where abortion is not an option raised by the parents themselves, should it be enforced by a governing authority? It must be vital for examination of home environments to be conducted on an equal level to ensure justice.

Finally, the health of a mother is important. The life of an unborn foetus should not be considered over the life of the woman. It is said that the right to life is of the utmost importance, hence this should be followed. When considering the health of the women, the physical and mental health must be considered equally. This is to ensure the safety of the unborn child as well as the mother.

I believe these are the circumstances that should be permitted. In turn this could reduce the crime rate, protests by those against abortion and can encourage safe sex, especially by teenagers. Although these circumstances may function in countries such as the UK, China, for instance, would permit abortion outside these guidelines due to the implementation of the 'One Child Policy'. However, I believe such policies reduce the freedoms of citizens which should be considered.

Examiner's Comments:

Introduction: The candidate points out that abortion should be allowed in three specific circumstances but does not consider why abortion shouldn't be allowed in any other circumstances (or be allowed generally). Other than this, the introduction is good, very clear, and sets the scene well for the essay.

Main Body: The third paragraph is unclear and does not consider the issue from enough perspectives to be balanced – what about the right of the child to live? Does the foetus not have that right? Or if it does, does the potential for the child to enter into crime outweigh that right? Consideration of such issues will add a greater depth to the essay and make one's argument more persuasive. It is crucial to consider alternative points of view to have a balanced essay. The candidate then digresses and considers whether abortion should be enforced on people and doesn't actually consider that issue properly – she implies that it's important (by saying that there should be 'home examination' but it's not clear what she is saying). The fourth paragraph could be improved by considering what rights, if any, should be given to the foetus and then whether the mother's right to life outweighs this. As it stands, the paragraph is a bit one-sided.

Conclusion: The conclusion is satisfactory but not great. It introduces a few new assertions (such as reducing protests and encouraging safe sex) which do not follow from the rest of the essay. It also introduces a completely new point regarding the One Child Policy in China: while this is an interesting point, the candidate has not demonstrated how it is/could be relevant to the question and so this point is a waste of space. The conclusion should be used to weigh up the pros/cons of the arguments you've already addressed in the main body and to bring everything together (and generally not to introduce new ones).

HSPSAA: SECTION B — ESSAYS

Example Essay 13

"The government should legalise the sale of human organs" Discuss.

With the lack of available organs for transplant in hospitals, many patients lost the change of survival for a longer period of time. To a large extent, government should legalise the sale of human organs, in order to boost the amount of organs available for replacement and might help the poor to gain some extra money as well.

Firstly, the sale of human organs involves buying and selling. One can gain money in exchange for given out extra/not necessary organs in their bodies (such as kidneys). This is also a more efficient use of resources while saving lives at the same time. However, it could be argued that the action creates bad incentives especially for the poor to sell as much organs as possible, without looking after their own health. This may cause serious damage to their health and even causing more deaths. On the other hand, monitory controls can be done before organs are sold. Compulsory health checks on the seller should be enforced to see whether he/she is capable of giving away the organs and also whether the organ is suitable for transplant at the same time.

Secondly, the selling of organs of organs generates tax revenue for the Government. This extra amount of revenue could be used on investment in healthcare to cure disease, which could in turn reduce the demand on organ transplants. It could also be used to hire more doctors to meet the increasing demand in the NHS. However, selling organs are morally wrong and our bodies are gifts from God and shouldn't be re-used for commercial transactions. Also, sellers might set high prices and widen the gap between rich and poor, as only rich people can afford the organs, thereby deepening inequality in society. Nonetheless, organs are property of individuals and we should full control on how we use them. We're allowed to engage in other potentially harmful activities, such as smoking and drinking. Furthermore, the government can set up a maximum price for organs to avoid the situation of overpriced organs. Accordingly, strong monitoring should be used in order to ensure everyone has an equal chance of getting suitable organs and organs should be arranged for those who are most in need of them.

In conclusion, the government should legalise the sale of human organs in order to increase the amount of organs available for transplant to save more lives, as people would have more incentive to give off their organs. This can also generate more revenue for the government under tax, which could be used in the NHS to help more people in need. Monitoring is also essential, such as setting up maximum prices and ensuring everyone has the equal chance of getting the organ they need.

Examiner's Comments:

Introduction: This is concise and the student directly addresses the question, which is good.

Main Body: The quality of written communication is not particularly good but otherwise, a number of interesting arguments are made and evaluated.

The point regarding tax was a bit remote (and, thus, did not seem entirely relevant in the context of the debate on human organs). It's not clear that would be taxed in the same way as goods (and would probably be too insignificant to make much of a difference to the government's tax revenues).

That time could have instead been used to delve deeper into evaluating the main pros and cons of legalising human organ sales. For example, the candidate raised the point that *"our bodies are gifts from God and shouldn't be re-used for commercial transactions."* This is a good point, but it could have been elaborated on further and critiqued on the basis that not all individuals follow a religion. This would have reinforced the candidate's conclusion and showed a greater depth of analysis.

Nonetheless, a variety of interesting and directly relevant arguments and counter-arguments are made, which makes this a very decent essay on the whole.

Conclusion: This is a good conclusion which directly addresses the question and the candidate elaborates on her view. However, the point about tax seems out of place as it is a new piece of information. The monitoring point would have fit well in the conclusion with a linking word, such as 'Nonetheless'. For example:
- ➤ *In conclusion, the government should legalise the sale of human organs in order to increase the amount of organs available for transplant to save more lives, as people would have more incentive to give off their organs.*
- ➤ *Nonetheless, this must be accompanied with an effective monitoring system, including the use of maximum prices, to ensure fairness.*

Example Essay 14

"The government should legalise the sale of human organs" Discuss.

The question as to whether the sale of human organs should be legalised in countries has always been a hot debate throughout the centuries. As far as I am concerned, this is illegal in most of the major countries and in this essay I am going to outline the reasons.

First and foremost, moral issues are raised in the sale of human organs because many regard it as inhumane and it is not morally acceptable. As I don't see it as a proper way to earn money in a civilised country, where people earn money by selling their organs. I believe life is sacred and should be treated with great care. The sale of human organs implies that money is more important than the protection of lives.

Personally, I am in favour of organ donations which is completely different from selling organs as this does not involve the transfer of money and the meaning behind it is people really want to help others out of compassion but not for the benefits they can receive afterwards.

In addition, legalising the sale of human organs can exploit the poor, particularly in developing countries because they are vulnerable groups which can be exploited by the rich. In developing countries, the majority are not fully educated and they are poor. There is a potential that the rich in educated countries will exploit their advantages to purchase organs from them. This is unjust and unequal. Allowed to continue, this can lead to dire consequences in the long run which cannot be easily stopped.

In my opinion, the government role is to protect the welfare of citizens, so especially in developing countries, the government should not legalise the sale of human organs.

Examiner's Comments:

Introduction: The introduction appears to miss the point slightly. The quote wants the candidate to consider whether the sale of human organs *should* or *should not* be legalised. The candidate, though, says that he is going to outline the 'reasons' why it is illegal in most countries, when actually, the question wants the candidate's view as to whether it should be legal or not (and not an explanation for the present state of affairs).

Main Body: This essay is very basic, considers arguments in little depth, and is only one-sided with no consideration of counter-arguments. The candidate highlights some serious issues about allowing organ sales but does not adequately consider the issues at stake – e.g. what can be done about the current organ shortage? Highlighting this point and then evaluating it, by arguing that you don't (for example) think legalising organ sales would solve it, would make for a more persuasive essay as it shows the reader that you have considered alternative perspectives. Merely stating a bunch of opinions such as "I believe…." and "I think...." is not helpful and does not advance an argument <u>unless</u> they're backed up with reasons.

Conclusion: The conclusion, though, is satisfactory and very succinct but since it does not follow from a balanced or well-argued main body, the essay as a whole is poor.

Example Essay 15

"Sufferers of anorexia nervosa should be force-fed" Do you agree with this statement? If so, evaluate at what point of an individuals' disease this measure should be taken.

Anorexia nervosa is a term used to describe individuals who are unhealthily skinny. Some may say that anorexia is a major issue which needs to be addressed and force feeding seems to be a solution to prevent anorexia. In this essay I will be looking at the points for and against force feeding people suffering with anorexia, and I will come up with a constructive conclusion giving my personal opinion on this controversial topic.

Particular diseases often have a domino effect which results in other diseases, meaning that sufferers from anorexia may have the risk of developing other diseases as well. If an individual's anorexia reaches a limit where their daily lives are impacted, then indeed, sufferers of anorexia should be force-fed

Similarly, sufferers from anorexia may be suffering from social anxiety and insecurity due to their body structure, so in order to help improve their quality of life, sufferers should be force-fed in order to prevent sufferers' life from deteriorating.

On the other hand, one would say that force feeding sufferers of anorexia would be unideal since you would be forcing someone to do something against their own will, even if it was benefiting the sufferers. Instead, other alternatives should be explored, such as psychiatric and medical help, or other programmes which could help track the progress of the sufferer's health, rather than force feeding them. This is why some people believe that force feeding sufferers of anorexia would be unideal.

In addition, it would be difficult to distinguish the severity of anorexia and hence force feeding would be unideal because some sufferers of anorexia would be force-fed, when they really didn't need to be. Finding the cut-off point to where sufferers would need to be force-fed would be unrealistic and so other alternatives such as medical help should be explored. This is why sufferers of anorexia should not be force-fed.

In conclusion, force feeding sufferers of anorexia would be a way to tackle this disease, however I personally believe that there are other better alternatives to tackle this disease such as receiving medical treatment or seeking long term help with a professional, which would benefit sufferers in the long run.

Examiner's Comments:

Introduction: The introduction starts straight off with an attempted definition of anorexia nervosa. It's not entirely correct but given that the HSPSAA exam is not a test of knowledge, it is a good enough approximation. It's really not necessary for the student to say: "I will be looking at the points for and against force feeding" or that "I will come up with a constructive conclusion giving my personal opinion" – these are both obvious and add zero marks, so the time could be better spent writing something more constructive to the essay.

Main Body: The second and third paragraphs (the beginning of the main body) are certainly valid points and they do indicate force feeding as a treatment, but the student uses the word 'should' as if it was a final conclusion in both of these paragraphs. This contradicts the student's actual conclusion at the end of the essay, which is a poor essay technique. Instead, as interim conclusions, the student should be more tentative within the main body and just say 'therefore, force feeding <u>may</u> be an option to resolve this' or 'some may, thus, argue that sufferers should be force-fed'. The fourth paragraph is very good.

A further point that links with the point on consent is that, since force feeding is against a person's free will, it would not solve the underlying problem of anorexia nervosa and a person may need to be continuously force-fed against their will, which surely does not respect their personal autonomy and capacity to think as a human being. Accordingly, alternatives such as psychiatric help to solve the underlying problem would both be more effective and accord with the patient's free will.

Conclusion: The conclusion is sufficient: it is comprehensive, clear and concise. On the whole, this is a very good essay.

Final Essay Advice

- Use linking words.
- Do NOT use long introductions – they just waste time.
- Answer the Question – a surprisingly common issue is where students don't answer the question. This is by either misinterpreting the question, answering a different question, or only answering part of it. It is absolutely <u>critical</u> to answer the question and it is not something you can just assume you are doing. At the end of each paragraph, it would be useful to ask yourself whether you're answering the question. A good plan would help with this. If you are not answering the question, you are not gaining marks on what you're writing and it will not be impressive to the admissions tutors reading your work.
- Give a judgement – if the question asks "Do you agree?" make sure that you say whether you agree or disagree with the quote. Feel free to take a midpoint and say that you agree with it in x, y, z circumstances but disagree with it in other circumstances.
- Do not give a rant of opinions – it is important to advance an argument throughout your response.
- Do not add completely new arguments in the conclusion – it is ideal to weigh up the pros and cons that you've raised in the conclusion.
- Consider counter-arguments – even when you're heavily committed to one side of the debate or argument, considering alternative arguments (and then rebutting the counter arguments) makes your essay more persuasive.
- Signposting language – using signposting language helps make your essay clearer and more readable for the admissions tutors. For example, using connectives such as 'however' or 'nonetheless' can be used to highlight contrasting points. Words such as 'therefore' help to indicate either an interim conclusion in the middle of the essay or the final conclusion at the end.

Example Essay Questions

- "There is a time and place for censorship of the internet" Discuss with particular reference to the right of freedom of expression.
- "Developed countries have a higher obligation to tackle climate change than developing countries" Discuss the extent to which you agree with this statement.
- "The EU is the only barrier to World War 3". Discuss
- "The government should legalise the sale of human organs" Discuss.
- "Sufferers of anorexia nervosa should be force-fed" Do you agree with this statement? If so, evaluate at what point of an individuals' disease this measure should be taken.

ANSWERS

THE ULTIMATE HSPSAA GUIDE — ANSWERS

Answer Key

Q	A	Q	A	Q	A	Q	A	Q	A
1	B	51	B	101	D	151	C	201	C
2	B	52	A	102	B	152	E	202	B
3	E	53	B	103	E	153	D	203	D
4	C	54	D	104	C	154	C	204	C
5	A	55	D	105	A	155	A	205	D
6	D	56	A	106	B	156	A	206	A
7	A	57	D	107	C	157	B	207	A
8	D	58	A	108	B	158	B	208	E
9	C	59	B	109	C	159	C	209	D
10	E	60	C	110	A	160	D	210	B
11	B	61	D	111	E	161	A	211	A
12	E	62	D	112	D	162	A	212	C
13	C	63	D	113	C	163	E	213	D
14	A	64	E	114	C	164	B	214	C
15	C	65	D	115	E	165	A	215	D
16	A	66	C	116	A	166	D	216	B
17	C	67	C	117	D	167	A	217	A
18	C	68	E	118	E	168	A	218	B
19	E	69	A	119	C	169	C	219	D
20	C	70	D	120	B	170	A	220	A
21	D	71	C	121	A	171	C	221	C
22	C	72	D	122	B	172	D	222	D
23	D	73	C	123	D	173	A	223	B
24	D	74	B	124	C	174	A	224	A
25	B	75	E	125	E	175	A	225	A
26	B	76	A	126	D	176	B	226	D
27	B	77	D	127	B	177	C	227	B
28	E	78	E	128	E	178	B	228	C
29	C	79	C	129	C	179	E	229	B
30	C	80	D	130	A	180	C	230	B
31	C	81	E	131	E	181	D	231	A
32	B	82	A	132	C	182	B	232	D
33	E	83	E	133	A	183	D	233	C
34	D	84	D	134	C	184	A	234	A
35	D	85	D	135	C	185	C	235	D
36	B	86	C	136	C	186	C	236	A
37	A	87	D	137	A	187	D	237	B
38	E	88	A	138	A	188	D	238	B
39	A	89	E	139	B	189	D	239	B
40	E	90	D	140	A	190	D	240	C
41	A	91	C	141	E	191	C	241	A
42	C	92	B	142	D	192	D	242	B
43	B	93	B	143	E	193	A	243	C
44	B	94	B	144	D	194	A	244	A
45	A	95	E	145	B	195	D	245	B
46	B	96	D	146	C	196	E	246	C
47	A	97	D	147	E	197	D	247	D
48	C	98	A	148	D	198	E	248	A
49	E	99	C	149	B	199	E	249	A
50	C	100	B	150	C	200	D	250	C

ULTIMATE HSPSAA GUIDE — ANSWERS

Q	A	Q	A	Q	A	Q	A
251	A	301	E	351	B	401	B
252	B	302	D	352	E	402	C
253	D	303	E	353	D	403	A
254	A	304	C	354	A	404	B
255	C	305	A	355	B	405	B
256	B	306	D	356	A	406	A
257	A	307	C	357	A	407	E
258	D	308	A	358	C	408	D
259	C	309	A	359	A	409	B
260	C	310	A	360	A		
261	D	311	C	361	C		
262	D	312	B	362	A		
263	A	313	A	363	A		
264	B	314	C	364	B		
265	B	315	C	365	C		
266	B	316	A	366	A		
267	A	317	D	367	B		
268	C	318	B	368	B		
269	B	319	E	369	D		
270	A	320	E	370	D		
271	C	321	B	371	B		
272	D	322	D	372	B		
273	B	323	A	373	D		
274	A	324	A	374	C		
275	C	325	A	375	D		
276	B	326	C	376	C		
277	A	327	A	377	B		
278	B	328	E	378	A		
279	D	329	A	379	E		
280	C	330	B	380	B		
281	B	331	B	381	D		
282	A	332	A	382	B		
283	D	333	C	383	A		
284	C	334	A	384	C		
285	B	335	D	385	E		
286	C	336	A	386	A		
287	A	337	C	387	E		
288	D	338	C	388	C		
289	D	339	A	389	A		
290	E	340	B	390	B		
291	B	341	D	391	A		
292	A	342	C	392	D		
293	B	343	B	393	A		
294	D	344	C	394	C		
295	A	345	D	395	D		
296	C	346	B	396	A		
297	A	347	B	397	B		
298	D	348	C	398	B		
299	C	349	A	399	B		
300	E	350	C	400	E		

THE ULTIMATE HSPSAA GUIDE ANSWERS

Worked Solutions

Passage 1

Question 1: B

The opponents said that drug consumption is criminogenic because a drug addiction 'can lead to other crimes'. Option A is incorrect as the passage already states that consuming drugs is in itself a criminal offence. Thus, it would be odd and circular if opponents were to argue this.

Question 2: B

It is close between A and B. In regard to A, the author merely points out a 'contrast', which may not necessarily indicate an inconsistency, whereas the author says, in the context of option B in the passage that there is 'incoherence', which clearly means there is an inconsistency. Therefore, the author *presented* B as being paradoxical.

Question 3: E

The entire article is based on the idea of controlled drugs being legalised. Each sub-argument provides an intermediate conclusion from which the main argument is inferred.

Question 4: C

The author does not argue that drug consumption would fall (as distinct from highlighting that it fell for one age group in Portugal) or increase, so A and B are incorrect. The author implied that drug consumption should be seen as a *present* public health problem in the passage – not that it would be a health concern once drugs were legalised so E is wrong. D is not a practical effect which the author believes would happen. C is explicitly stated in the passage.

Question 5: A

The author has based his argument on the fact that there aren't third party effects to taking drugs (e.g. no third party health effects & that the fact of criminalising increases secondary offences). However, if drug consumption increases one's propensity for violence, it contradicts that argument.

Passage 2

Question 6: D

The passage attacks a generalisation and shows an example that refutes one given to the 'musical' genre. Nothing is mentioned of Sondheim's talents, or what his role was in creating the musical, nor are there claims made in relation to Wheeler's literary tastes (he may just like ONE penny dreadful). This musical may deal with morbid themes, but that's not to say that most do - it could be only a select few that do.

Question 7: A

The pies make the crimes 'culinary' in nature, the mention of revenge shows Todd's illegal acts to be 'vengeful', the word 'macabre' indicates it's disturbing and the judge's rape is a 'sexual' crime. There is nothing explicitly suggesting the crimes of any party are funny, or to be considered funny.

Question 8: D

This option is essentially synonymous in the quoted belief, 'we all deserve to die', which includes both bad and good people and makes no significant reference to gender exclusion/inclusion.

Question 9: C

There are four mentioned themes, but that does not mean there are only four themes, nor does 'legal corruption' get named as the central theme. As the entirety of Sweeney Todd is not discussed in the passage, only a central plot line, one could not exclude the potential of something positive happening in the play - even a minor incident. Sadness in itself, therefore, cannot be considered the focus of the play. The themes mentioned are, however, indeed macabre.

THE ULTIMATE HSPSAA GUIDE — ANSWERS

Question 10: E
Though the original title 'A String of Pearls: A Romance' may appear to suggest a romantic relationship within the narrative, nothing in the passage states the two are a couple so A is incorrect. The passage only suggested that *some* of the songs were removed, not all of the songs, so B is incorrect. We can't be sure about D as the passage does not refer to the critical acclaim of the film. In regard to C, while some changes were made to the film, we aren't told whether the main storyline changes. Finally, E is explicitly stated in the passage, so that must be true.

Passage 3

Question 11: B
This is mentioned as an impact on the country in the passage and not mentioned as having a personal impact, whereas all others are mentioned as personal impacts. Also, as is evident from the term itself, an increase in government spending affects the government. The focus of the point was on the government's spending (rather than on any welfare benefits derived).

Question 12: E
This option is explicitly stated in the passage.

Question 13: C
This is implied as the author states the numerous benefits of high-quality education provision but also notes how 'more emphasis' should be placed on it. Crucially, it says that vocational education is 'second rate' and that it must change. A clear implication of these sentences is that more should be done to encourage vocational courses. E is already stated in the passage (as the author highlights the negative consequences). The author also explicitly states A, B, and D. Therefore, since they are all stated in the passage, they are incorrect.

Question 14: A
While the author does argue for B, it is only part of the main argument and is in the context of increasing high-quality vocational provision for young people. The skills shortage was used more as a reason to argue for A. Given the emphasis on raising vocational education, it is clear that A is the correct answer. The author does not argue for C and actually points out that the jobs are already there, it's just that young people need to be trained more. D was not argued for and E was an assertion (and, thus, not an argument, let alone a main argument).

Question 15: C
This is explicitly stated in the passage. A is not stated in the passage. While Dulux was increasing young people's skills, the author did not advocate this for businesses generally and, thus, B is incorrect. The author suggested that D and E should be done by the government, rather than by businesses.

Passage 4

Question 16: A
B, C, and D are all stated as influences in the passage but option A is stated as underlying all those reasons and thus, A is the 'ultimate' influence.

Question 17: C
The passage mentions that a son was required to secure the Tudor dynasty. Therefore, there is something familial relating to all of this. Therefore, B and E are incorrect. D doesn't follow from the sentence so it has to be either A or C. A doesn't make sense in this context as it's not clear how having a son would secure his family but C fits in well.

Question 18: C
Royal Supremacy was merely the process of getting control over the church and was not a reason for getting a son (it was the means to getting the son) so A is wrong. B is incorrect as it should be the other way round – he wanted to divorce Catherine to get a son (and not get a son to divorce Catherine). C fits in with the passage and, thus, is correct.

THE ULTIMATE HSPSAA GUIDE | ANSWERS

Question 19: E

A and D were stated in the passage, so are incorrect. Even if B and C were true, they would not weaken any of the conclusions, so they are not correct. However, E is correct as if he believed that he could get a divorce from Rome, he would have tried to get that as it was the 'straightforward' option. The author also stated that without Henry's desire for a break from Rome, it wouldn't have happened. Therefore, point E would be a necessary assumption to support the author's points.

Question 20: C

The passage never suggests that the Act of Supremacy is the royal supremacy, so E is incorrect. The passage states that the Royal Supremacy was established once Henry became the only head of the church, so C is, thus, correct as it means the King had become the leader of the church. D is, therefore, obviously incorrect as the Pope isn't the head of the English church. B is too vague and while option A had to occur for the Royal Supremacy to take place, the passage pointed out that C was, in fact, the royal supremacy.

Passage 5

Question 21: D

The passage explicitly states that charities may not need to pay corporation tax. A is not true based on the passage – as you can provide a public benefit but have not registered to be a charity. It is only after registration as a charity that an institution gets the fiscal benefits; this does not happen automatically. B and C are not proved in the passage, and E is an opinion, which can't be true or false. In regard to C specifically, it cannot be assumed that just because event X is required for event Y to occur that if Y does not occur, X does not occur – in the context of the passage, you can still provide a public benefit and not be a charity. Therefore, C is incorrect.

Question 22: C

The passage explicitly states that it's "necessary" for an institution to demonstrate that its purposes are for the public benefit.

Question 23: D

Both C and E are easily eliminated as neither of these institutions were part of the trial, which is where the argument was advanced. We're told that tribunal judges didn't consider the argument and it is, thus, clear by implication that they didn't bring it forward (therefore, B is incorrect), so we're left with either A or D. It's not A as the argument weakens their position (being independent schools) so it's unlikely they would advance it. By elimination, therefore, it must be the Education Review Group, D.

Question 24: D

Whether the law should or should not allow a free-for-all is not a point that can be tested – it is a person's opinion and cannot be true or false. All the other options can be tested.

Question 25: B

In the passage, it is stated that the tribunal said that children who couldn't afford the fees of private schools must benefit from them for there to be a 'public benefit'. Accordingly, providing scholarships to others who can't afford the fees would help with this. A is insufficient to meet the tribunal's definition. C, D, and E do not support the argument that there's a public benefit.

Passage 6

Question 26: B

Amazon is more powerful. The author said that one is more powerful than the other at the beginning of the passage and it later becomes clear that Amazon is more powerful as they were able to restrict the sales of Hatchette's books in negotiations, thus, indicating a stronger bargaining position.

Question 27: B
There is irony because Hatchette have done aggressive things, just like Amazon have and yet, they are now complaining about Amazon.

Question 28: E
This option draws all of the points expressed in the passage together. Even though Amazon engaged in aggressive tactics, others have done it too and Amazon have done beneficial things. It gets to the heart of the passage, which is considering the actions of Amazon.

Question 29: C
The word 'monstrous' implies not only that there is a big task, but that the task is too big as the word implies some dissatisfaction with all the work that authors have to do.

Question 30: C
If Hachette had offered the same services as Amazon had, it would directly contradict what the author has said – Amazon's services wouldn't be an 'innovation', Hachette (one of the 'big publishers') would not have been acting unfairly in the past and Hachette would have been acting to the benefit of small authors: this would all be contrary to the author's points in the final paragraph; therefore, point C most undermines the author's argument.

Question 31: C
The author has been positive about what Amazon has done throughout the article. Therefore, the author would most likely disagree with the suggestion that Amazon has abused their market position. The author has acknowledged A, B, and E in the article. The author isn't likely to agree with D because Hachette had engaged in a conspiracy.

Passage 7

Question 32: B
The answer here is between A and B, both undermine the author's argument that the court system limits access to justice. B *most* undermines the author's argument because if these cases are normally settled out of court, the court system's high cost does not limit access to justice as people would already be getting justice, albeit outside the court system. Option A doesn't undermine it as much because it just says that there are different options for small claimants, whereas B directly cuts at the option. C, D, and E don't necessarily undermine the author's argument.

Question 33: E
This question necessitates being able to deduce the correct information from the passage and shows whether you've understood the passage. 1 hour of legal advice is £200 and the court fee for each is £35. Therefore, the cost for each side is £235. Therefore, the cost for both sides together is £470. As the passage stated that the losing side pays the winning side's costs (as well as their own), the losing side would have to pay a total of £470. N.B. there have been similar questions to this in recent HSPSAAs.

Question 34: D
This is a statement that cannot be tested as true or false and is a normative statement. Therefore, it is an opinion.

Question 35: D
A and B are true but they are explicitly stated in the passage, so are incorrect (the question explicitly asks for an option which is *not stated*). Neither C nor E can be implied. The passage states that the TV show 'resembles' a courtroom, thereby implying that it is not actually a real courtroom but some kind of mock courtroom that looks similar.

Question 36: B
Despite discussing the Judge Rinder show, the author never advances an argument that an online court should be modelled on it – just that the TV show shows that lawyers aren't needed.

Question 37: A

B doesn't even relate to whether the justice system is inefficient or not, so that's incorrect. Again, D and E don't relate to whether the *current* justice system is efficient. On the other hand, option A points out that the author has only referred to a subset of claims (i.e. small claims) and not considered the justice system generally. In particular, no reference was made to the criminal justice system. It doesn't follow that just because one part of it is inefficient, that the rest of it is inefficient. Therefore, A is correct as it highlights why that argument was weak.

Passage 8

Question 38: E

The author made the analogy in order to demonstrate that even though the driverless car may seem strange, people will still adapt to it. Therefore, E is correct. A is wrong as the author only says that at the first part of the analogy. C doesn't necessarily follow. While D is, in essence, what the author is saying, he's applied it to driverless cars. Therefore, his *main* point is that the public will adapt to the driverless car. Since the author was not arguing that the public *should* take up the driverless car with the analogy, B is incorrect.

Question 39: A

The assumption made is that people adapt to new things.

Question 40: E

The Top Gear test doesn't suggest any of A, B, C or D in respect of the use of autonomous cars *on roads*. A, B, C are obviously not demonstrated by the passage. D is not relevant to the question and would be a generalisation as well.

Question 41: A

Throughout, the author describes different aspects of the take-up of driverless cars by car companies and governments and only considers the benefits of it to drivers in the final paragraph. The author does not point out arguments for and against, so E is incorrect. Indeed, the author's view is that the public will want to drive such a car, but this does not underlie the entire piece, so C is incorrect. The same is true with option B. Again, while D is true, it is not the underlying theme of the article.

Question 42: C

E is incorrect as it doesn't relate to the author's main argument in the final paragraph – indeed, the author even acknowledged point E in respect of luxury cars. In regard to B and D, which relate to how cars are currently (B) or the current views on it (D), the author argues that there will be an uptake of it *in the future*. B and D just relate to the present and, thus, don't undermine the author's argument. If C were true, though, this would undermine the author's argument as the public may not take it up in that case. A doesn't necessarily show that people won't take up driverless cars. Therefore, A is incorrect.

Passage 9

Question 43: B

The Society suggest that one's autonomy involves a condition to act ethically and, therefore, if one restricts euthanasia/assisted suicide (an intentional killing), it wouldn't infringe autonomy. Hence, it is assumed that euthanasia/assisted suicide is unethical so that one is not infringing another's autonomy by restricting the unethical act. Looking at it from the reverse view – if we said that an intentional killing is ethical, the conclusion above wouldn't necessarily follow from the premises.

C and E are not necessarily assumed in the argument – i.e. the argument would hold even if they are untrue. Again, in contrast to A and D, the Society actually states that acting ethically is a part of being autonomous. Therefore, it does not infringe autonomy to stop an unethical act. Hence, A and D are incorrect.

Question 44: B
A clear difference, as stated in the first paragraph, between assisted suicide/euthanasia and suicide is that the former options involve a third party, whereas the latter only involves one person. The Society just argued that euthanasia/assisted suicide should be restricted and not necessarily suicide in itself. While D is true, it does not explain the gap in the logic (which is what the question is asking for). C and E are irrelevant as the author suggested the Society argued that suicide *should* be illegal, which is suggesting an opinion, so it's not relevant that it's in fact currently legal.

Question 45: A
It's implicit that assisted suicide and euthanasia should not be allowed – the society already assumed that it's unethical and said not allowing it wouldn't restrict one's autonomy. B is an assumed assertion, but not an implied *argument*. C and D are incorrect as the Society isn't considering what the current state of the law is. E is incorrect as it did not follow that the Society made this and the author explicitly suggested this.

Question 46: B
This is a question asking for a factual response. The author has pointed out that the court has given more weight to non-maleficence and, thus, that clearly has priority. Although the arguments initially suggest the author may be in favour of autonomy, the question is not asking what the author's opinions are, but which principle, in fact, has priority. C and D are wrong as they're not principles in this context and E is wrong as it has already been shown that non-maleficence has priority.

Question 47: A
In the final paragraph, the case of Miss B was explained on the basis that the doctors were not actually harming the patient, which satisfies the definition of non-maleficence given in the passage. The author also states that non-maleficence was given a significant weighting in the case. B, C, D, and E may well have been relevant to the court's decision but the author only referred to A when discussing the case of Miss B.

Passage 10

Question 48: C
The author never suggested that the IMF should be replaced throughout the passage.

Question 49: E
Benefits of giving the loan to Ireland was explicitly stated.

Question 50: C
Some of the other options were indeed factors in the Greek debt crisis but those other factors were, according to the author, caused by the government spending more money than what it had.

Question 51: B
The author would not agree with the view that the IMF have *only* been beneficial in the world because of the issues the author has stated that they've caused. D and E follow directly from the passage, so the author would agree with those. Given the issues of the IMF in the past, the author would likely agree with A. Even though the author didn't explicitly suggest C in the passage, he is less likely to agree with B compared to C because there have been issues with the IMF, so it is more plausible to agree with C, when compared to B (in particular because B directly contradicts the passage, whereas C does not).

Question 52: A
Incompetence suggests that something was not done *as it should have been done* – accordingly, option A fits in well with the passage and more so than options B and C. Although point E was stated in the passage, it was mentioned in a different context. D is explicitly pointed out, so is incorrect.

Passage 11

Question 53: B
This was not explicitly stated but is quite clearly true as the passage states that since 1953, a UK citizen could take the UK government to the European Court.

Question 54: D
In the third paragraph, the author explicitly stated that UK citizens could sue from 2000 onwards, when the Human Rights Act came into force. While the ECHR was in force since 1950, the author never said that UK citizens could sue in domestic courts then. It was only after the UK Human Rights Act was passed that, as the author said, they could sue in domestic courts.

Question 55: D
The author makes an argument in the final paragraph, citing examples of 'positive cases' and argues that they're some of the examples of the Convention giving rights to people. Therefore, a clear argument is that the Convention is benefiting UK citizens. The author doesn't argue for A and takes the opposite position to B and C. While E is true, it is merely an assertion as opposed to an argument.

Question 56: A
C and E are clearly incorrect as they aren't stated or implied at all in the passage. D was a reason for the European Court of Human Right's decision to block the deportation but the UK still wanted to deport Qatada – they just couldn't do so legally – it was the European Court that blocked the deportation and thus, A is the correct answer.

Question 57: D
The author makes the point that the benefits of the Convention outweigh the negatives as it is pointed out that there are more positive cases than negative cases. The author acknowledges that there are sometimes bad outcomes (so B is incorrect) but that the good ones outweigh this.

Question 58: A
In the final paragraph, the author was suggesting that being a signatory to the ECHR was beneficial to the UK (as there are many more 'good' cases). Accordingly, B doesn't follow. While the author may agree with D or E, they would be inconsistent as a *main* conclusion given that the author's primary contention was that there are many more positive aspects of the system than the negative and doesn't touch on altering it (so C is incorrect).

Passage 12

Question 59: B
C is incorrect as there's no mention or implication of an organisation (and it's not a literary technique), D is incorrect as no irony (when what *appears* to be the case is not *actually* the case) is present and the author does draw a similarity between anything so E isn't correct. The author does not suggest that the invisible hand was 'like' anything, so it can't be a simile (A is incorrect). It is in fact a metaphor, option B.

Question 60: C
A is wrong as while employees are stakeholders, it was stated in the passage (and the question related to an unstated implication). People generally are not stakeholders – the passage defined stakeholders as only those who are significantly affected by a business' decision. Again, this was not implicitly suggested in the passage, so B is incorrect. Neither D nor E is implied either. Shareholders are a stakeholder that is implicitly mentioned in the passage. In paragraph 5, the author discusses moving call centres abroad when considering the impact of business decisions on 'stakeholders'. The author says that the increase in profits benefits shareholders. As shareholders are significantly affected by this (in getting more profit), they are stakeholders. Further, immediately after the profit point, the author states: "However, it negatively harms other stakeholders"; using the word 'other' also implies that shareholders are stakeholders.

THE ULTIMATE HSPSAA GUIDE ANSWERS

Question 61: D
The author brings up the call centre example to show the effects of it but also to show that it is based on profit maximisation and what the impact of profit maximisation is (i.e. that it can lead to call centres going abroad but it might not, as in the case of BT). The author does not argue for either A, B or C and it is not clear that the author takes a position against moving call centres abroad. Therefore, E is incorrect.

Question 62: D
The author considers throughout that profit maximisation is a relevant objective but that other objectives should also be taken into account and explicitly states this. Accordingly, A and B are incorrect: the author never suggests those points. While C may be broadly true, the author points out that it isn't always beneficial. The author does not argue for or consider point E in much detail.

Question 63: D
As stated in the passage (2nd paragraph), if an individual tries to maximise profits, that will maximise the welfare of society because of the market (or the invisible hand of the market). Accordingly, Smith's view is that profit maximisation maximises the welfare of society. A is in the wrong order (profit maximisation occurs *before* the invisible hand), B and C are wrong because the invisible hand appears to discuss the automatic mechanism of the market and these options do not espouse Smith's ultimate view, which is point D. D more precisely equates with the view in the passage than E, so D is correct.

Passage 13

Question 64: E
A and C are clearly wrong as those groups are harmed. The passage doesn't mention B so that is incorrect. The choice is between D and E, both of whom receive benefits. However, according to the passage, law firms will lose out on fewer oil exploration projects, whereas the consumers have no immediate loss – just the benefit of lower prices. Therefore, E is the correct answer.

Question 65: D
A number of the options are potential reasons but the loss of £4.5 billion was cited as the *immediate* reason in the passage. Low revenues don't necessarily mean a loss is incurred and the passage cites losses as the reason for job cuts generally. Therefore, E is incorrect. Both A and B are factors but not the immediate factors and C just describes the way in which the workers were made unemployed.

Question 66: C
Obviously, to claim unemployment benefits, one cannot have a job. Therefore, it is assumed that those 7,000 individuals would not have a job if they're to seek unemployment benefits. Hence, C is correct. B is not a necessary assumption as the passage just says that the individuals would *seek* unemployment benefits – this does not require that the government actually do have benefits to give. This is a very fine distinction and you're doing very well if you have understood this. Hence, C is a necessary assumption but B is not necessary to support the statement. A, D and E are not relevant as they merely explain or describe the unemployment that has already occurred.

Question 67: C
The first paragraph explicitly attributes the reduction in oil price to the shale boom in the US, which increased supply and ultimately lowered oil prices. A and B are not cited as reasons. E is just a descriptor for the hard times that oil companies are experiencing and not a reason. The whole part of D was not suggested in the passage.

Question 68: E
The author simply points out that the oil companies will go bust if they continue to make losses, which is happening to *some* due to the oil price. Low oil prices are not a reason in and of itself to make redundancies – it is when a company is making a loss that it may need to sack workers.

Passage 14

Question 69: A
All other options are stated in the passage and this is explicitly not true based on the passage – as nuclear power is stated as a non-renewable energy source but the passage also states that it doesn't emit carbon. Therefore, A is correct as not *all* non-renewables emit carbon.

Question 70: D
The author explicitly argues for this at the end of paragraphs one and two. Option A is an assertion and not an argument. B, C and E are plainly not argued for in the passage. The author also appears to disagree with E.

Question 71: C
The author has already argued for a focus on renewable energies and has also expressed concern and doubt as to whether nuclear power is economical given the dangerous waste it produces. Therefore, C is the answer. E is incorrect as the author said that nuclear power is now mostly safe. A and B are not considered. While the author would agree with D, he would be more likely to accede to C as he said at the end of the final paragraph that nuclear power is not economical for the UK.

Question 72: D
This is clearly correct. Earlier in the passage, the author brought up the importance of effective government planning and then the High Court decision showed that the government hadn't undertaken effective planning.

Question 73: C
As the passage highlights the fact that there are issues with fossil fuels emitting carbon, just because a form of energy is cheaper in itself does not mean it will be more beneficial than nuclear power (if the cheaper form pollutes). Therefore, A doesn't necessarily weaken the author's argument based on the passage. B is too vague. While D is true, the author states that there are new safeguards now, so it doesn't necessarily apply in the present day nuclear power stations, so D is incorrect. E is incorrect as all it shows is that the government didn't do enough consideration of waste disposal – i.e. it does not indicate that nuclear power is *not* or is *less* beneficial. Either way, option C weakens the government's argument the most as other options may well be more beneficial if C is true.

Passage 15

Question 74: B
Neither A nor D is suggested in the passage. The author does suggest C, but only if B doesn't work. The author explicitly endorsed option B in the passage and believes that this would stimulate the culture change required in the final paragraph. The author did suggest E at the end of the second paragraph, but this only applies to direct wage discrimination, which the passage says does not account for the entirety of the gender pay gap. The author clearly believes that a reporting obligation would be effective to help the gender pay gap and help with direct discrimination (as stated in the final paragraph). Therefore, it is clear that option B is the preferred option of the author.

Question 75: E
The author clearly argues for this at the end of the second paragraph. B, C and D are not argued for. A is stated in the passage as an *assertion* and not an argument.

Question 76: A
In contrasting both a reporting obligation and the mandatory minimum, the author states that the mandatory minimum may not lead to a culture change and may cause resentment whereas the author states that the reporting obligation will lead to a culture change. So it is, thus, clear that this is the reason for the author's choice. D is not relevant here and E is not the main reason why the author preferred the reporting obligation – it was the culture change. The author doesn't suggest in the passage that B or C will occur from choosing the reporting obligation.

Question 77: D
Each of A, B, and C are cited as reasons for differences in the pay between genders. E is not stated as a reason for a difference.

Question 78: E
The high cost is the author's concern. While the author would agree with B, which is not the author's *concern* but merely the way in which the author would *address his concern*. A and D are not argued in the passage.

Passage 16

Question 79: C
"Oddly, even in spite of a weakening currency, the country is nowhere near to having a trade balance". The use of the words 'oddly' and 'in spite' suggest that the opposite should normally be happening. Since the country is nowhere near to having a trade balance, the opposite would be that the country would be nearer to (or have) a trade balance. Therefore, C is the correct answer as that fits in with this idea the most. E is wrong as that is the current position. A and B are wrong as they fit in with the current position as well. D is not suggested in the passage.

Question 80: D
This is explicitly explained in the passage (fourth paragraph – "As long as Britain exports to the rest of the world as much as it imports…").

Question 81: E
In the final paragraph, the author points out that de-industrialisation and a poor skills base are the wider problems linked with being a net importer. Based on the definition within the passage, being a net importer means the country doesn't have a trade balance. Thus, it is clear that the author is saying that de-industrialisation and poor skills are the reasons for the lack of exports (which mean the UK doesn't have a trade balance). B is incorrect as it means the same thing as not having a trade balance – it does not explain why there is no trade balance.

Question 82: A
This is most consistent with the entire passage. The author explicitly states that our import levels would be OK, but we just need to export more. The final paragraph also indicates that the UK's problem is too few exports as opposed to too many imports. Therefore, B is incorrect. C, D, and E do not underlie the entire passage either.

Question 83: E
A, B and C are irrelevant as they are not referred to in the last paragraph. While both D and E are true, an individual would choose the German goods because they're cheaper (as stated in the last paragraph). They wouldn't have a reason to base their choice on the lack of investment in the UK. Therefore, D is incorrect.

Passage 17

Question 84: D
The author explicitly said this is due to concerns about ESPN, a different part of the Disney Company, so D is obviously the correct answer.

Question 85: D
Ultimately, whether something is 'successful' can be a matter of opinion – some cinema goers did not particularly like the film, even though most did. All other options were facts.

Question 86: C
A prediction is, of course, an estimation of a future result. A is wrong as other companies already have produced such products and the author does not argue for D or E. While B is mentioned in the passage, the author did not predict that it would happen – the author simply stated that some analysts said it would happen. Therefore, B is incorrect. On the contrary, the author expressly predicted C in the passage.

Question 87: D
The author talks about how success does 'not stop' at the success of the box office alone but how merchandising has a role to play. Throughout the passage, the author also pointed out how the merchandising was successful. Therefore, D is the correct answer. E does not follow. Although the author asserts that an important part of *most* successful films is merchandising, that does not mean all – therefore, C is incorrect. The author did not argue for either A or B as well.

Question 88: A
This option is definitely false because the fifth paragraph explicitly states that Disney created products. It also said that Disney did not create all of the products themselves, thus implying that they created at least *some* of the products themselves and that others created some of the products.

Passage 18

Question 89: E
The author does not evince a belief as to whether society should adopt same-sex or opposite-sex marriage. The author just argues (by the end) that marriage is a social construct and, arguably, implies that adopting same-sex marriage is a reflection of society. This does not mean that the author argues for same-sex marriage – he could still disagree with society's position. The passage just doesn't refer to his personal view.

Question 90: D
The author explicitly states that the argument of the opponents (in the second paragraph) was circular and only criticises their argument, but does not take a view as to either side of the debate in the process.

Question 91: C
The author was arguing that while marriage was originally a religious construct, it was still a social construct in the 12th Century as much as now. It's just that religion had a greater role in society then.

Question 92: B
The basis for saying that marriage did not require a religious ceremony since 1837 would be that there had to be a religious ceremony before 1837.

Question 93: B
The author states that marriage has continued to evolve, even 'now' to reflect society, thereby suggesting that the recent reform which allowed for same-sex marriage (mentioned at the beginning of the passage), was a reflection of society. It is important in such questions to take a 'global' look at the whole passage while also referring to specific details when required.

Passage 19

Question 94: B
The author argues throughout that sugar should be taxed and considers potential counter-arguments, but rebuts them. E is incorrect because, while the author does consider the pros and cons, the author argues for a sugar tax throughout and thus, C is also incorrect. Indeed, the author does point out that D should be done, but that it should be done as well as a sugar tax and this was an incidental point at the end of the article, rather than underlying the entire article. Although the author does allude to point A, that is not the main point of the article, which is to reduce sugar consumption by a sugar tax – the author just deployed point A to suggest that a sugar tax is fair.

Question 95: E
If people were not to reduce consumption of sugary drinks, it would directly undermine the author's argument because imposing the sugar tax (which would increase prices) would not reduce sugar consumption, which the author highlighted as the reason for imposing the tax in the first place. D does not contradict the argument – it is, in fact, intended that prices would increase. A and C don't undermine the author's argument. While B may be an issue, the author potentially reconciles with this on the basis that those who consume it should bear the consequences of it. Therefore, E is the correct answer.

Question 96: D
This question was limited to the sixth paragraph only. If people don't get health problems from consuming sugar, they're not causing problems for society (i.e. costs to NHS); therefore, it would not be fair to tax them extra given that they aren't causing additional health costs to society. Although the author suggests that people are ignorant of the health consequences, it's not an intrinsic part of the argument that a sugar tax is fair – a sugar tax is meant to be fair (according to the author) because the people who cause the social costs would pay for it. Therefore, E is incorrect. Again, A, B, and C don't take issue with the argument that the people who cause health costs should pay for them. Accordingly, they're incorrect. While B would undermine the author's main argument, it does not undermine the argument he advanced in the sixth paragraph.

Question 97: D
While the passage implies that excess sugar consumption can cause obesity, it does not suggest that all cases of obesity are due to excess sugar consumption. Therefore, we cannot say that option D is true based on the passage. All other options are stated in the passage.

Question 98: A
A is not explicitly stated but is clearly assumed as the link between excess sugar consumption and the health consequences that the author cites (if we said option A was false, then the author's argument would be undermined - option A is a necessary assumption). None of the other options are unstated assumptions.

Question 99: C
The final sentence effectively says that prevention is better than cure, and option C is the only one which illustrates this. E is incorrect because the final sentence does not suggest that anyone is falling.

Passage 20

Question 100: B
Whether something is the 'toughest' sporting challenge is open to debate and can't be tested as being true or false.

Question 101: D
The team leader has the support of his teammates (according to the passage) and, thus, is more likely to win the race compared to if he was just one of the supporting teammates. The team leader also benefits from saving energy. This is also supported by the example stated in the passage, where the leader of Team Sky won in 2012. A, C, and E are incorrect as they don't denote an additional benefit – in particular, A and C are pre-conditions to becoming a team leader. While B is true, it's not correct as it's not necessarily a benefit that the team leader alone gets – in the passage, it was stated that the supporting rider in Team Sky came second in the race (and, by implication, beat all the other team leaders).

Question 102: B
When discussing the slipstreaming effect, the passage explicitly says that this is why cyclists tend to stay together. C is wrong because the passage says that the fact of the cyclists being in a bunch influences team strategy (not the other way round).

Question 103: E

A and B are clearly not implied in the passage. Team Sky's choice was correct for them because their rider won the race. C is stated in the passage ('it would not be possible to say that the result would have been the same') and D does not follow from the passage – the passage never said that the slipstreaming effect would make someone a better rider (just that it's a natural phenomenon that increases one's speed). Therefore, by elimination, E is the only one left. The author seems to believe this based on the fact that the supporting rider did something historic (by coming 2nd) and something 'unheard of' and that the author doubts the result if they were both equals. Hence, E is the correct answer.

Question 104: C

This is the only option that follows from the passage. In the final paragraph, it is explicitly stated that the supporting cyclist used extra energy to help his team leader. As the passage states, helping out a team leader involves keeping the team leader behind the supporting cyclists so that the team leader uses *less* energy – or conversely, the result is that the supporting cyclist may use *more* energy.

Passage 21

Question 105: A

Whether something requires *urgent* attention cannot be tested as true or false and is, therefore, an opinion as opposed to an assertion of fact. B, C, D, and E are all assertions of fact.

Question 106: B

Option A doesn't necessarily follow. The fact that there is a greater proportion of ethnic minorities in prison when compared to their proportion in the population indicates that there's a disproportionate number of ethnic minorities in prison. The government does indeed need to find out about it, but this was explicitly stated in the second paragraph (rather than being implicit) and so was the fact the statistics aren't ideal. Therefore, C and D are incorrect. E does not follow from the statistics so it is incorrect.

Question 107: C

The passage explicitly states that ethnic minorities are more likely to receive longer sentences. The passage doesn't indicate whether there is conscious discrimination, so D is incorrect. Judges don't have discretion for the guilty plea discount and it's not argued that the higher sentences are a breach of the rule of law. Finally, E is incorrect as the passage indicates that socio-economic factors are relevant.

Question 108: B

The passage states that there are a number of factors that judges consider when deciding their sentences and these form part of their discretion when deciding the sentence. The author uses this to explain why there may be different sentences for the same offence so B is the correct option. C and E show specific instances of different sentences but option B explains all the circumstances. Finally, option A does not, according to the author, appear to always explain the differences in sentences, although it sometimes might. Option D does not have an impact on sentencing so is not relevant.

Question 109: C

This option fits in best with the final paragraph and explains the higher number of ethnic minorities in the prison population. A doesn't follow from the paragraph. D doesn't explain the increase in prison population and E is just a policy suggestion (it's not an explanation) so it's not relevant.

Question 110: A

This is implicit in the final paragraph as the author cites researchers who have found that racial stereotypes do exist in the police force. B and C are explicit (and not implicit). While D is noted in the passage, it is not implied in the final paragraph and the author, if anything, would likely argue against point E and there's nothing to imply that in the paragraph, so E is incorrect as well.

Passage 22

Question 111: E
The definition of a tax inversion, according to the passage, is that a company buys another company in a different country (different jurisdiction). Therefore, the two companies have to be in different countries.

Question 112: D
The passage explicitly states that the purpose of a tax inversion is for a company to move its headquarters to get a lower tax rate. Therefore, D is the essential element. A and B are just a means to an end (the end being D). C doesn't necessarily follow (although it may be the aim of the company) as the defining feature and E doesn't follow either.

Question 113: C
Simply, the aim is to lower their tax liability, as stated in the passage.

Question 114: C
A is wrong as that isn't a benefit to society. D doesn't follow and E was not stated in the passage. However, C was explicitly stated as a potential benefit.

Question 115: E
Buffett was explicitly stating the benefits, with the implication being that businesses should pay their taxes. Therefore, C is incorrect as that is explicit. D does not follow (he was saying that there are benefits from *existing* tax rates). Neither A nor B was argued either.

Passage 23

Question 116: A
The third paragraph was saying that the Black Death transformed the position of peasants *because* ('as') they could now move to different manors. Therefore, a 'transformation' necessitates the assumption that the peasants could not move to different manors before the Black Death. Therefore, A is correct. The passage doesn't say that peasants transformed society, so B is incorrect. D is contradicted and E does not follow. While C is not contradicted, it does not fit in with the discussion in the 3rd paragraph.

Question 117: D
The passage refers to the shortage of the workforce when explaining why women's wages increased. None of the other options follow from the explanation.

Question 118: E
Although peasants moved around, that doesn't necessarily mean that they had permission to do so.

Question 119: C
This is a necessary assumption since the author points out that the population started decreasing before the Black Death due to the Great Famine.

Question 120: B
Both views agree on the point that the Black Death had a *role*.

Question 121: A
This would mean that manorial discipline did not weaken and the author's intermediate conclusion would be false.

Passage 24

Question 122: B
The passage explicitly makes the point that legal rights and obligations are lower for a cohabitation than for a marriage. While A may sometimes be true, it doesn't always hold and the passage doesn't argue for this.

Question 123: D
The fourth paragraph explicitly states that the cohabitee wouldn't receive such property "unless it was stated in the will" and the author says it's easy for a cohabiting couple to get round it by creating a will.

Question 124: C
This is the likely argument of the campaigners as their statistic was a 'retort' to the author's point on the infringing couples freedom and the statistic does provide some support (albeit weak) to point C because it shows that a number of couples would consent to the additional legal rights and responsibilities.

Question 125: E
The author expressly disagrees with A and B. C doesn't make sense as the author already stated that it is not a legal concept, so it can't really be banned. The author does not argue for D either. In the final paragraph, though, the author refers to improving the public's understanding, so it is likely that the author would agree with E.

Question 126: D
The author expressly disagrees with giving additional legal rights and responsibilities to cohabiting couples on the basis of absence of consent.

Passage 25

Question 127: B
This naturally fits in the context. Higher costs are not a benefit so point A doesn't make sense. D and E do not easily fit in the sentence either. B makes the most sense as the author is trying to say that the higher costs are resultant from the change in regulations.

Question 128: E
It is open to debate whether Mercedes should or should not be criticised and it, thus, cannot be a fact as it is not something that is provable to be either true or false.

Question 129: C
This is the best answer as the passage explicitly discusses the impact on smaller teams who have been hit by the increase in engine costs. The author does not believe A is the case. B, D and E do not directly relate to whether competition has been hampered so they are incorrect.

Question 130: A
The author simply states that Mercedes built the best car and should get the credit for that. It was not the change in the rules that caused it, but they simply exploited the new rules best.

Question 131: E
The author was not referring to Mercedes specifically, but to other teams dominating previous seasons as well. Therefore, B is wrong and so is C, as that's a recent phenomenon. Ultimately, the author points out that rule changes can increase overtaking (and, thus, competition) and explicitly states that the nature of some rules and regulations is a reason for the dominance.

Passage 26

Question 132: C
Germany paid the victims of the Nazi war crimes themselves whereas the author brings up the contention that the victims of the slave trade are no longer with us. Hence, option C is the relevant distinction between the two.

Question 133: A
This option best fits in with the argument. The company can be equated to the country and the employee being the individual victim. While the individual victims should be compensated, the passage's argument doubts whether the country as the overarching institution should benefit.

Question 134: C
The author considers arguments both for and against giving reparations throughout. It does not appear that the author takes up positions A or B.

Question 135: C
The author does not disagree with Hartley-Brewer's point but merely states that the responsibility of one of the main antagonists (i.e. the UK) should hold. D is an assumption but does not highlight the author's view.

Passage 27

Question 136: C
The passage explicitly states that the government considers the costs and benefits of animal research when deciding whether to give a license to allow it. A and E are wrong as the author was actually saying that no reasonable scientist would make animals suffer *unnecessarily*.

Question 137: A
The author seems to take the position that animal testing is beneficial by highlighting many of the positive examples of it. The author does indeed point out issues and says that a blanket allowance should not be given but that's consistent with allowing animal testing in certain circumstances.

Question 138: A
What counts as reasonable is not something that can be definitively proven to be true or false. Accordingly, it is an opinion – different people can validly disagree on the issue.

Question 139: B
This seems to be the main concern of the author.

Question 140: A
Option A undermines the author's view as, if it is true, this would mean that the government's licenses are given too frequently and that the harm to animals is not minimised.

Passage 28

Question 141: E
This was explicitly stated by the writer.

Question 142: D
This was implied by the writer when stating that unauthorised use would increase.

Question 143: E
As everyone has a natural right in what they produce, it shouldn't be used without their permission.

Question 144: D

Incentivising the production of intellectual works was explicitly stated by the author as a justification for copyright laws.

Question 145: B

This is implied in Hettinger's argument.

Question 146: C

Locke argues for natural rights, which would require copyright protection and Hettinger wants copyright protection to encourage the production of intellectual works.

Passage 29

Question 147: E

The passage explicitly states that tax evasion is illegal and that tax avoidance is legal.
It is true that Google/Starbucks have engaged in tax avoidance in the past, but that point does not indicate the difference between avoidance and evasion.

Question 148: D

The passage says that Starbucks paid zero tax. It also says that the tax rate is 20% on all declared profits. This means that Starbucks both enjoyed a declared profit and evaded tax *or* it had zero declared profits and may have avoided tax. Given that the writer explicitly stated that Starbucks were within the law, they can't have evaded tax. Therefore, they must have declared zero profits in the years they paid zero tax.

Question 149: B

Starbucks engages in tax avoidance and the author explicitly stated that this 'led' to boycotts.

Question 150: C

It is simply that companies should pay tax because they receive a benefit. The writer also points out an example of a company's use of a public service, thereby implying that companies should pay tax.

Question 151: C

Tax avoidance is where not as much tax is being paid as what should be paid. The author says this can be subjective as well. Accordingly, whether a tax payment is as it *should* be cannot be tested to be true or false. Indeed, most people may think that 20% is the correct amount to be paid but others think that as long as the law is being followed, the company is fine (and those individuals would not call it tax avoidance).

Question 152: E

The author discusses both the responsibilities of the government and the companies.

Question 153: D

This question refers to the tax system *generally* as opposed to just Starbucks' tax arrangement and the author refers to this at the final paragraph when comparing the different groups of taxpayers (large business, small business, and individuals).

Passage 30

Question 154: C

The passage explicitly states that 14 women were arrested and so were the 3 inspectors, thereby making it to a total of 17 arrests.

Question 155: A

It is clear that Anthony was brought to trial but it is not clear whether any other women or whether the 3 inspectors went to trial.

THE ULTIMATE HSPSAA GUIDE ANSWERS

Question 156: B
Hall dissented, so it's clear that the election officers were not united but were divided, so B is the correct response. Neither, C, D nor E follow from the passage.

Question 157: A
It was explicitly discussed in the third paragraph that Anthony believed she had a lawful right to vote due to the advice from her counsel.

Question 158: B
This follows from what is stated in the passage. The passage does not say that the judge believed the jury were biased and there is nothing to suggest that either A or D follows.

Passage 31

Question 159: C
Women in Illinois, not across the USA, were subject to the law, and the passage does not state either a change in fashion or actual arrests, only the potential for arrests.

Question 160: D
The pulling out of feathers from live birds was seen as the negative alternative to using osprey feathers.

Question 161: A
They could be possessed only 'in their proper season'.

Question 162: A
The problem cited is that the article was already in use in the clothing of numerous military men. The authority of the princess/sexist politics does not feature in the passage, and 'D' is patently false.

Question 163: E
None of those are precluded, as only 'harmless' and 'dead' birds (in their entirety) were prohibited. Wearing a living bird was not explicitly banned.

Passage 32

Question 164: B
He thought it was 'a pity that only rich people could own books', and from this, he 'finally determined to contrive' of a new way of printing. The passage does not state that he wished to make money, found books too expensive to get a hold of, or was impatient himself when it came to the production of books.

Question 165: A
The need to be careful is mentioned, as is the fact that the process takes a long time both in creating the block and due to the fact one block can only print one page. That it may tire a carver to make the block is possible, but it is not cited in the passage.

Question 166: D
The statement says it is 'very likely' he was taught to read but is not definite. The fact that his father comes from a 'good family' does not mean he is a member of the aristocracy, necessarily. Though block printing was used as the boy grew up, it does not state this was the most popular process. The mention of Gutenberg's family's 'wealthy friends' indicates that they were sociable.

Question 167: A
The paper was laid on top of the block, not underneath.

Question 168: A
There is nothing written in the passage praising the craftsmanship of manuscripts. The appropriateness of the titles for both book production processes is explained, and the 'wealthy friends' are described as a source to borrow books from, and, thus, a way of expanding one's reading. The boy was 'very likely' taught to read as well which implies that he was probably educated.

Passage 33

Question 169: C
Nowhere does it state that all European countries have similar creatures (though certain types can be found in both British Isles and Norway) nor does it state that the array of animals is limited to this one nation. Sharing animals and birds does not necessitate sharing geographical features, but it is said that a country with forest and moorlands is likely to have a variety of birds and animals, so one can see the link between forests and creatures.

Question 170: A
There was a time when the English dreaded wolves and bears, but that indicates the past, or at least does not include the present. Norwegians being superior is not suggested here.

Question 171: C
Bears are called destroyers, which is sufficient to conclude that they cause damage.

Question 172: D
They are ruthlessly hunted by farmers in country districts, but numerous only in the forest tracts in the Far North.

Question 173: A
The word 'fortunately' implies that it is good that the wolves are no longer central. The children are under no threat, as the threat of wolves belongs to a bygone time, there is no mention of regret that such a time is gone and Norsemen are not presented in the above passage as having respect for Nature, but instead, they are said to interfere with it through hunting and driving wolves farther afield from their current homes.

Question 174: A
This is not based on evidence and can vary from person to person. It can't be tested as being true or false and, therefore, is an opinion.

Passage 34

Question 175: A
Most requires over half by definition, and "most" of the people living in this area were the descendants of immigrants who moved to the country a "full century ago".

Question 176: B
Hall only makes a claim for New England, not the entirety of America, being the descendants of 20,000 immigrants. The 'one million' figure comes from Franklin, not Hall. Less than 80,000 ("under" 80,000) people led to the population boom of one million. One million is over ten times more than 80,000, so "B" is correct.

Question 177: C
It is said to be "distinct" to older aristocracy "of the royal governor's courts". It is not similar to any European aristocracy. There is no specific reference to it not being a system based on lineage.

Question 178: B
"A", "C" and "D" are cited in the passage (the journey took 'the better part of the year', it was 'hazardous' and 'expensive'), whereas 'B' is not referenced at all.

Question 179: E
The word 'reference' best fits in as the author is referring to the lack of citation of Shakespeare and the Puritan poet Milton.

Passage 35

Question 180: C
It would be a massive assumption to state that just because two characters in a book are 'vicious', all of them will be, so 'A' is not necessarily correct. 'B' also believes in a despair that is described to belong to the Comedian, but not Rorschach. The argument of the passage is that 'D', which Moore may believe, is not the case - the beloved character is not simply worshipped for his violence, but for his belief in justice. 'C' is correct, as Moore describes how he did not wish for Rorschach to be a favourite character, but rather a warning.

Question 181: D
Rorschach is considered as a hero, despite using violence. Therefore, A and B are wrong. The author then goes on to highlight that the issue with the Comedian is that he has no purpose but at least Rorschach does have a purpose, even if he does use violence. Accordingly, D naturally follows from this. C and E do not follow from what is discussed.

Question 182: B
He does not mention madness ('D'), or invoke shame ('C'), or simply state it is good to be good ('A') - specifically, he states we must act as if the world is 'just', even when it is not, in order to attain dignity.

Question 183: D
No value judgment is made regarding violent actions or on the Comedian's jokes so 'A' and 'B' are false. The passage also acknowledges Rorschach's violence, showing 'C' is wrong but does state that his actions are due to the fact he believes that he is acting in the name of justice, which lends him an ethical justification for his actions.

Question 184: A
The lack of meaning in anything is what leads him to treat everything as a joke - it is not hatred, but the inability to see 'purpose' in himself or his fellow man.

Passage 36

Question 185: C
This is the most accurate definition of a fallacy. Indeed, the first paragraph discusses that the gambler's fallacy is indeed a falsehood.

Question 186: C
The Monte Carlo fallacy and the Gambler's fallacy are labels for the same phenomenon. Accordingly, the events in Monte Carlo are not the definition of the fallacy, but merely why it has its name. Answer C fits in best with the explanation provided in the first paragraphs. It is the fact that there have already been lots of (previous) black rolls that people believe that there will be a red due.

Question 187: D
People were betting before the 26th spin so C is incorrect. E is incorrect as the passage does not indicate that they knew of the gambler's fallacy. A is impossible as it's not possible to know with certainty that a future event will happen and there's no evidence to suggest that B was the case. As explained in the passage, the gambler's fallacy operated to engender a false belief that one's odds of getting an *independent* future result (i.e. a red) increased because of the fact that there were lots of blacks beforehand.

Question 188: D
This can be assumed as the gambler's fallacy as it involves at least two independent events – that because one (or more) previous events occurred in a given way means that it's likely that a future event will occur in a particular way.

Question 189: D
Since the experimental group did not differ from the control group, it is clear that teaching probability alone may not change things. It does not prove A as not all possible methods of alleviating the gambler's fallacy were used in the study. B and C don't follow, and E is explicitly mentioned in the passage.

Question 190: D
The gambler's fallacy appears to operate whether or not one has a belief in it (based on the study in the preceding paragraph) therefore, B and C are incorrect. While A is true, it doesn't explain *why* those in the first group tended to predict tails more. Also, point A was the same for both groups. E is too vague. Thus, D has to be correct. It also follows from the author's explanation of the gambler's fallacy in the beginning of the passage that that is what was being tested here in the final paragraph.

Passage 37

Question 191: C
The essence of the libertarian argument is that people should do what they want so long as they're exercising 'free will' (according to the passage). Therefore, A, B, D, and E are all incorrect. It doesn't matter if there is some risk to the provider or if it is against nature, as long as people consent, it's fine. Accordingly, when one does not give informed consent, arguably one is not exercising free will. Therefore, the libertarian argument would not be relevant in those circumstances.

Question 192: D
It is explicitly stated in the passage that people in Wales are presumed to consent *unless* they have indicated otherwise, so it is thus clear that people in Wales still have a choice as to whether to donate their organs.

Question 193: A
The author throughout has based the arguments in the passage on the case for allowing the sale of human organs, so point A is correct.

Question 194: A
Whether the poor are exploited through a system for organ sales is open to debate and arguments on either side can be equally valid. This can't be tested as being true or false. Therefore, it is an opinion. All other options are assertions of fact.

Question 195: D
This is never suggested in the passage – while the author believes that there wouldn't be exploitation of the poor, it is never suggested or implied that the poor should donate their organs as opposed to the rich.

Passage 38

Question 196: E
This is the only option that has to be true in order to sustain the author's argument. The author based his point on the fact that the officer didn't want to speak with Tatchell. However, if the students unions would have been fine with Tatchell speaking, then the author would, in fact, have a platform to speak.

Question 197: D
It is clear that the author's assertions and arguments point towards Tatchell being allowed to speak but the question was asking what the author's views were as to freedom of speech generally. Option D, thus, better describes the author's main position as adopted throughout the passage.

THE ULTIMATE HSPSAA GUIDE — ANSWERS

Question 198: E
Whether such censoring is concerning or not is simply an opinion – some may find it wrong but others may legitimately find it OK because it might offend people. It cannot be tested as it can't be true or false. On the other hand, all other options are assertions of fact. In regard to B, while the question of 'offensiveness' in itself is an opinion, the statement that "Offensiveness has a number of different meanings' is a factual assertion – we can simply have a look at whether there's more than one meaning of offensiveness or not. Therefore, point B taken as a whole is an assertion of fact.

Question 199: E
This is the only point that logically follows from the passage. It is not suggested that any students are extremists (so A is incorrect), it is not suggested or implied that students generally are against free speech (so B is incorrect), it is not clear that many students are against it (so C is incorrect) and finally, the passage does not assume or imply that student unions express the views of the student body.

Passage 39

Question 200: D
While A is true, it is not the main reason for the US bringing the case against Great Britain. B isn't correct as it's not clear that the seals were the US' and C isn't correct as it's neither stated nor implied in the passage that the Canadian ships breached US waters. The passage explicitly states that the depletion of seal stocks led to the conflict.

Question 201: C
The passage explicitly says that Great Britain's counsel persuaded the tribunal. Therefore, it's clear that Great Britain won the case. Canada was not a party to proceedings as Great Britain was representing them (so B is incorrect).

Question 202: B
This explains why the US' argument was convenient because this means that Canada was acting illegally while the US was acting lawfully and would have supported the US' case. A does not provide an explanation. C is not true and D, in fact, makes the US' argument less convincing. The author did not use the word 'convenient' in the context of E.

Question 203: D
This is true as while both sides could seal in the exclusion zone, the tribunal held that they were both restricted in the extent of their sealing.

Question 204: C
The regulation didn't refer at all to the Pribilof Islands. Accordingly, the US would still be free to seal there as they always had done (so long as there were enough seals there).

Passage 40

Question 205: D
A is obviously incorrect as opponents and supporters disagree on the existing wage rates. B is incorrect – we don't know whether opponents and/or supporters believe that fairness has different meanings in different contexts. The author seems to imply this, but the author does not imply that opponents and supporters think that it can have different meanings. However, the author points out that the supporters have one view of fairness (market-based wage rate) and opponents have another view (based on differences in wages). Therefore, both sides consider fairness and so D is correct. E is obviously incorrect because opponents of footballers' wages do not believe that the current outcome is fair.

THE ULTIMATE HSPSAA GUIDE ANSWERS

Question 206: A
This is a tricky question involving the use of two negatives ('not' and 'inconsistent') in the question. Simply put, which of the following responses doesn't contradict both the opponents and supporters arguments? Opponents and supporters all disagree on B, C, D, and E. Therefore, A has to be correct. Indeed, supporters of footballers' high wages never deny that luck played a part.

Question 207: A
This is because the passage never says that hard work is unimportant or not a factor. It's perfectly logical for hard work to be a factor alongside one's birth talents. B is wrong because it's not obvious – the author says that 'careful' political debate is required to determine whether there should even be reform. C is wrong because two different formulations of fairness are highlighted in the passage. D is wrong because the author states that luck has a role to play. E is obviously incorrect.

Question 208: E
It is clear that this sentence is introducing a contrasting point because of the author's use of the word 'however'. Accordingly, having just brought up the possibility of a wage cap, it means that the author is suggesting some kind of limitation to that in this sentence. E is the only choice that fits in with this.

Question 209: D
The author does not argue that the footballers' wages are correct or incorrect but *considers* the arguments as to whether they are *fair*. Therefore, A and B are incorrect. C and E are incorrect as they are merely assertions in the passage as opposed to arguments. D is correct because that is an intermediate conclusion, backed up by reasons immediately preceding it.

Passage 41

Question 210: B
The author asks readers to 'consider how you might feel if your employment contract was suddenly changed without your consent. The author also states: I would further ask how you would feel if that contract was changed such that your working hours became significantly less convenient without additional remuneration. Both of these statements invite readers to empathise with the tube workers.

Question 211: A
The doctors' strikes are the only one of the answers mentioned in the passage. They are mentioned in a way which contrasts the position taken (by the public) on their strikes with the position taken towards tube workers. As such, the answer is A because the author is highlighting an inconsistency in the way in which the industrial action of both groups is received by the public.

Question 212: C
The author states we should hesitate before using social media as a useful poll of public opinion. This indicates that it may offer a skewed view of public opinion. The other answers are not mentioned in the passage.

Question 213: D
In the passage, 'conservative' is used to describe newspapers, rather than people. As such, A & C cannot be correct. B cannot be correct because the passage does not indicate a view as to how conservative individuals view or interact with other people. Therefore, D is the correct answer.

Question 214: C
The author states that many of us may have unwittingly taken on the views promulgated in such media and that we might benefit from rethinking such views'. As such, she is suggesting that we should re-evaluate some of our beliefs.

Passage 42

Question 215: D
The author does not state any political views. Although the Labour Party is used as an example, and the Conservative Party briefly mentioned, the author does not comment on whether or not their views align with them. The Liberal Democrats are not mentioned. As such, there is not enough information to tell.

Question 216: B
This is explicitly given as a reason why people should join political parties in the introduction. Although the other answers are mentioned in the passage, they are not used to demonstrate why people should join political parties.

Question 217: A
The whole piece assumes that it is a good thing to engage with politics. If that were not the case, the whole piece falls down. B and C are mentioned explicitly so they cannot be correct. D is not an assumption of the piece – most of the piece is not about young people.

Question 218: B
'Untenable' means not able to be maintained or defended against attack or objection. It is a word which especially applies to a position or viewpoint.

Question 219: D
The statement that a large proportion of the UK population are completely disengaged from politics is one of the three arguments which follows directly from the statistic given. Although the other points are mentioned in the passage, they are not connected by the author to the statistic given.

Passage 43

Question 220: A
To perpetuate something is to cause it to continue, perhaps indefinitely.

Question 221: C
The author says 'only' 7% and that it was not clear whether this increase was caused by the policy. The use of the word 'only' indicates the answer cannot be A, and we do not have enough information to determine whether it could be D.

Question 222: D
The author states that 'if such privileges are given only to women, the idea that only women should be responsible for childcare may be perpetuated'. Answers A and B are not mentioned.

Question 223: B
The author states that 'the aim of this policy was to allow women to continue working, rather than leaving their jobs after having a child'. This is distinct from C because the author uses the word 'allow' rather than 'make'.

Question 224: A
The author says 'emphasising women's differences and adjusting for them may actually have done more harm than good in this case', indicating that it may not have helped gender equality.

Passage 44

Question 225: A
This statement is made without any evidence to support it and does not follow from any other arguments made in the piece. The other statements have evidence to support them.

Question 226: D
Although A is mentioned in the passage, it is not in the first paragraph. Peel's Metropolitan Police is discussed in the first paragraph but there is no mention of it being old fashioned. Visible patrol is mentioned but there is no indication that it wasn't working. The idea that governments were keen to secure value for money is explicitly mentioned, however.

Question 227: B
This is the only option, which is actually given as evidence. C is not present at all; although D and A are present, they constitute merely a further explanation of the point. B is given to support the original statement and, as such, is being given as evidence for the claim.

Question 228: C
Although this might be useful evidence for the statement, it is not present in the passage. A, B, and D are all referred to in the final paragraph.

Question 229: B
The passage is not designed to persuade the reader of anything. Persuasive language is not used and, as such, A and D are wrong. Although C is mentioned, it is only part of the last paragraph and is not the main point of the piece. The idea expressed in B runs through the entire extract.

Passage 45

Question 230: B
Is the central point of the first paragraph. A and C are not paradoxes at all; they are merely pairs of facts. D is incorrect because there is no suggestion that people are not interested in the law.

Question 231: A
The key phrase to understand this answer is "although many treaties now", indicating that the situation was different in the past. The other answers are not mentioned in the passage.

Question 232: D
A and B are not mentioned in the passage. C is only briefly mentioned. D is frequently referred to and runs throughout the passage and is the central argument of the extract.

Question 233: C
This option is not mentioned in the passage. The other answers are all contained in the last paragraph.

Question 234: A
The sentence on 'rules on international postage and telephone calls' is followed by the statement that 'this shows that the legislative process does work reasonably well'. B is the opposite and is, therefore, wrong. D and C are entirely separate points and mentioned elsewhere in the passage.

Passage 46

Question 235: D
C is not given as a reason for why it's important to find an answer to the question of whether or not law is coercive. A and B are both mentioned but there is no indication given as to which is more important. As such, the question cannot be answered with the information available.

Question 236: A
This is the only mention of Hart in the passage so we cannot know what he thinks about the other statements. The passage says "The criminal law is the clearest example of law being like commands (Austin), and despite Hart's criticism of Austin, he too concedes this", indicating that Hart and Austin agree on this point.

Question 237: B

C and D are not correct statements at all and misinterpret the 'puzzled' idea in the extract. There is no indication that lawmakers actually enjoy the use of sanctions so A cannot be correct. B is stated in the first paragraph.

Question 238: B

Coercive means using force or threats to make someone do something. The other answers do not relate to this idea at all.

Question 239: B

C is not mentioned at all. D cannot be correct because the passage states "serious sanctions are needed". B is correct because the passage states "a substantial portion of society obeys the law because of fear of sanction." A is an unconnected statement.

Passage 47

Question 240: C

Paragraphs two and three provide different perspectives on the new management structures. One offers an advantage and one offers a disadvantage and the author does not come down on either side.

Question 241: A

This is the only idea which is presented as a positive consequence of the new management structures. B is not mentioned. C and D are presented as potential negatives of the new structures.

Question 242: B

The introduction tells you that consultancies have been advising big companies on hiring fewer people from outside their companies and the second paragraph provides statistics to show that this is what Sahara have been doing.

Question 243: C

A is mentioned in the last paragraph, B in the second paragraph and D in the introduction. Although staff is discussed, they are management level, not entry level.

Question 244: A

The author says avoiding another financial crisis would "mean that we all avoid a great deal of misery". This suggests that there was a great deal of misery this time round.

Passage 48

Question 245: B

The final line of the passage is "There is no place to argue they are treated too leniently". The author tries to correct the ideas expressed in A, and D. C is not expressed in the passage.

Question 246: C

This might be very useful information to have but it does not appear in the passage. A, B, and D are all mentioned at different points in the passage.

Question 247: D

The enduring belief is discussed but not explained. C is not mentioned. A and B are included in the passage but not in connection with the enduring belief.

Question 248: A

The author states that these programmes "emphasise dependency and traditional femininity, and most crucially, fail to aid rehabilitation".

Question 249: A

We know that 70% of women have addiction problems, which is double the amount for men.

Passage 49

Question 250: C

B is not mentioned at all. A and D are mentioned as minor pieces of evidence. C is a repeated theme throughout the passage.

Question 251: A

The author states "prison has in fact been found to have an overall negative effect", which rules out B, C, and D which are all positive outcomes.

Question 252: B

The author states "making people miserable is not the way to bring about reform", meaning both that people are sad and that rehabilitation is, therefore, not being achieved.

Question 253: D

A and C are explicitly stated so cannot be unstated assumptions. B is incorrect – the passage repeatedly explains that prisons do not have a positive effect. The passage criticises the prison system for not achieving rehabilitation without ever explicitly saying that rehabilitation should be a goal, making it an unstated assumption.

Question 254: A

This might be a valid criticism but it does not appear in the passage. All the other answers are contained within the passage.

Passage 50

Question 255: C

All the answers are mentioned in the passage. However, readers are warned to be careful so as not to knock the water over, so it is not an advantage.

Question 256: B

This is the only contradiction. It cannot actually be true that everyone is sleeping badly if the author herself is doing well with sleep.

Question 257: A

To say 'we all are these days' is clearly an exaggeration. The other statements are literally true and not hyperbolic.

Question 258: D

Although the author says that the third piece of advice is important, she does not say it is the most important. There is no way of knowing which she thinks is the best piece of advice.

Question 259: C

The author tells us explicitly she is not a doctor. The final line, "I hope this helps you all sleep much better. Leave your comments below with tips and tricks which work for you!" indicates the piece may well be from a blog.

Passage 51

Question 260: C
In the introduction, the author states "It is submitted that all four are useful and are relatively complete as a set, meaning the criteria do not need to be re-written." B and D are not stated at all.

Question 261: D
The author tells you that Taiwan lacks independence. Prior to that, she has explained that capacity to enter into legal relations is essentially the same as independence.

Question 262: D
The author merely states that "The government need not be 'legitimate' or 'democratic' – it just needs to be in effective control". She does not state what she thinks about this.

Question 263: A
In the second paragraph, the author writes that "States are necessarily legal entities made up of people." B and C are not present. D is mentioned but is an explanation, rather than an argument in favour of the permanent population requirement.

Question 264: B
The author states that "it is self-evident that we expect states to be territorial entities and it is clear that this is an appropriate criterion for statehood". The other criteria are explained much more thoroughly.

Passage 52

Question 265: B
Although A and C are mentioned, they are only briefly referred to. B runs throughout the passage. D is not contained in the passage.

Question 266: B
Although A is made as a concession, this is not in the second paragraph. C and D are not concessions. The phrase "if it's really necessary" indicates a concession is being made.

Question 267: A
This might be a good argument but the author does not make it. B, C, and D and E are all referred to in the passage.

Question 268: C
The author states "the whole system ought to be built around teaching healthy and happy relationships, with the biology section firmly as a secondary point." This shows that the author thinks that biology should be taught but it's less important than relationships.

Question 269: B
Although A, C, and D could lead to the problem highlighted, the author does not connect them to the issue. She states in the introduction "children are going to the Internet or their peers to glean more information and this is leading to unstable adolescents."

Passage 53

Question 270: A
We know this because she says it would be "no bad thing" if "all businesses (were) required to have this policy" in the final paragraph.

Question 271: C
We know this because, in the first paragraph, the author states that it is "especially useful for new parents, who want to return to work but not do as much as they had previously".

Question 272: D
When discussing this option, the author writes that "this is unlikely, however, because businesses which offer flexi-time have largely invested in the scheme wholesale."

Question 273: B
The author states that "one of the major benefits from the perspectives of businesses is that their employees become much more productive." C is discussed as a possibility but not something of which we can be certain.

Question 274: A
This piece is not aimed at persuading anyone of something. It is written as a news article, reporting on a changing business practice.

Passage 54

Question 275: C
We know this because the author states "More significant, however, is that they employ even more people in the planning and sales of such projects."

Question 276: B
The author states that "One wonders, then, why the government is choosing not to invest much further. The economic recovery will not happen by itself." The unstated assumption behind this is that it is the responsibility of the government to stimulate the economy.

Question 277: A
The author offers criticism of the other groups. She also states that "One wonders, then, why the government is choosing not to invest much further."

Question 278: B
A and D are mentioned but would not impact the economy. C is incorrect because the author repeatedly states that the reason we need big infrastructure projects is to stimulate the economy.

Question 279: D
The author says that this group has a "selfish attitude". Although she disagrees with the environmental groups, she acknowledges they are thinking of people's welfare.

Passage 55

Question 280: C
The author states that "We discovered that London is the world's most popular tourist destination!" This necessarily means that London receives more visitors than anywhere else in the UK.

Question 281: B
We know this because the author states "councils should not be investing in tourism. This is because it is such a high-risk industry."

Question 282: A
All the other ideas are mentioned in the passage. Although it might be interesting to know how many tourists go to the beach, the author does not discuss it.

Question 283: D
The author expresses a great deal of surprise that people want to go for Madame Tussauds and queue for it. She goes as far as to call it 'bizarre'.

Question 284: C
It might be reasonable to think the other answers could be true but they would be going beyond what the author tells us. All seasonal means here is that the income is dependent on the seasons.

Passage 56

Question 285: B
The author states "Tax, it seems, makes all the difference." She alludes to Americans tweeting that Europeans are alcoholics but does not give credence to this claim.

Question 286: C
We know this because the author states "There is more sugar in American fizzy drinks than their European equivalents. In fact, there is even less in Asian markets." This necessarily means the American market has more than both the European market and Asian market.

Question 287: A
We know this because earlier in the paragraph, we read that "American senators have had very little joy in trying to tackle this problem because drinks companies provide financial support to so many of those in politics in the US."

Question 288: D
We know this from the following sentence: "The French – very meritoriously – take children with them to dinner parties and slowly allow them to start drinking alcohol in a sensible way."

Question 289: D
We know this because when the author discusses the tax, she says "but this appears to have made little difference to those in their twenties."

Passage 57

Question 290: E
The other options could happen and are discussed in the passage. However, none of the options are presented as definite results of the ageing population. D would only occur if governments do indeed struggle to pay for their ageing populations; however, the passage tells us only that they are 'likely' to struggle.

Question 291: B
All the other answers are perfectly credible reasons, but the author does not, in fact, choose to explain why there is a difference.

Question 292: A
We know this because although the author expresses concern for all the countries mentioned, she uses the phrase "Most alarmingly, in countries such as Niger…" indicating that this is the place she is most concerned about.

Question 293: B
A and C are stated explicitly in the passage so cannot be unstated assumptions. D is not relevant at all. The paragraph discusses the limits on development as being problems in themselves, meaning B is the right answer.

Question 294: D
We know this is the answer because the paragraph discusses different ways of paying for an ageing population as well as how to save costs. Thus, we can infer that they cost a lot of money.

Passage 58

Question 295: A
We know this because she uses phrases such as "swan around thinking they are so on trend and yet most of them produce nothing of value whatsoever", indicating an attitude of derision towards them.

Question 296: C
We know this because the author criticises tech for being 'dull in practice' and states that jobs in arts are 'more interesting' – and therefore, better.

Question 297: A
The sentence "Jobs in finance may seem like good ideas for graduates but jobs in publishing actually offer more opportunities for the truly talented" is a direct comparison.

Question 298: D
The author states that "publishers are much more rigorous in their hiring procedures – and rightly so" indicating the hiring procedures are tough. She does not think they are too hard, however – as we know from the use of the word 'rightly'.

Question 299: C
This is only revealed in the final paragraph when the author says, "The point here is that although I'm sure you've been told that jobs in the industries that graduates typically go into have a lot to offer, you should not close your mind to other options. Think a little bigger!"

Passage 59

Question 300: E
The passage begins by speaking of 'social convulsions' and quickly switches to speaking of 'revolutions' without any indication that the author is changing the topic. 'Social convulsion' must, therefore, refer to revolutions. Option C is incorrect as although a revolution necessarily brings about change, the notion of change is not synonymous with that of revolution (given that change can come about otherwise than through a revolution).

Question 301: E
The author writes that 'This skin, or envelope, however, does not expand automatically.' This suggests that law and institutions (which are represented by 'skin') do not change by themselves or without much pain/suffering.

Question 302: D
The author argues that Washington was able, because of his genius and because of the men who supported him, to postpone revolution. If, therefore, one could prove that the men around his were not particularly remarkable, it would weaken the argument that they contributed to his success. Option B is incorrect because even if intelligent men opposed Washington, this has no effect on the author's argument that some intelligent men also supported Washington.

Question 303: E
All the other options appear in the second and third paragraphs in relation to Washington. Option E is used in relation to the men who supported Washington.

Question 304: C
The author writes that: 'Yet even Washington and his adherents could not alter the limitations of the human mind'. This immediately precedes the statement to the effect that Washington could postpone but could not prevent revolution, suggesting that the natural limitations of the human mind were to blame.

Passage 60

Question 305: A
The first line of the piece hints at option A as the correct options: 'the whole scope of the essay is to recommend culture as the great help out of our present difficulties.' Later on, the author makes clear the fact that the value he places on culture lies in its ability to give us 'a fresh and free play of the best thoughts'. Options B, C, and D are just used to support the main argument. Option E is an argument advanced by the author only to further elucidate the nature of culture (the fact that it is inward).

Question 306: D
The author emphasises the fact that his critics have lost sight of 'the essential inwardness of the operation of culture, and that 'it is just our worship of machinery, and of external doing' that led to the bringing of the charge. This suggests that the entire example is designed to illustrate our focus on external actions.

Question 307: C
The third paragraph suggests that the effect of culture is to bring about a change inwardly in our thoughts – hence, we need not follow a specific set of outward actions to obtain culture, if we can obtain these same effects without following that set of outward actions.

Question 308: A
The author emphasises that an academy constitutes 'outward machinery', whilst culture is 'inward', suggesting that an academy is unhelpful because it is outward.

Question 309: A
The lines which immediately follow that line suggest that people can obtain culture through different means and need not necessarily do so by reading. The author, however, does not suggest that the meaning of culture itself is open to individual interpretation – only the means by which one strives to obtain it.

Passage 61

Question 310: A
The question which follows the line in which 'basal' is used ('what common ground…') sheds light on the sense in which it is being used by the author. If a feature is common to many different situations in which laughter occurs, it suggests that the feature is the 'essential' element in the laughable.

Question 311: C
In the second paragraph, the author suggests that his exploration of the topic of laughter cannot fail to throw light on the way the human imagination works and that it must have something to tell us about life. Although A, B, D, and E are mentioned in the passage, nothing in the author's language suggests that these are the goals of his investigation – and they seem to relate to the method of the investigation A, background information about the topic E, and mere observations on the topic D and B.

Question 312: B
All the examples in the paragraph are geared towards demonstrating that, as stated in the penultimate line, 'the comic demands something like a momentary anaesthesia of the heart'. The use of 'then' in the penultimate line affords strong evidence that what is to follow is a summary of all that has been discussed earlier in the paragraph and is, therefore, the conclusion of the paragraph.

Question 313: A
A metaphor involves the representation of one thing with another. A is the correct answer as the other options are either not figurative, or even if they do employ figurative language, do not concern the representation of one thing with another.

Question 314: C
The fourth paragraph states that laughter demands an anaesthesia of the heart, suggesting that the absence of sentiment is a precondition for laughter. (A) can be found in the penultimate paragraph, B is derived from the statement in the final paragraph that laughter has a social function, D is derived from the statement in the second paragraph that laughter can throw light on human life/imagination and E is stated in the first paragraph ('we regard it as a living thing'). Therefore, C is the only answer not used to characterise laughter.

Passage 62

Question 315: C
A premise of the author's argument that the patriarchal nature of a society influences their conceptions of God is that the Jewish God embodies masculine qualities and is to be found in a patriarchal society. However, for this premise to support her argument, she must assume that the Jewish conception of God stemmed from the people themselves (and, thus, from the patriarchal society), and not through divine revelation (which would have been completely unrelated to the people, and, thus, unrelated to the patriarchal society). Options A and B are incorrect because whether or not there is a god or whether or not the Jewish God exists has no direct bearing on whether the conceptions of God *endorsed by a society* are endorsed because of the structure of that society. Option D is incorrect because it is the writer's argument, rather than an assumption of her argument. Option E is an implication of her argument, not an assumption of it.

Question 316: A
This question requires the student to pick up on the word 'special' and to identify the subtle distinction between the motive for subjecting religious conceptions to examination, and the intended outcome of such an enquiry. The question, which asks 'why' the author believes that religious conceptions should be examined, relates only to the former. The author states: '*as* the forms and habits of thought connected with worship take a firmer hold on the mental constitution than do those belonging to any other department of human experience, *religious conceptions should be subjected...*' - suggesting that this is the motive for her subjection of religious conceptions to examination.

Question 317: D
The author's argument is that as society evolved into a patriarchal society, the religious ideas endorsed by society came to reflect a more masculine conception of God. The author, therefore, argues that society's conceptions of God follow changes in the structure of society. It is true, of course, that different societies have different conceptions of religion, but this doesn't come *closest* to describing the author's stated views on the relationship between religion and society – hence E is incorrect.

Question 318: B
The author offers no reasoning to support this view – it is merely stated – hence it is a mere assertion. D is supported by the reasoning in the first paragraph (that as society became more masculine, conceptions of God changed) and E is merely an application of D to a specific society – it is, therefore, supported by the same reasoning which supports D. C is supported by the statement that 'every branch of inquiry is being subjected to reasonable criticism', and A is supported by the reasoning in the second paragraph.

Question 319: E

The author mentions that with the rise of male dominance came the valuing of male qualities over female qualities. Both these factors were necessary for producing the contemporary (masculine) ideas of God. The answer is to be found in the final paragraph: 'After women began to leave their homes at marriage, and after *property, especially land, had fallen under the supervision and control of men,* the latter, as they manipulated all the necessaries of life and the means of supplying them, began to *regard themselves as superior beings, and later, to claim that as a factor in reproduction, or creation, the male was the more important.* With this change, the ideas of a Deity also began to undergo a modification.'

Passage 63

Question 320: E

Independence is not attributed to goodness, as the author states that the idea of goodness appears only as an '*element*' in other things, and we must ourselves strive to '*give goodness an independent meaning*'. The other options are to be found in the first and second paragraphs. Option D is incorrect because, at the start of paragraph two, goodness is described as being somewhat paradoxical in that it is familiar and yet remote and, therefore, curious.

Question 321: A

The author states: '*But while thus familiar and influential when mixed with action, and just because of that very fact, the notion of goodness is bewilderingly abstruse and remote.*' The other options are not stated as reasons for which the notion of goodness is difficult to understand. Option E is a restatement of the problem, not an explanation of its origin.

Question 322: B

A statement to this effect comes immediately after the author's declaration that '*familiarity obscures*' – this gives the student a strong hint that B constitutes an explanation of the phrase '*familiarity obscures*'. The next closest option is A, but this is not stated as an explanation for the phrase '*familiarity obscures*'. It is presented, rather, as the false belief of most people (which the phrase '*familiarity obscures*' is intended to correct).

Question 323: D

Immediately after making this statement, the author uses another example: '*To determine beforehand just how polite we should be would not facilitate human intercourse*' which reiterates the idea that understanding the theory of a topic does not help in its practical everyday application.

Question 324: A

Although the author does mention that understanding goodness will not necessarily help and may hinder everyday life, that statement acts merely as a caveat to the central point – which is that understanding the idea of goodness is necessary for ethical students (but if we mean to be ethical students and to examine conduct scientifically, we must evidently at the outset come face to face with the meaning of goodness). The entire text concerns coming to grasp the idea of goodness, so it is also likely that the main conclusion of the final paragraph will relate to the importance of understanding the idea. Option E is incorrect because the statement that the goodness is the ethical writer's chief tool is a premise which is designed to support the idea that students need an understanding of goodness; in critical thinking, it cannot, therefore, be the ultimate conclusion.

Passage 64

Question 325: A

In the final paragraph, the author is speaking against the idea that women ought to have children only in wedlock. This suggests that when she encourages having children '*in freedom*', she means having children outside of marriage.

Question 326: A

The fifth paragraph speaks of the fact that women are taught to only consider money in determining who to marry. This suggests that they employ a flawed criteria in determining who to marry, and the author suggests at the beginning of the paragraph that this is in fact the reason why '*Nora leaves her husband*'. Option B is the next closest option – however, it is not the <u>ultimate</u> cause of unsuccessful marriages, as the use of a flawed criteria temporally and logically precedes the marriage to an unsuitable person.

Question 327: C

The author makes it clear at the beginning of the passage that '*Marriage and love have nothing in common*', suggesting that there is no relationship between the two. She goes on to mention that love doesn't spring from marriage (paragraph 3).

Question 328: A

If the parents of destitute children are unmarried, then the author's' argument in that paragraph (that marriage does not protect children) completely falls apart. The other options do nothing to damage the argument in that paragraph – e.g. option D, or, in fact, contradict the author's argument (option B), or are explicitly argued by the author – i.e. option C (see the final line of the paragraph).

Question 329: E

The examples and arguments advanced by the author all support the idea that marriage is a failure – i.e. it is a failure because it cannot protect children, and because it cannot bring about love and because divorce statistics are so high. The main argument does not concern children as only one paragraph is devoted to children, and that paragraph is itself designed to support the idea that marriage is a failure.

Passage 65

Question 330: A

The author mentions that '*the multitude, the mass spirit, dominates everywhere, destroying quality*'. She then goes on to give one example of how this has occurred, mentioning that mass goods are now being produced (quantity), which are generally injurious to us (reductions in quality). This example is given to support the idea that we prioritise quantity over quality nowadays, so the other options cannot be the main conclusion (as they support option A). Option E is not mentioned in the first paragraph.

Question 331: B

A metaphor is the representation of one thing with another. Only option B satisfies this criterion (a '*god*' is used to represent success).

Question 332: A

The main argument is that art is successful only if it appeals to the majority of people. The author then states that this is the cause of the ugliness of the art that can now be seen around the city. If, however, a minority are responsible for that art, it would undermine the author's argument that the prevalence of majority taste produces ugly art. Option E is irrelevant to the author's argument, as is option D. Option B is just a reiteration of what the author mentions already and supports her argument. Option C doesn't do much damage to the author's argument as the idea that for most of their lives artistic geniuses are unable to thrive as they don't appeal to the vulgar majority taste still stands.

Question 333: C

This statement supports the idea that the oft-repeated slogan is incorrect as it suggests that individuals are only successful due to the majority, and cannot obtain that success on their own. The other options do not give reasons for us to take seriously the author's rejection of the oft-repeated slogan and are mere assertions.

Question 334: A

The author suggests that even when politicians engage in disgraceful behaviour, they need only '*muster up their minions*' to ensure that they stay in power nonetheless. This suggests that democracy helps those with poor morals to hold on to power. Options E and B are incorrect because the author nowhere suggests that democracy actively encourages corruption. Option C is incorrect as it is the opposite of what the author is saying.

THE ULTIMATE HSPSAA GUIDE ANSWERS

Passage 66

Question 335: D
That is the only option which is not supported by extra reasoning – e.g. the statement that the purpose-novel proposes to serve two masters is supported by the idea that the novel aims to entertain as well as to instruct.

Question 336: A
The author mentions that the bishop may be the best preacher there is, but the viewer is still entitled to get their money back because they came to watch a play, not a sermon. This idea is encapsulated by option A. Option D is incorrect as the purpose-novel is said to be a failure in that it fails to entertain and fails to instruct; however, the bishop example is an expression of the author's view even in the event that the purpose-novel is successful in providing excellent instruction for the reader.

Question 337: C
In paragraph 2 the author mentions that *'it is often said that the novel should instruct as well as afford amusement'*, before branding this species of novel a *'purpose-novel'* and going on to state that such novels propose to *'serve two masters'*. The two masters are, therefore, likely to represent the two purposes of a purpose-novel. Option D is incorrect as the author says *'besides procuring…'* and this suggests that providing an income for the author is a separate function of the purpose-novel in addition to its service of *'two masters'*.

Question 338: C
A novel about politics is most likely to be aiming to instruct readers, and the author views instruction or education in serious topics as unsuitable objects of a novel. He would, therefore, believe that topics/themes which are more entertaining are more suitable (i.e. options A, B, D or E). Option D could be considered trivial, and, therefore, appropriate for a novel.

Question 339: A
This would strengthen the idea that the purpose-novel is a fraud because it tricks people. Option B would weaken the author's argument. Option C is irrelevant, as are option E and option D (as they do not relate to the topic of books which purport to be works of fiction but which, in reality, are not).

Passage 67

Question 340: B
This is the only option that can be directly implied from the line quoted. Option A is close but incorrect because it is expressed in absolute terms 'no one', whilst the quote is not ('no one <u>who was older than a baby</u>). Option C is incorrect because the statement itself doesn't tell us anything about how widespread the destruction was. Option D is incorrect as the opposite is implied by the quote.

Question 341: D
Option D provides a reason for abandoning Big Media. Options A, B, and E are merely factual statements with no normative content. Option C is an argument in favour of Big Media.

Question 342: C
At the end of the fifth paragraph, the author mentions that the changes were inevitable because of *'new publishing tools available on the internet'*, suggesting that this was the principal trigger for the changes. The changes were manifested after 9/11 – but 9/11 didn't itself trigger the changes, and option D constitutes a result of the changes, not a trigger for the changes.

Question 343: B
The author mentions that the evolution *'will force the various communities of interests to adapt'*. Option C is incorrect as it constitutes merely a repetition of the idea that there has been an evolution. Options D and A are not mentioned.

Question 344: C

The meaning of the phrase *'we can't afford'* is that we cannot continue in our present state – this suggests that the author repeats the phrase to reinforce the idea that change is necessary. Option B is incorrect as repetition of an idea does not make it any more convincing; it is, therefore, unlikely that the author employs repetition to this effect. Option D is incorrect as finance is only mentioned towards the end of the paragraph in question. Option A is vague – so option C is the better option.

Passage 68

Question 345: D

This option is merely an assertion of fact, not an argument (it has no normative content), although it later constitutes a part of the author's argument that intellectual property rights shouldn't be tradable. The other options are all arguments (premises) found in the text. Option E can be found in the final paragraph where the author suggests that knowledge is power and that the abolition of copyright laws would enable the education of more people.

Question 346: B

This can be found in the following line: *'There is no cost for materials and the same labour that went into making what I bought also went into what everyone else bought'*. The idea that intellectual property is not physical merely sets the stage for the invocation of the argument found in option B (i.e. it is because intellectual property is not physical that there is no extra cost involved in the sales of the produce of intellectual property).

Question 347: B

The protectionism example states that we try to improve transportation but immediately offset any gains by using tax laws. The author is, therefore, trying to make the point that *'we have advanced methods of storing and promulgating information, we replace any advantage gained in that respect with legislation that restricts the flow of information'*.

Question 348: C

An assertion is a statement that is unsupported by evidence or reasoning. Option E is the only statement which fits that description; all the other statements are supported by reasons given by the author – e.g. option C is supported by the idea (in the first paragraph) that we can use *'information as a framework for future advances'*. Option B is supported by the statement that *'all the knowledge of the world could be given away freely in a digital format'* (i.e. it would be easy to educate people.)

Question 349: A

The author argues, effectively, that intellectual property rights should not be tradable for value because, for instance, it doesn't cost the seller anything extra to sell one more e-book and no extra labour goes into it. It would follow that whenever the provision of a good or service doesn't cost the seller anything extra, and no extra labour goes into it, they should not be able to charge for it. Only option A fits this criteria, as it doesn't cost anything extra (beyond the initial cost of building the house) to rent out a house, and no extra labour is involved.

Passage 69

Question 350: C

The tenor of the author's argument is that humans are all similar such that we may *'see [our] own vices without heat in the distant persons of Solomon, Alcibiades, and Catiline'*. Options E and A are incorrect as the author focuses on learning not just on seeing what historical figures have done – e.g. *'...we shall learn nothing rightly'*.

Question 351: B

Most of what comes after this statement consists of examples of the way in which humans have shared characteristics – e.g. *'What Plato has thought, he (any other man) may think; what a saint has felt, he may feel'*; *'All that Shakespeare says of the king, yonder slip of a boy that reads in the corner feels to be true of himself'*. Option D is merely another example of this broader idea.

Question 352: E

The author uses an encyclopaedia to represent a man. He, therefore, employs a metaphor. None of the other options involve the representation of one thing with another.

Question 353: D

The author dedicates a large part of the passage to showing that humans all have shared characteristics. However, for him, the significance of having shared characteristics lies in the fact that we can then study history and, through the study of men in the past, learn about ourselves in the present. The title – '*History*' – also hints at option D as the correct answer.

Question 354: A

The use of '*we*' seems to suggest that it is indeed possible to make generalised statements, yet it doesn't go as far as to suggest that humans are '*identical*' in every respect other than in the respects alluded to in the statement. Option B is also a step too far and cannot be directly inferred from the use of 'we' alone.

Passage 70

Question 355: B

In the first paragraph, the author writes: '*it is easy in solitude to live after our own; but the great man is he who in the midst of the crowd keeps with perfect sweetness the independence of solitude*' – i.e. it is harder to live amongst other people and '*live after*' one's own opinions. Option D is incorrect as not all forms of contempt are necessarily difficult to handle, according to the author (e.g. '*the sour faces of the multitude, like their sweet faces, have no deep cause, but are put on and off as the wind blows and a newspaper directs*').

Question 356: A

The answer is to be found in paragraph three, where the author suggests that the rage of the '*multitude*' is more fearsome than that of the upper classes. Options C and D are incorrect as the author argues the opposite. Option E is not mentioned.

Question 357: A

This is the argument advanced by the author against reverence for past acts; he states: 'suppose *you should contradict yourself; what then?*' The next closest option is option E, but a close reading of the final paragraph will reveal that the author is not saying that reflecting on the past is in itself <u>always</u> unhelpful.

Question 358: C

In the passage, the author argues that a person must follow their own opinion. It follows from this that social conventions should only be followed if a person personally considers them worth following. It does not follow that they should never be followed since the point is that an individual should think for themselves, and not that social conventions should be shunned per se. The same reasoning applies for option D.

Question 359: A

The use of the word 'corpse' emphasises the fact that the events which are the subject of memories have already passed and are of little relevance to life in the present. Nothing else in the passage seems to suggest that memories are unpleasant – so option D is incorrect. The phrase '*corpse.*' doesn't itself suggest that memories are burdensome – hence options B and C are incorrect. Portraying memory as '*the ghost of past events*' does little to add to the author's argument or support that argument – therefore, option E is incorrect.

Passage 71

Question 360: A

The author states: '*The student receives at one glance the principles which many artists have spent their whole lives in ascertaining*', suggesting that the student is able to gain an insight into the principles of art without going through the same lifelong process as the great masters. This is the main advantage – although the implication may be that students need not think for themselves; this is not stated by the author as an advantage. Option C, D, and E are also incorrect, as they are not stated by the author.

THE ULTIMATE HSPSAA GUIDE — ANSWERS

Question 361: C
The author states: *'he who begins by presuming on his own sense has ended his studies as soon as he has commenced them'*, suggesting that no sufficient progress can be made by those who already think they are enlightened enough to criticize the great masters. Option A is incorrect, as the author is not necessarily arguing that the works are themselves infallible – just that they should be *'treated'* as being infallible. Options B and E are not mentioned. Option D is also a departure from what the author says (which is that principles only constitute a fetter to students who have no talent – not that such students focus on criticism).

Question 362: A
The author's argument is that men of great natural abilities can improve through observing the works of the great masters. He uses Rafaelle as an example of this process. However, if Rafaelle produced his best work before gaining access to the work of great masters, it would suggest that observing those works did not improve him. Option B is incorrect as it is irrelevant to the main argument. Option D is incorrect because the author is already speaking of talented artists, and never disputes that artists may be talented before viewing the works of great masters. Option E is incorrect because the author argues only that exposure to such works improves the artist and it may not be necessary for the artist to value the art highly (it may suffice that they view the art as a repository of art principles/rules) for the improvement to occur.

Question 363: A
The author writes that armour is *'an ornament and a defence'* for the strong, but is a *'load'* for the weak. The illustration, therefore, highlights the point that rules give additional strength or help to those with talent, whilst constituting a *'load'* – i.e. a hindrance for the students who lack artistic talent.

Question 364: B
The argument is that students can and should learn from the works of the great masters in order to produce good work and progress. The author must, therefore, assume that art has an objective value and is not purely subjective, otherwise, it would make little sense to speak of improvement in one's art. Options C and E are incorrect as they are more or less explicitly argued by the author, and cannot, therefore, constitute assumptions. Options A and D are not strictly relevant to the argument that studying the works of the great masters is a means to improvement.

Passage 72

Question 365: C
In the first paragraph, the author declares that the value of art is to be measured by 'the mental labour employed in it, or the mental pleasure produced by it'. The most mental labour involved in the painting of the scene is likely to be the most, especially given the amount of time it takes. It would, therefore, be of most value.

Question 366: A
The author insists that only general topics (topics to which people can relate generally) are appropriate subjects of art. He implies, therefore, that the recording of a subjective experience through art would be inappropriate. Option D is incorrect as it does not necessarily follow that the scope of choice for artists is very narrow (i.e. there may be many topics which fall under the requirements laid out by the author). Options B and E are explicitly stated. Option C is incorrect because the majority of people can relate to the subject without enjoying the piece of art.

Question 367: B
The author does not stipulate that art must embody a grand style to constitute valuable art – he just mentions *'grand style'* as one form of art. All the other options are described as features of good art – e.g. in speaking about an appropriate topic for works of art, the author writes: *'there must be something either in the action or in the object in which men are universally concerned'*.

Question 368: B

The author argues that works of art should focus on the broad picture and not on tiny details because when people picture a story in their minds, they see only the broad picture. The author must, therefore, assume that the purpose of art is not to show tiny details (and, therefore, not to record reality as it really is). Option D is irrelevant to the author's argument. Option A is stated. Option C is not really relevant to the argument – it only offers to explain why people only remember the big picture in their minds. Option E is irrelevant because the paragraph focuses on situations in which we are concerned with stories, and doesn't speak of what should prevail in other situations; the author, therefore, doesn't assume that the situations of which he speaks (where a story is involved) are the only situations in which art is produced.

Question 369: D

The author states: '*The power of representing this mental picture in canvas is what we call invention in a painter*', making it clear that the answer is D.

Passage 73

Question 370: D

The author writes that unlike the '*superstition of religion*' which resulted organically from man's experience with unexplained natural phenomena, the superstition of patriotism is man-made. Options C and E are not used to distinguish between religion and patriotism. Option A is not used to characterise the 's*uperstition of religion*'. Option B is only used to characterise patriotism.

Question 371: B

Gustave Herve, and not the author, refers to patriotism as a superstition.

Question 372: B

The author says that the rich are perfectly at home in every land. This is a matter of opinion as there are no objective means of proving this statement true or false. The other statements are statements of fact, not of opinion, given that they can be proven to be either true or false.

Question 373: D

The author mentions that the money used to fund the army and war is '*taken from the produce of the people*', suggesting that the people bear the financial burden of patriotism. The author does mention factory children and cotton slaves but this is in relation to the wealth that the rich are able to accumulate, not in relation to the cost of patriotism, and, in any case, it is not argued that only those two groups bear the burden of patriotism.

Question 374: C

The rich are presented as hypocrites in that, whilst they endorse patriotism '*theirs is the patriotism*', they are still able to send messages to foreigners and live abroad (i.e. they do not act in accordance with patriotism because they do not promote the interests of their country above that of other countries). Hypocrisy consists in endorsing or promoting an idea but not acting in accordance with it – hence, option C comes the *closest* to the author's description of the rich.

Passage 74

Question 375: D

The context in which the phrase is found sheds light on its meaning. The author states afterward that '*We doubt that we bestow on our hero the virtues in which he shines*', suggesting that we almost worship our friends and attribute many '*virtues*' to him. This suggests that we have an extraordinarily positive outlook on our friends. Options C and E are incorrect as the focus of the first paragraph is not on our expectations of our friends or our expectations of friendship – its focus is on how we currently view our friends.

Question 376: C

The author compares friendship to the immortality of the soul by saying that they are both too good to be believed. None of the other options involve the comparison of one thing (or of a feature of one thing) to another. Option E is a metaphor.

Question 377: B

'*The slowest fruit*' is a reference to fruit which takes a long time to grow. The fact that we '*snatch*' at it signifies that we are impatient and don't want to wait for the fruit to ripen. Similarly, the author is arguing that we don't take the time to explore and cultivate deep friendships, and want a '*swift and petty benefit*'.

Question 378: A

The benefit at which people '*snatch*' is described as being both '*swift and petty*'. These two are not, therefore, contrasted. The other contrasting pairs are to be found in the text. Eternal laws and sudden sweetness are contrasted in the lines: '*The laws of friendship are great, austere, and eternal, of one web with the laws of nature and of morals. But we have aimed at a swift and petty benefit, to suck a sudden sweetness.*'

Question 379: E

This is the author's main argument because all the other points raised in the paragraph are designed to support the idea that we need to explore our friend's true characteristics. For example, options B and D attest to the need to explore our friends' true characteristics. Moreover, option A is incorrect as the statement '*friendship is too good to be believed*' merely suggests that we do not view our friends as they really are – which itself lends support to the idea that we need to explore their true characteristics. Therefore, option E, and not A, is the main argument.

Passage 75

Question 380: B

The author states that receivers of gifts wish to assault givers and that receiving a gift is a very '*onerous business*', suggesting that givers of gifts ought not to expect gratitude on the part of recipients. Option E is not really stated by the author. The other options support the idea encapsulated in option B, and cannot, therefore, constitute the main argument. Option A is incorrect as it is not stated by the author who is likely to use the term '*mean*' to mean '*poor*' or '*mean-spirited*' – rather than unkind.

Question 381: D

'*generous*' is the meaning of the term '*magnanimous*' which best fits in this context; a magnanimous person is said to put us in his debt – suggesting that he himself gives to us, such that we feel that we owe him.

Question 382: B

The author states in the final paragraph that: '*our action on each other, good as well as evil, is so incidental and at random, that we can seldom hear the acknowledgments of any person who would thank us for a benefit, without some shame and humiliation*'. The third paragraph doesn't really consider our entitlement to thanks and is more focused on reasons why we cannot expect thanks from beneficiaries – hence option E (which could possibly be derived from the third paragraph) is incorrect.

Question 383: A

The meaning of the expression is that receiving a gift well is a particularly rare quality. This suggests that most people do not possess it – hence option A is the correct answer. Option B is incorrect as '*good*' is not being used in the sense of moral status – as evidenced by the author's suggestion that we may be wronged by gift giving (hence we would incur no moral obligation to receive a gift well in the first place). Option E is incorrect as the author speaks only of one particular instance in which we could be gracious – and not generally. Option D is incorrect as it cannot be inferred directly from what the author says.

Question 384: C

This answer can be derived from the explanation by the author of why gifts are offensive. He suggests that we are offended because the giver aims to '*bestow*' on us and we don't like the idea being provided for by another person: '*We sometimes hate the meat which we eat, because there seems something of degrading dependence in living by it*'. It would follow that gifts out of love, which are acceptable, lacks this feature which makes other gifts undesirable.

Passage 76

Question 385: E

Irony is the expression of one's meaning through saying the opposite. Options A, B, C, and D are incorrect because the author really means what he explicitly says – e.g. he says '*We write from aspiration and antagonism, as well as from experience. We paint those qualities which we do not possess*', to suggest that he really means that he has no prudence, and is only writing about it because of his '*aspiration*' towards prudence.

Question 386: A

This illustration is immediately preceded by: '*We paint those qualities which we do not possess*', suggesting that the illustration is designed to support the idea that we esteem qualities which we do not possess. Option B is incorrect because even though the illustration might suggest that sometimes we want our children to have different careers to us, that isn't the purpose of the illustration.

Question 387: E

The author states: '*A third class live above the beauty of the symbol to the beauty of the thing signified*'. He then describes that class as having '*spiritual perception*' and being able to reverence: '*reverencing the splendour of the God which [they] see bursting through each chink and cranny.*' These two statements suggest that to live above the beauty of the symbol means to focus on the spiritual significance of physical things. It involves an appreciation of nature, however, option E is the fuller description of what the statement means.

Question 388: C

Most of the author's reasoning is designed to support the idea that prudence involves spirituality. The second paragraph speaks of prudent people as being spiritual, and the third paragraph criticises a view of prudence as relating to physical matters. Although option B is implied in the introduction, it doesn't feature anywhere else in the argument. Option E does not feature in the piece. Option A is not mentioned by the author either (he speaks of a different form of prudence in the last paragraph, but it is clear that he does not view it as being really prudence at all).

Question 389: A

The author refers to the false idea of prudence as being '*a disease like a thickening of the skin until the vital organs are destroyed*', clearly manifesting his disapproval. The other terms aren't themselves used to convey disapproval, even if they appear in disapproving statements.

Passage 77

Question 390: B

The author states that '*these sacrifices are by far not the only standard of measurement of Russia's participation in this gigantic struggle*' before going on to the other means of gauging Russia's role in the war. All the reasoning in the paragraph is, therefore, designed to support the conclusion that the losses sustained by the Russian Army should not be the primary means of gauging their role in the war.

Question 391: A

The answer is to be found in the following quote: '*The final catastrophe of the Central Powers was the direct consequence of the offensive of the Allies in 1918, but Russia made possible this collapse to a considerable degree, having effected, in common with the others, the weakening of Germany*'. Option E is not stated in the text. Options C and D are incorrect because they do not constitute descriptions of the significance of Russia's contributions to the defeat of Germany. Option B is not stated by the author.

Question 392: D

The fact that Russia acted in self-sacrifice tells us nothing about the effect of her self-sacrifice on the course of the war. That statement, therefore, unlike the other options, does nothing to advance the case that Russia played a significant role in the defeat of Germany.

Question 393: A

If the German's lost very few men in the conflict with Russia, it might suggest that Russia did not do very much to weaken the German army. Options C and d are incorrect because the author does not deny the relevance of the other allies to the defeat of Germany. Options B and D are irrelevant to the argument that Russia weakened the German army.

Question 394: C

The author's statement suggests that it is only the recognition of those facts that is necessary for forming the conclusion that Russia played an enormous role in the victory against Germany. It is implied, therefore, that the facts alone are very compelling. Option D cannot be inferred directly from the author's statement – especially as historians may fail to concede Russia's enormous role due to ignorance of the facts, not only due to bias. Option E cannot be inferred from anything in the statement, and neither can option B. Option A is incorrect as it constitutes a mere repetition of the explicit statement.

Passage 78

Question 395: D

The answer is to be found in the author's statement to the effect that: *'finding, however, that the alterations this would have involved would have been incompatible with a clear and connected view of the author's statements, he preferred giving the theory itself entire'*.

Question 396: A

This is added by the writer as a reason for the unfavourable treatment of Goethe's work – it is not stated by Goethe himself. The other options, which are stated by Goethe, can be found in the second paragraph.

Question 397: B

The author's main argument is that Goethe's ideas were not accepted because of the way in which he presented them. This argument would be strengthened by option B because the option suggests that in Goethe's days, the manner in which ideas were presented had an effect on how they were received. Options A, C, D, and E tell us nothing in relation to the main argument – e.g. it may well be the case that all of Goethe's work was expressed in uncompromising language, but we would need to know of the success of those pieces of work to form any sort of judgment in relation to the main argument.

Question 398: B

Immediately after using this phrase, the author states *'the translator begs to state once for all, that in advocating the neglected merits of the "Doctrine of Colours," he is far from undertaking to defend its imputed errors'*. This suggests that he doesn't want to accept Goethe's views just because opinions about them are changing, unless there is reason to accept the views – hence, he refuses to deny the errors in Goethe's doctrine. All this suggests that *'fashion in science'* refers to changes in opinion which are not based on reason.

Question 399: B

The author speaks in favour of *'a due acknowledgment of the acuteness of [Goethe's] views'*. In this context, 'due' signifies approval as the author, in using it, portrays the *'acknowledgement'* as being fitting or appropriate. Option E is not used to portray approval or disapproval. Option D is simply a description of an alternative to the harsh treatment Goethe received, but the author expresses neither approval nor disapproval. Options A and C are also neutral.

Passage 79

Question 400: E
The author mentions servitude to the aristocracy but that is preceded by the line *'With the loss of their municipal independence went the loss of their political authority'*, which suggests that the loss of municipal independence is the trigger for everything else that happened.

Question 401: B
A principality is a state. The phrase *'little principality'* is likely to be used in this sense here as the towns which are described as little principalities are also described as having political/governmental independence – e.g. they *'elected their own rulers and officials'*. A little principality differs from local government in that local government is often still subject to central control – however, the text doesn't suggest that any central control was imposed on the people.

Question 402: C
The phrase *'this free and vigorous life'* refers back to the three paragraphs which precede it. The life described in those paragraphs comes closest to what is described by option C. Option D is incorrect as the text does not say that the treaties established were peace treaties. Option A is incorrect as there is no suggestion that the reform bill itself negatively affected the towns. Option B is incorrect as the mayors are stated as defining the boundaries, not the citizens.

Question 403: A
The author's main argument is that the loss of municipal independence led to political apathy in towns. If A is correct, this severely damages the author's argument. Option C is incorrect as it is already conceded by the author. Options D and E do not really relate to the author's main argument, neither does option B.

Question 404: B
Given that the author speaks of ordinary townspeople in a generally positive manner, he is likely to use quotation marks around *'mean people'* – a derogative term – in order to make it clear that he is not endorsing the term.

Passage 80

Question 405: B
The author states that there was a shift from 'attention on the punishment of terrorists and the criminalisation of new offences following their occurrence' to greater emphasis on the *'management of anticipatory risk'*. Option C is wrong as it relates only to how the Terrorism Act 2000 differs from its predecessors, not to legislation post 9/11.

Question 406: A
This is the only option that can be directly derived from the statement quoted. No extra information is given to support B or D. Options C and E do not necessarily follow from the statement.

Question 407: E
The author mentions that the Terrorism Act 2000 set aside article 5 of the HRA; however, the author doesn't really contrast the two acts with each other. In contrast, all the other options involve each part of the pair being presented as an alternative.

Question 408: D
The author's main argument is that terrorism laws, in general, are discriminatory. However, if only one Act has been found to have been discriminatory, this would erode the author's main argument. Option A is incorrect as the fact that one specific group has not been affected doesn't make terrorism legislation any less discriminatory. Option C supports the author's argument. Options E and B in no way affect the main argument.

Question 409: B
This is the only option which is stated in the text (*'the government felt that in order to prevent mayhem their actions needed to be swift and decisive'*).

Final Advice

Arrive well rested, well fed and well hydrated

The HSPSAA is an intensive test, so make sure you're ready for it. Ensure you get a good night's sleep before the exam (there is little point cramming) and don't miss breakfast. If you're taking water into the exam then make sure you've been to the toilet before so you don't have to leave during the exam. Make sure you're well rested and fed in order to be at your best!

Move on

If you're struggling, move on. Every question has equal weighting and there is no negative marking. In the time it takes to answer on hard question, you could gain three times the marks by answering the easier ones. Be smart to score points- especially in section 1B where some questions are far easier than others.

Make Notes on your Essay

You may get asked questions on your essay at the interview. Given that there is sometimes more than four weeks from the HSPSAA to the interview, it is really important to make short notes on the essay title and your main arguments after the essay. You'll thank yourself after the interview if you do this.

Afterword

Remember that the route to a high score is your approach and practice. Don't fall into the trap that *"you can't prepare for the HSPSAA"*– this could not be further from the truth. With knowledge of the test, some useful time-saving techniques and plenty of practice you can dramatically boost your score.

Work hard, never give up and do yourself justice.

Good luck!

Acknowledgements

I would like to express my sincerest thanks to the many people who helped make this book possible, especially the 5 HSPSAA Cambridge Tutors who shared their expertise in compiling the huge number of questions and answers.

Rohan

About UniAdmissions

UniAdmissions is the UK's number one university admissions company, specialising in **supporting applications to Medical School and to Oxbridge**.

Every year, *UniAdmissions* helps thousands of applicants and schools across the UK. From free resources to these *Ultimate Guide Books* and from intensive courses to bespoke individual tuition, *UniAdmissions* boasts a team of **300 Expert Tutors** and a proven track record of producing great results.

To find out more about our support like intensive **HSPSAA courses** and **HSPSAA tuition**, check out our website www.uniadmissions.co.uk/HSPSAA

Your Free Book

Thanks for purchasing this Ultimate Guide Book. Readers like you have the power to make or break a book – hopefully you found this one useful and informative. If you have time, *UniAdmissions* would love to hear about your experiences with this book.

As thanks for your time we'll send you another ebook from our Ultimate Guide series absolutely FREE!

How to Redeem Your Free Ebook in 3 Easy Steps

1) Find the book you have either on your Amazon purchase history or your email receipt to help find the book on Amazon.

2) On the product page at the Customer Reviews area, click on 'Write a customer review' Write your review and post it! Copy the review page or take a screen shot of the review you have left.

3) Head over to www.uniadmissions.co.uk/free-book and select your chosen free ebook! You can choose from:
- The Ultimate UKCAT Guide – 1250 Practice Questions
- The Ultimate BMAT Guide – 800 Practice Questions
- The Ultimate TSA Guide – 300 Practice Questions
- The Ultimate HSPSAA Guide – 400 Practice Questions
- The Ultimate LNAT Guide – 400 Practice Questions
- The Ultimate NSAA Guide – 400 Practice Questions
- The Ultimate ECAA Guide – 300 Practice Questions
- The Ultimate ENGAA Guide – 250 Practice Questions
- The Ultimate PBSAA Guide – 550 Practice Questions
- The Ultimate FPAS SJT Guide – 300 Practice Questions
- The Ultimate Oxbridge Interview Guide
- The Ultimate Medical School Interview Guide
- The Ultimate UCAS Personal Statement Guide
- The Ultimate Medical Personal Statement Guide
- The Ultimate Medical School Application Guide
- BMAT Past Paper Solutions
- TSA Past Paper Worked Solutions

Your ebook will then be emailed to you – it's as simple as that!

Alternatively, you can buy all the above titles at **www.uniadmisions.co.uk/our-books**

Oxbridge Interview Course

If you've got an upcoming interview for Oxford or Cambridge school – this is the perfect course for you. You get individual attention throughout the day and are taught by specialist Oxbridge graduates on how to approach these tricky interviews.

- Full Day intensive Course
- Guaranteed Small Groups
- 4 Hours of Small group teaching
- 4 x 30 minute individual Mock Interviews +
- Full written feedback so you can see how to improve
- Ongoing Tutor Support until your interview – never be alone again

Timetable:

- **1000 - 1015:** Registration
- **1015 - 1030:** Talk: Key to interview Success
- **1030 - 1130:** Tutorial: Dealing with Unknown Material
- **1145 - 1245:** 2 x Individual Mock Interviews
- **1245 - 1330:** Lunch
- **1330 - 1430:** Subject Specific Tutorial
- **1445 - 1545:** 2 x Individual Mock Interviews
- **1600 - 1645:** Subject Specific Tutorial
- **1645 - 1730:** Debrief and Finish

The course is normally £295 but you can get £35 off by using the code "*BRK35*" at checkout.

www.uniadmissions.co.uk/oxbridge-interview-course

£35 VOUCHER: BRK35